Study Guide

Contemporary Business

ELEVENTH EDITION

Louis E. Boone

University of South Alabama

David L. Kurtz

University of Arkansas

Prepared by

Kathy Daruty

Pierce College

THOMSON

SOUTH-WESTERN

Australia · Canada · Mexico · Singapore · Spain · United Kingdom · United States

Study Guide to accompany Contemporary Business, 11e

Louis E. Boone and David L. Kurtz

VP/Editorial Director:
Jack W. Calhoun

VP/Editor-in-Chief:
Michael P. Roche

Senior Publisher:
Melissa S. Acuña

Senior Acquisitions Editor:
Steve Hazelwood

Senior Developmental Editor:
Rebecca von Gillern

Marketing Manager:
Nicole Moore

Production Editor:
Chris Hudson

Manufacturing Coordinator:
Diane Lohman

Printer:
Globus Printing
Minster, Ohio

For permission to use material from this
text or product, contact us by
Tel (800) 730-2214
Fax (800) 730-2215
http://www.thomsonrights.com

For more information
contact South-Western,
5191 Natorp Boulevard,
Mason, Ohio 45040.
Or you can visit our Internet site at:
http://www.swlearning.com

Preface

The *Study Guide* to accompany *Contemporary Business,* eleventh edition, by Louis E. Boone and David L. Kurtz consists of eighteen chapters and four appendices that follow the sequence of the text.

Design of the Study Guide

Each chapter follows a basic format:

Chapter Summary: Key Concepts: The key concepts are a summary of the major ideas covered in the chapter.

Business Vocabulary and Applications: The key terms from the chapter are listed alphabetically, and the application section uses fill-in questions to enable the user to master the vocabulary.

Learning Goals: Each learning goal is listed in the order in which it appears in the text. The learning goal is followed by multiple choice, true or false, completion, comparative concepts, or short-answer questions. These exercises are designed to cover major points and give a quick review of important information.

Self Review: This section tests the user's overall comprehension of each chapter and consists of true or false and multiple choice questions.

Application Exercises: This section consists of a hypothetical situation, problem, or decision-making opportunity. Exercises are designed to expand knowledge and understanding of the text material. In some cases there are no definitive answers, giving the user an opportunity to analyze various ways of viewing a given situation.

Short Essay Questions: Each chapter contains at least two short essay questions, designed to allow the user to write on major chapter topics in essay form.

Solutions: Solutions to all sections of each chapter and appendices of the *Study Guide* are found in the Solutions section at the end of this book.

Using the Study Guide

The *Study Guide* is designed to enhance understanding, comprehension, and application of the material presented in the text, and to give users an opportunity to develop their writing and critical thinking skills. Learning styles differ, and different students will no doubt use this *Guide* differently. One recommended procedure is to read the chapter in the text, then work the exercises in the *Guide*. Check your answers in the Solutions section at the back of the *Guide*. Mark those questions you've had difficulty answering. Review all the exercises, particularly the questions you've marked, before an exam. Keep in mind that this *Guide* is designed as an aid to learning that should allow you to master the material in the text while you enjoy learning.

Personal Acknowledgments

My thanks go first to the text authors, Louis E. Boone and David L Kurtz, whose text this *Guide* accompanies. I have used this text since its second edition, largely because students love learning from it, and I am delighted to have an opportunity to make some contribution to that learning process. I am also grateful to the staff of Thomson Learning., and especially to Rebecca von Gillern and Melissa S. Acuna.

A special note of thanks goes to my husband, Ron, whose constant support and great sense of humor have made this project more enjoyable than it might have been.

Kathy J. Daruty
Pierce College
Woodland Hills, California
September 2003

Contents

CHAPTER 1

BUSINESS: 2005 AND BEYOND

Chapter Summary: Key Concepts

What Is Business?:

Business	All profit seeking activities and enterprises that provide products and services needed or desired in an economic system.
Not--for-profit organizations	Establishments that have primary objectives other than returning profits to their owners. Included are all government agencies as well as private-sector non-profits like trade organizations, charitable and religious organizations, and private educational institutions.
Factors of production	The inputs to operational effectiveness include a combination of natural resources, human resources, capital and entrepreneurship.

Private enterprise system

Capitalism	Capitalism is another name for the Private Enterprise System. Capitalism minimizes government interference in economic activity and rewards businesses for their ability to perceive and serve the needs of customers.
Basic rights in the private enterprise system	There are four basic rights. The first and most fundamental is the right to private property: the right to own, use, buy, sell, and bequeath most forms of tangible and intangible property. The second is the business owners' right to after tax profit. The third is the freedom of choice in employment, purchases, and investment. The fourth basic right is the right to fair competition: allowing the public to set rules for competitive activity.

The entrepreneurship alternative	Entrepreneurs are risk takers who recognize marketplace opportunities and use their skill and capital to seize and profit from those opportunities. The spirit of entrepreneurship drives the fast pace of new business creation in America. It also contributes to innovative behavior in large organizations.

Six Eras in the History of Business

The colonial period	Prior to 1776, our economy was rural and agricultural, and relied on England for manufactured items and for the financing needed to develop.
Industrial revolution	Between 1760 and 1850, the industrial revolution saw mass production by semiskilled workers, aided by machines.
The age of the industrial entrepreneur	The 1880s was an era of industrial entrepreneurship. Advances in technology and increased demand for manufactured goods led to enormous entrepreneurial opportunities.
The production era	Between 1900 and the 1920s the focus was on producing more goods faster. Every effort was made to meet growing demand leading to production innovations like the assembly line.
The marketing era	During the 1950s marketing grew to mean much more then selling. Since ability to produce was not enough, businesses began to focus on producing just what customers wanted. That is, customer orientation became the center of business thinking.
The relationship era	Since the 1990s we have been in the relationship era: using information technology to build lasting relationships with customers, employees, suppliers, and other businesses.

Managing the Technology Revolution

Technology	Business success today depends on the application of technology to streamline production, increase organizational efficiency, and provide better information for management's interactions both inside and outside the firm.

The Internet   A worldwide network of interconnected computers that generally allows individuals with computing devices to send and receive images and data anywhere.

World Wide Web   Sometimes known simply as the Web, it is an interlinked collection of graphically rich information sources known as sites.

From Transaction Management to Relationship Management

Relationship management   Rather than focusing on finding enough business for existing products, known as transaction management, firms increasingly rely on relationship management. This approach seeks to build and maintain ongoing, mutually beneficial ties with customers and other parties.

Strategic alliances and partnerships   Firms increasingly seek to build partnerships and strategic alliances to assist in meeting common goals and in creating competitive advantages.

Creating Value through Quality and Customer Satisfaction

Value   The customer's perception of the balance between the benefits and the price paid for a product or service.

Quality   Quality generally means the degree of excellence or superiority of a firm's goods and services. It also includes customer satisfaction, which is the ability of a good or service to meet or exceed buyer needs and expectations.

Competing in a Global Market

The global market   Since the world's economies are developing increasing interdependence, firms must now focus on opportunities both inside and outside their national boundaries.

Productivity   A measure of the efficiency of production generally found by dividing outputs (goods or services produced) by inputs (human or natural resources, capital, etc.).

Gross domestic product   The sum of all goods and services produced within a nation's boundaries in a given year.

Developing and Sustaining a World-Class Workforce

A changing workforce Human resource management must meet the challenges of an aging population and a shrinking pool of workers who are more mobile and more diverse than ever before.

Reaping the benefits of diversity Blending individuals of different ethnic backgrounds, cultures, religions, ages, genders, and physical mental abilities has been shown to produce benefits for firms. These include more creative solutions to business problems and more effective task performance.

Wanted: A new Type of Manager

Vision The ability to perceive marketplace needs and what an organization must do to satisfy them.

Critical thinking The ability to analyze and assess information to find problems or opportunities.

Creativity The capacity to develop novel solutions to organizational challenges.

Ability to steer change Technology, marketplace demands, and global competition bring many changes. Managers must be aware of both internal and external causes for change, and they must be good at helping the organization and its people adapt.

Managing Ethics and Social Responsibility

Business ethics The standards of conduct and moral values involved in distinguishing right from wrong actions in the work environment.

Social responsibility Managers today must take into account the social and economic effects of managerial decisions.

What makes a company admired? Profitability, stable growth, a safe and challenging work environment, high-quality goods and services, and business ethics and social responsibility all contribute to a company's reputation and long-term success or failure.

Name_____ Instructor_____

Section_____ Date_____

Business Vocabulary

branding
business
capital
competition
competitive differentiation
consumer orientation
creativity
critical thinking
customer satisfaction
diversity
entrepreneurs
entrepreneurship
fair competition
freedom of choice
gross domestic product (GDP)
invisible hand of competition

Internet
human resources
natural resources
not-for-profit organizations
outsourcing
private enterprise system
private property
profit
productivity
quality
relationship management
strategic alliances
technology
transaction management
value
vision

Application of Vocabulary

Select the term from the list above that best completes the statements below. Write that term in the space provided.

1. List the basic rights guaranteed to the public in the private enterprise system:

   a.   c.

   b.   d.

2. List the four factors of production in the private enterprise system:

   a.   c.

   b.   d.

3. The sum of all the goods and services produced within a nation's boundaries is called the _____.

4. The measure of efficiency of production is termed _____.

5. The _____, first discussed by Adam Smith in his *Wealth of Nations,* assures the best product and price since less efficient producers are driven from the market.

6. The battle among businesses vying for consumer acceptance is known as _____.

7. _____ is the unique combination of organizational abilities and approaches that sets a firm apart from competitors in the minds of consumers.

8. In the Marketing Era of business development firms adopted a _____, which means they find out what customers want and need and then design products to meet those needs.

9. In capitalism, also known as the _____, success or failure depends on how well firms can perceive and meet customer needs and wants.

10. _____ is the process of creating an identity for a good, service, or company which is readily recognized by the firm's intended market.

11. The profit-seeking activities that produce the goods and services needed by society are collectively called _____.

12. Firms engaged in _____ hire outside firms who are specialists to perform operations that were formally handled by the company's own employees.

13. _____ is the term used to describe the business application of knowledge based on science, inventions, and innovation.

14. The _____ is a worldwide network of interconnected computers that, within limits, lets anyone with access to a personal computer send and receive images and data anywhere.

15. _____ is the managerial quality of being able to perceive marketplace needs and what an organization must do to satisfy them.

16. The customer's perception of the balance between the positive traits of a good or service and its price is called _____.

Name _____ Instructor_____

Section _____ Date _____

17. _____ are long term partnerships of firms designed to improve overall competitiveness.

18. _____ is the degree of excellence or superiority of a firm's goods or services.

19. Perhaps he best measure of quality is _____, defined as the ability of a good or service to meet or exceed buyer needs and expectations.

20. Risk takers who initiate economic activity in the private enterprise system are known as _____.

21. The _____ of the U.S. workforce enhances innovation, creativity, and sensitivity to the multicultural marketplace by blending individuals of different genders, ethnic backgrounds, cultures, religions, ages, and physical and mental abilities

22. _____ include all public sector government agencies as well as many private sector organizations such as labor unions, museums, and religious organizations.

23. _____ is the collection of activities that build and maintain ongoing, mutually beneficial ties with customers and other parties.

24. Before the 1990s, businesses tended to rely on _____. This approach focused on current sales and profits instead of thinking about the future benefits of creating long term customers.

25. _____ is the capacity to develop novel solutions to perceived organizational problems and to see better and different ways of doing business.

26. _____ skills include the ability to analyze information and assess its authenticity, accuracy and worth, to evaluate arguments, and to identify crucial issues and solutions.

Analysis of Learning Goals

Learning Goal 1.1: Distinguish between business and not-for-profit organizations and identify the factors of production.

True or False

1. ___ In the private enterprise system, businesses are the primary providers of the goods and services needed by society.

2. ___ Business and not-for-profit organizations both have as their primary objective the return of profits to the owners.

3. ___ While religious and charitable organizations are not-for-profits, government agencies are not.

4. ___ Only profit-seeking organizations face competition.

Learning Goal 1.2: Describe the private enterprise system and explain how competition and entrepreneurship contribute to the system.

True or False

1. ___ Over the long run, competition ensures that organizations who provide superior customer satisfaction will be more successful than those who do not.

2. ___ People who take the risks of pursuing a business opportunity are called entrepreneurs.

3. ___ Profits are both the reward and the incentive for risk taking.

4. ___ The invisible hand of competition ensures that only the most efficient producers will survive in the marketplace.

Learning Goal 1.3: Identify the six eras of business and explain how the relationship era influences contemporary business.

True or False

1. ___ The colonial era was characterized by a factory system and the growth of large cities.

Name_____ Instructor_____

Section _____ Date _____

2. ____ The production era focused on mass production while increasing productivity of manufacturing processes.

3. ____ Since entering the marketing era, producers make what they do best, and marketing is simply selling that product.

4. ____ The relationship era is driven by advances in information technology that allow businesses to form deep, ongoing links with their customers, employees, suppliers, and other organizations.

Learning Goal 1.4: Describe how technology is changing the way businesses operate and compete.

Multiple Choice

1. The worldwide network of interconnected computers is known as:

    a. the World Wide Web.
    b. e-mail.
    c. transaction management
    d. the Internet.

2. Sites that offer interactive opportunities to receive information, known as Web sites, are found:

    a. on the World Wide Web.
    b. on a typical roadmap.
    c. off the Internet.
    d. all of the above.

3. The ability to electronically deliver messages, documents, spreadsheets, and pictures anywhere in the world makes use of:

    a. e-mail.
    b. express delivery trucks.
    c. snail-mail.
    d. all of the above.

4. Managing technology will mean:
    a. using technology to provide new goods and services for customers.
    b. using technology to improve customer service while lowering prices.
    c. being aware of new questions about business ethics and social responsibility.
    d. all of the above.

Learning Goal 1.5: Relate the importance of quality and customer satisfaction to efforts to create value for customers.

Short Answer

1. What is value?

2. What is quality? How is it best measured?

Learning Goal 1.6: Explain how productivity affects competitiveness in the global market.

True or False

1. ___ While many U.S. firms are important exporters, the U.S. is rarely an attractive market for foreign competitors.

2. ___ Productivity is a measure of efficiency and is found by dividing inputs into outputs.

3. ___ Gross domestic product (GDP) is equal to the sum of all goods and services produced within a nation's boundaries.

4. ___ Since the U.S. has the largest GDP in the world, it makes sense for firms to focus exclusively on the domestic market.

5. ___ Recent investments in technology have dramatically increased U.S. productivity.

Name_____ Instructor_____

Section _____ Date _____

Learning Goal 1.7: Describe the major trends in the workforce that challenge managers' skills for managing and developing human resources.

True or False

1. ___ The growing use of technology makes it less important for organizations to make effective use of human resources.

2. ___ Outsourcing refers to the increased globalization of business.

3. ___ Experts predict a decline in the number of available adult workers in the coming years.

4. ___ Each year more American workers are employed in goods producing industries, while employment in service industries is declining.

5. ___ Employers are increasingly developing employer-employee partnerships that recognize and encourage worker creativity and contribution to customer satisfaction.

Learning Goal 1.8: Identify the skills that managers need to lead businesses in the new century.

Short Answer

Name and define the four most important qualities that will be required of managers in today's organizations.

1.

2.

3.

4.

Learning Goal 1.9: Discuss the importance of good business ethics and social responsibility in business decision making.

Multiple Choice

1. The standards of conduct and moral values involving right and wrong actions arising in the work environment are known as:

    a. social responsibility.   c. creativity.
    b. business ethics.   d. vision.

2. The call for greater social responsibility of business means:

    a. businesses should focus exclusively on short-term profit goals.
    b. businesses should focus exclusively on the interests of the owners and managers.
    c. management should consider the social and economic effects of management decisions.
    d. management should consider giving away all the firm's profits for good causes.

3. Failure to behave ethically:

    a. can be costly in the long-run.
    b. can spoil a company's image.
    c. will damage efforts to build long-term customer relationships.
    d. all of the above.

Name _____ Instructor _____

Section _____ Date _____

Self Review

True or False

1. ___ A simplistic definition of business would be: All profit-seeking activities and enterprises that provide products and services needed or desired in an economic system.

2. ___ The majority of businesses in the United States are owned by the government.

3. ___ Each factor of production generates a financial return.

4. ___ The factor payment for the use of capital is profit.

5. ___ The most basic freedom under the free enterprise system is the right to private property.

6. ___ The industrial revolution involved mass production, the specialization of labor, and the development of machines and the railroads.

7. ___ Even today, marketing is synonymous with selling.

8. ___ The United States is moving away from manufacturing as a basis for its economy and toward an economy based on service industries.

9. ___ Studies indicate that diverse employee teams and workforces tend to be less effective and creative than groups made up of people who are all alike.

10. ___ Total productivity of a nation's businesses has become a measure of its economic strength, standard of living, and ability to compete.

11. ___ In the 21st century, managers will have to find the best way to connect people, technology, and ethics in order to form strong partnerships with customers, employees, and other organizations.

12. ___ Managers can expect the rate of change to slow in the future.

13. ___ The marketing era introduced the idea that a firm should identify and satisfy consumer wants and needs.

14. ___ Government agencies, public schools, and labor unions are all good examples of organizations in the not-for-profit sector of the U.S. economy.

15. ___ Karl Marx is the Father of Capitalism.

Multiple Choice

1. The *Wealth of Nations* was written by:

   a. Paul Samuelson.
   b. Karl Marx.
   c. Adam Smith.
   d. John Galbraith.

2. A capitalist economic system could also be called:

   a. a community interest system.
   b. a utopian system.
   c. a futile system.
   d. a private enterprise system

3. The factor payment that rewards entrepreneurship is:

   a. profit.
   b. interest.
   c. wages.
   d. rent.

4. Gross Domestic Product (GDP):

   a. is higher in the United States than in any other country.
   b. is the sum of all goods and services produced within a nation's boundaries.
   c. is used to calculate per capita output in our economy.
   d. all of the above.

5. The U.S. workforce in the 21st century can be expected to:

   a. be less diverse.
   b. be less mobile.
   c. require greater skill and flexibility.
   d. include fewer older workers.
   e. do less telecommuting.

Name_____ Instructor _____

Section _____ Date _____

6. An entrepreneur is defined as a(n):

    a. government employee.   d. monopolist.
    b. risk taker.   e. executive.
    c. professional manager.

7. Laws that prohibit price discrimination and deceptive advertising practices are included in the right to:

    a. private property.   c. freedom of choice.
    b. profits.   d. fair competition.

8. The right of the risk taker to retain his or her after-tax earnings is the right to:

    a. private property.   c. freedom of choice.
    b. profits.   d. fair competition.

9. In the free enterprise system, the individual's right to select a career is one example of:

    a. private property.   c. freedom of choice.
    b. profits.   d. fair competition.

10. Which of the following is *NOT* one of the factors of production?

    a. natural resources   d. entrepreneurship
    b. human resources   e. wages
    c. capital

11. Profit is defined as:

    a. the difference between receipts and expenditures.
    b. a firm's sales revenues.
    c. the cost of production.
    d. net sales.
    e. assets minus debts.

12. The "invisible hand of competition" refers to:

    a. Uncle Sam's taxation of your earnings.
    b. the problem of shoplifting in American retailing.
    c. the way competition in a market economy produces high quality and low prices.
    d. the need for government regulation to ensure high quality and low prices.

13. A partnership formed to create competitive advantage for the businesses involved is called a:

    a. strategic alliance   c. vision.
    b. social responsibility.   d. global market.

Application Exercises

The history department at your college requires that each student enrolled in History 201 give a five-minute oral presentation. Tamar Seigel decides to give her presentation on the history of business in the United States. To cover the time span from the colonial society to the current business era, she decides to mention two important aspects of each stage of development. Tamar has not had a business course, and she asks you to be her "expert consultant." List two main aspects she should include for each era.

1. The colonial society.

2. The Industrial Revolution.

3. The age of industrial entrepreneurs.

Name_____ Instructor _____

Section _____ Date _____

4.   The production era.

5.   The marketing era.

6.   The relationship era.

Short Essay Questions

1.   What is the global market, and why is it important?

2. Define the four basic rights awarded to citizens living in a private enterprise economy. How important are these rights?

3. What is Relationship Management, and how can it enhance business prospects?

CHAPTER 2

Business Ethics and Social Responsibility

Chapter Summary: Key Concepts

Concern for Ethical and Societal Issues

Business ethics

Standards of business conduct and moral values as they apply to the business environment.

Awareness of social issues

Businesses try to consider the social as well as economic effects of business decisions since those decisions can affect the environment, employees, customers, investors, and the general public. Today's businesses seek to balance doing what is profitable with doing what is right.

The New Ethical Environment

Business ethics in the spotlight

While most companies and their leaders are highly ethical, it is clear that not all companies successfully set and meet high ethical standards. Fraud and corruption have cost employees their jobs and retirement savings, and hurt investors. In response, more companies are carefully articulating ethical guidelines.

Individuals make a difference

Executives, managers, and employees bring their own ethical values into the workplace, but they can also face pressure to compromise those values. Top management may set the ethical tone, but employee's own choices in the workplace matter as well.

Three stages in the development of individual ethics

In the first, preconventional stage, individuals mainly look out for themselves and follow rules only out of fear. In the second, conventional stage, individuals are aware of and act in response to their obligations to others. In the third, postconventional stage, individuals follow personal principles for resolving dilemmas, considering personal, group, and societal interests.

On-the-job ethical dilemmas   Common business ethical dilemmas include honesty and integrity in business dealings, whistle-blowing, the interplay between loyalty to the organization and truthfulness in business relationships, and conflict of interest.

How Organizations Shape Ethical conduct

Ethical awareness   Ethical awareness can be heightened through the development of a code of conduct.

Ethical reasoning   Employees also need to develop ethical reasoning ability, including the skill to evaluate options and spot ethical issues in day to day decisions.

Ethical action   Means must be developed to translate ethical decisions into ethical action. Examples include company ethics hotlines, or a set of ethics questions to guide decision making.

Ethical leadership   Perhaps most important, executives must demonstrate ethical leadership in their own actions. They also encourage ethical behavior in an organization by insisting that each employee be an ethical leader.

Acting Responsibly to Satisfy Society

Social responsibility   Management's acceptance of the obligation to consider profit, consumer satisfaction, and societal well-being of equal value in evaluating the firm's performance.

Responsibilities to the general public   These responsibilities include reducing dangers and promoting public health, protecting the environment, and developing the quality of the workforce. Many would also argue that businesses should support charities and social causes through corporate philanthropy.

Responsibilities to customers	Consumerism is the idea that businesses should consider and safeguard certain customer rights. Businesses are obligated to protect the consumers' right to be safe, to be informed, to choose, and to be heard.
Responsibilities to employees	In addition to pay, employees today expect a safe working environment, consideration of quality of life issues like family leave, and equal opportunity on the job. The workplace should also be free of age discrimination, sexual harassment and sexism.
Responsibilities to investors and the financial community	Businesses must be honest in reporting their profits and financial performance to avoid misleading investors. When firms fail in meeting these responsibilities thousands of investors, employees and customers can suffer. Therefore, government agencies exist to insure that businesses follow proper accounting practices and to investigate alleged fraud and other financial misdeeds.

Business Vocabulary

boycott
business ethics
code of conduct
conflict of interest
corporate philanthropy
consumerism
Equal Employment Opportunity
  Commission (EEOC)
family leave
genetic engineering
green marketing

integrity
pollution
product liability
recycling
Sarbanes-Oxley Act of 2002
sexism
sexual harassment
social audit
social responsibility
whistle-blowing

Application of Vocabulary

Select the term from the list above that best completes the statements beginning on the following page. Write that term in the space provided.

Name _____ Instructor _____

Section _____ Date _____

1. Employers with 50 or more employees must provide _____,
   an unpaid leave of up to 12 weeks to deal with new births, adoptions, or illness of
   workers or their relatives.

2. _____ is the tainting or destroying of the natural environment.

3. _____ is reprocessing of reusable materials.

4. A _____ is a formal statement that
   defines how the organization expects and requires employees to resolve ethical
   questions.

5. _____ is the term used to describe a firm's formal examination of
   its social responsibility programs.

6. _____ is the demand that business give proper consideration to
   consumer wants and needs when making decisions, and is based on the belief that
   consumers have certain rights.

7. The _____ is the federal commission created to
   aid in the elimination of job discrimination while increasing job opportunities for
   women and minorities.

8. Employees should be careful to avoid the appearance of any _____
   _____, that is, any situation where a business decision benefiting one
   person has the potential to harm another person.

9. Many argue that social responsibility to the general public means businesses should
   give back to the communities in which they earn profits through _____
   _____.

10. In addition to making a profit, there are obligations businesses have to the wider
    society, known as _____.

11. _____ deals with standards of conduct and moral values
    that arise in any work environment.

Name _____ Instructor _____

Section _____ Date _____

12. _____ has occurred when an employee discloses to the media or government authorities any suspected illegal, immoral, or unethical practices of the organization.

13. _____ can include unwelcome sexual advances, requests for sexual favors as a condition of employment or promotion, and/or the creation of what feels like a "hostile" work environment due to unwelcome flirting, lewd comments or obscene jokes.

14. Congress enacted the _____ to further protect investors from unethical accounting practices. Among other things, this law requires a special oversight board to regulate public accountant firms that audit the financial records of corporations.

15. _____ is demonstrated by people who adhere to deeply felt ethical principles in business situations.

16. _____ is a type of discrimination in which people are treated differently in the workplace due to their gender.

17. _____ involves altering crops or other living things by inserting genes that provide them with more desirable characteristics.

18. When consumers refuse to buy a company's goods or services, they are engaged in a(n) _____.

19. The responsibility manufacturers face for injuries or damages caused by their products is called _____.

20. Companies who work to promote environmentally safe products and production methods are engaged in _____.

Analysis of Learning Goals

Learning Goal 2.1: Explain the concepts of business ethics and social responsibility.

True or False

1. ___   Social responsibility refers to management's consideration of the social as well as economic effects of its decisions.

2. ___   Business ethics refers to standards of conduct and moral values applied in business decision making.

3. ___   Social responsibility and ethical conduct generally cost more than they create in business value.

4. ___   Lack of social responsibility may lead to increased government intervention.

5. ___   Employees, customers, government, and the general public all have a stake in the performance of modern organizations.

Learning Goal 2.2: Describe the factors that influence individual ethics.

Multiple Choice

1. Individual ethics in the workplace are influenced by:

   a. past experiences and peer pressure.
   b. the organization's culture.
   c. family, cultural, and religious standards.
   d. all of the above.

2. A firm's ability to behave ethically depends upon:
   a. the ethical values of the firm's executives.
   b. the ethical values of the firm's employees.
   c. a climate within the organization that promotes ethical conduct.
   d. all of the above.

3. The legal environment of business:
   a. can help clarify and promote ethical expectations.
   b. is useful primarily to punish wrongdoers.
   c. does little to regulate unethical business practices.
   d. all of the above.

Name _____ Instructor _____

Section _____ Date _____

4. The social responsibility of business:
    a. is determined entirely by businesses themselves.
    b. is simple to understand and implement.
    c. is molded in part by societal forces.
    d. is restricted to simply obeying the law.

Learning Goal 2.3: List the stages in the development of ethical standards.

Fill-in

1. In the _____ stage of ethical development, individuals primarily consider their own needs, desires, and personal consequences in making ethical decisions.

2. Those who are aware of and respond to their duty to others have achieved the _____ stage of ethical development.

3. An individual who can move beyond self-interest and duty, who considers the needs of the wider society, and who can employ ethical principles in a variety of situations, has attained the _____ stage of ethical development.

Learning Goal 2.4: Identify common ethical dilemmas in the workplace.

Multiple Choice

1. A situation where an action benefiting one person has the potential to harm another is called:

    a. a conflict of interest.   c. a loyalty dilemma.
    b. whistle-blowing.   d. integrity.

2. When an employee discloses illegal, immoral or unethical practices of an organization to outside parties, it is called:

    a. a conflict of interest.   c. a breach of honesty.
    b. whistle-blowing.   d. integrity.

3.   Adhering to ethical principles is business decisions demonstrates:

   a.   a conflict of interest.   c.   a loyalty dilemma.
   b.   whistle-blowing.   d.   integrity.

4.   Loyalty to one's employer:

   a.   means saying anything that will promote the firm's interests whether it is true or
        not
   b.   can create an ethical dilemma if the truth about the firm is not favorable.
   c.   means always telling bosses what they want to hear even if it stretches the truth.
   d.   has nothing to do with being truthful.

Learning Goal 2.5: Discuss how organizations shape ethical behavior.

True or False

1. ___   Top management plays a crucial role in developing an organizational culture
         that encourages ethical behavior.

2. ___   Most companies today don't bother with a code of conduct.

3. ___   A code of conduct gives guidance on how the organization expects employees to
         resolve ethical questions.

4. ___   A firm whose managers set unrealistic goals for employees invites unethical
         behavior.

Learning Goal 2.6: Describe how businesses' social responsibility is measured.

True or False

1. ___   If a business practice is legal, it is surely ethical.

2. ___   Quantitative economic measures such as employment levels, sales, and profits
         are irrelevant in evaluating a firm's social performance.

3. ___   Conducting a social audit can help a firm measure its progress in meeting social
         responsibility objectives.

4. ___   Consumers and public-interest groups have played an active role in helping
         firms recognize and meet their social responsibilities.

Name _____ Instructor _____

Section _____ Date _____

Learning Goal 2.7: Summarize the responsibilities of business to the general public, customers, and employees.

True or False

1. ___   Environmental protection, avoiding pollution, and promoting recycling are the responsibility of government, not the business community.

2. ___   American firms have found a significant competitive advantage in developing a culturally diverse and highly skilled work force.

3. ___   In our current high skill work environment, businesses need to encourage education and skill development among their employees.

4. ___   According to President John F. Kennedy's consumer bill of rights, consumers have the rights to safety, to be informed, to choose, and to be heard.

5. ___   The EEOC was created to increase job opportunities for all members of society and to help end discriminatory practices in employment.

6. ___   Family leave is a benefit companies may choose to offer, but no American firm is legally required to provide family leave.

7. ___   Sexism, or discrimination based solely on a person's gender, has been completely eliminated in today's global business environment.

8. ___   Businesses have both a legal and an ethical requirement to eliminate sexual harassment in the workplace.

9. ___   Corporate philanthropy involves businesses getting as much as possible from the communities in which they earn profits for the sole benefit of their shareholders.

Learning Goal 2.8: Explain why investors and the financial community are concerned with business ethics and social responsibility.

True or False

1. ___ Since investors are risk takers, there are no ethical requirements for managers to protect investor interests.

2. ___ Investors who believe management has not dealt honestly with them have legal recourse.

3. ___ Unethical business practices can have adverse effects on the financial community as a whole, both nationally and internationally.

4. ___ The Securities and Exchange Commission is the federal agency responsible for investigating alleged unethical or illegal financial behavior of publicly traded firms.

Self Review

True or False

1. ___ Distribution of information about dangerous products and other public health issues is the sole responsibility of government, and there is no need for business to be involved.

2. ___ Social audits measure a firm's performance relating to such issues as employment practices, environmental responsibility, and philanthropy.

3. ___ While managers may conduct internal audits on social responsibility, public opinion rarely has any real impact on business practices.

4. ___ Consumerism is becoming an antiquated concept because of the rise in imported products.

5. ___ Smoking and alcohol use are legal and private matters, and do not impact business responsibility to the wider society.

6. ___ Green marketing targets consumers who care whether or not businesses demonstrate environmental responsibility.

Name _____ Instructor _____

Section _____ Date _____

7. ___ Business ethics deal with the right and wrong actions that arise in any business environment.

8. ___ A firm must be able to prove that any claim made about the quality or superiority of a good or service has been substantiated.

9. ___ Before you accept a job, it is a good idea to review your new employer's code of ethics.

10. ___ It makes good sense to have all employees aware of the firm's stands on social and ethical issues.

11. ___ Most new jobs in developed countries require college educated workers.

12. ___ All charges of sexual harassment involve unwelcome sexual advances.

13. ___ Today we find no significant differences between the average pay of men and women.

14. ___ Programs that increase social responsibility and ethical practices in a firm may be good for public relations, but they generally cost more than they create in economic benefits.

15. ___ Social responsibility and business ethics reach beyond national borders and are a factor of growing importance in global business.

Multiple Choice

1. In order to promote ethical behavior in an organization:

   a. ethical guidelines should be clearly stated and communicated to employees.
   b. managers must show a personal commitment to ethical values and a willingness to enforce them.
   c. the organization may design training programs to help employees develop ethical reasoning skills.
   d. the organization's structure and business practices should reflect and reinforce ethical values.
   e. all of the above.

2. The agency charged with insuring the accuracy of financial statements provided by publicly traded companies is the:

    a. EEOC.   c. SEC.
    b. FTC.   d. EPA.

3. In a social audit:

    a. a firm attempts to measure its own performance relating to social responsibility.
    b. outside auditors are called in to evaluate business practices.
    c. the FTC audits the ethical practices of a firm.
    d. the government estimates the social costs of individual business actions.

4. Business responsibilities to the general public include:

    a. dealing with public health issues.   c. developing a quality work force.
    b. protecting the environment.   d. all of the above.

5. The Family and Medical Leave Act of 1993:

    a. affects firms with more than 100 employees.
    b. requires firms with 50 or more employees to provide up to 12 weeks of paid leave for workers who need to attend to family matters.
    c. requires firms with 50 or more employees to provide up to 12 weeks of unpaid leave for workers who need to attend to family matters.
    d. does not include a guarantee that employees will be returned to an equivalent job when they come back to work.

6. Discrimination based on gender:

    a. is known as sexual harassment.
    b. is known as sexism.
    c. is to be expected in a culturally diverse work force.
    d. was outlawed by the Sarbanes-Oxley Act.

7. The federal agency charged with ensuring universal access to jobs and ending discrimination in the workplace is the :

    a. FTC.   c. EPA.
    b. SEC.   d. EEOC.

Name _____ Instructor _____

Section _____ Date _____

8. In the U.S. economy, the social responsibility of a firm is evaluated:

    a. by consumers who may patronize or avoid a firm based on its behavior.
    b. on the basis of the firm's contribution to economic growth and employment opportunities.
    c. by outside groups who create and monitor standards of corporate performance.
    d. by the firm itself doing a social audit.
    e. all of the above are methods for evaluating social responsibility.

9. After graduating from trade school, Ann accepted a position as a mechanic in a shop where she is the only woman. After a few months she complained to her supervisor about lewd jokes and sexually explicit posters in the workplace. Her supervisor should:

    a. tell Ann to relax and try to be one of the boys.
    b. listen to Ann and help her to adjust to the environment.
    c. realize that these occurrences can be construed as sexual harassment and need to be addressed.
    d. realize that women have no place in a work environment that was previously all male.

10. In the highest level ethical and moral behavior, the individual is able to move beyond mere self-interest and duty and take the larger needs of society into account as well. This stage of ethical development is the:

    a. preconventional stage.   c. postconventional stage.
    b. conventional stage.   d. metaethical stage.

Application Exercises

The following situations deal with ethical issues in business. Write a short explanation of why you think the participants did nor did not act in a socially responsible or ethical manner.

1. Two sales representatives from competing companies regularly have lunch together and discuss corporate decisions about new products that their companies are developing.

2. A wheelchair bound secretary is denied a job because the employer has no rest room that can accommodate a wheelchair.

3. Jill is an executive secretary and John an assistant administrator for the same company. They both oversee large budgets, handle some contract negotiations, deal with customers, and have otherwise similar responsibilities. The company pay scale for assistant administrators is significantly higher than its pay scale for executive secretaries. Hence, John makes a lot more than Jill does.

4. Patty is the owner of her own small business. She is a smoker, and has always felt free to smoke in her own office. She hires a worker who objects to cigarette smoke in the work environment, since the EPA has identified second-hand smoke as a public health risk.

Name _____ Instructor _____

Section _____ Date _____

Short Essay Questions

1. Aside from earning a profit for owners, what responsibilities should business managers have?

2. How can firms and their employees promote ethical business practices?

Notes

CHAPTER 3

Economic Challenges Facing Global and Domestic Business

Chapter Summary: Key Concepts

Opening Overview

Economics	The social science that studies the allocation of scarce resources in both the private and public sectors.
Microeconomics	Focuses on the economic activities of an individual economic unit, such as an individual or a firm.
Macroeconomics	Overall operation of economies. Includes issues like maintaining adequate supplies of needed resources, improving productivity, government monetary and fiscal policies, and the resulting effects on the standard of living.

Microeconomics: the Forces of Demand and Supply

Demand	The willingness and ability of buyers to purchase goods and services at different prices.
Supply	The willingness and ability of sellers to provide goods and services for sale at different prices.
Factors driving demand	A demand curve is a graph of the amount of a product that buyers will purchase at different prices under a given set of conditions. Generally, as price goes up, demand goes down and visa versa. However, the entire curve can shift to the right or left depending on changed conditions. These changes reflect factors such as customer preferences, number of buyers, buyers' incomes, prices of substitute goods, prices of complementary goods, and how optimistic or pessimistic future expectations become.

Factors driving supply

A supply curve graphically shows the relationship between different prices and the quantities that sellers will offer for sale, regardless of demand. Generally, as prices rise, the quantity sellers are willing to produce increases, and vice versa. The entire curve can also shift right or left depending on such factors as costs of inputs, costs of technologies, taxes, and the number of suppliers.

How demand and supply interact

The equilibrium price identifies the prevailing market price and is found at the intersection of the supply and demand curves.

Macroeconomics: Issues for the Entire Economy

Capitalism and competition

Capitalism (also called market economy or the private enterprise system) depends upon competition. In this kind of economic system, different industries exhibit different competitive market structures. The four market structures are pure competition, monopolistic competition, oligopoly, and monopoly.

Planned economies: communism and socialism

In a planned economy, governments control business ownership, profits and resource allocation based on the government's goals. Under communism, there is no private property, and government plans and controls the nation's economic activity. Under socialism, government owns and operates the major industries.

Mixed market economies

In practice, most countries implement mixed market economies, economic systems that display characteristics of both planned and market economies in varying degrees.

Evaluating Economic Performance

Flattening the business cycle

A nation's economy tends to flow through various stages of a business cycle: prosperity, recession, depression, and recovery. While the business cycle is normal, a major U.S. goal is to manage the cycle to reduce the severity and duration of recessions, and to prevent depressions.

Productivity and the nation's GDP	Increased productivity generally leads to economic growth and rising wealth, because fewer inputs are needed to produce goods and services. The measure of these goods and services upon which productivity is calculated in the Gross Domestic Product (GDP), defined as the total dollar value of goods and services produced within a nation's boundaries in a given year.
Price-level changes	Inflation is a sustained rise in prices that devalues a nation's currency. It is a result of increased costs (cost-push) and/or excessive demand (demand-pull). It is commonly measured by the Consumer Price Index (CPI). Nations must also guard against deflation, a period of falling prices when customers put off purchases, business slows, jobs are lost, and the economy weakens.
Employment levels	People need incomes to be consumers, so low unemployment is a sign of economic health. The unemployment rate measures people who are actively looking for work but unable to find jobs. Unemployment can arise in four ways: it can be frictional, seasonal, cyclical or structural.

Managing the Economy's Performance

Monetary policy	Action to increase or decrease the supply of money in the economy. An expansionary policy increases the money supply to stimulate business activity. A restrictive monetary policy reduces the money supply to curb excessive and potentially inflationary economic growth.
Fiscal policy	Government taxation and spending decisions can also affect the economy. Increased spending or lower taxes are stimulatory, while reduced spending or higher taxes can reduce overall economic activity. The U.S. government plans its expenditures in a budget. If tax receipts equal expenditures, the budget is balanced. When tax receipts exceed expenditures, a budget surplus occurs. If tax receipts fall below spending levels, a budget deficit arises. These deficits accumulate into the national debt.

The U.S. economy: a roller coaster ride	The government can use fiscal and monetary policy to stimulate the economy and manage the business cycle. Factors to monitor include unemployment, inflation/deflation, productivity, and consumer spending.

Global Economic Challenges of the 21st Century

Creating a long-term global strategy	There are many challenges to be managed in the growing global economy. Among them are international terrorism, a shift to a global information economy, the aging of the world's population, improving quality and customer service, and enhancing competitiveness of every country's work force.

Business Vocabulary

balanced budget
budget deficit
communism
consumer price index (CPI)
cost-push
cyclical unemployment
deflation
demand
demand curve
demand-pull
deregulation
economics
equilibrium price
fiscal policy
frictional unemployment
gross domestic product (GDP)
inflation
macroeconomics
microeconomics

mixed market economy
monetary policy
monopolistic competition
monopoly
national debt
oligopoly
private enterprise system
privatization
producer price index (PPI)
productivity
pure competition
recession
seasonal unemployment
socialism
structural unemployment
supply
supply curve
unemployment rate

Application of Vocabulary

Select the term from the list above that best completes the statements beginning on the following page. Write that term in the space provided.

Name_____ Instructor_____

Section _____ Date_____

1. The science of allocating scarce resources is known as _____.

2. The term used to describe the study of the overall operations of an economy and its various components is known as _____.

3. _____ refers to the study of the economic activities of a firm or an individual.

4. _____ refers to people who are temporarily out of work but who are looking for a job.

5. _____ refers to the type of inflation that is caused by increased production costs.

6. In the United States, changes in price levels are tracked by the _____, which measures the monthly average changes in prices of goods and services.

7. When the federal government spends more than it gets from tax revenues, a _____ is the result.

8. When prices continue to increase due to costs or demand, the economy is said to be experiencing a period of _____.

9. _____ counts people like farm laborers or ski instructors who are out of work due to the time of year.

10. _____ refers to governmental measures designed to affect the level of economic activity through changes in the money supply.

11. The _____ depicts the difference in the amount of a good that a seller will produce at various prices.

12. The _____ depicts the relation between different prices and the quantity of a good that buyers will purchase.

13. When people are out of work during a recession or other economic downturn, their job loss is referred to as _____.

14. The _____ is the price at which the demand curve and the supply curve intersect.

15. Governmental actions concerning tax revenue and expenditures of public funds are referred to as _____.

16. The _____ measures the number of people who are looking for work but are unable to find jobs.

17. The _____ type of inflation occurs when there is more demand than goods and services available.

18. _____ counts those people who are unable to find work for a long period of time because their skills fail to match those needed in the work force.

19. The ability and willingness of buyers to purchase goods and services in the economy is known as _____.

20. When demand increases, prices will also increase unless producers also increase _____.

21. When the federal government generates enough revenues through taxation to cover the total proposed spending for the year, a _____ has been attained.

22. The _____ is the total cumulative borrowing by the federal government to finance budget deficits.

23. Six months or more of economic contraction counts as a _____.

24. Under the economic system known as _____, the means of production are owned and controlled by the government.

25. Under _____, the government owns and operates the key industries that are considered vital to the public welfare.

26. Nearly all of the world's economies today blend private and public ownership into what is known as a _____.

27. A(n) _____ is a market situation that features few sellers and substantial entry restrictions.

Name_____ Instructor_____

Section _____ Date_____

28. A supplier in a market situation where there are not direct competitors is said to have a_____.

29. The market situation in which a large number of buyers and sellers exchange well-differentiated products is known as _____.

30. In _____, a large number of buyers and sellers exchange homogeneous products so no single participant has a significant influence on price.

31. A capitalist or market economy, in which competition regulates economic life, is also called the _____.

32. In a mixed market economy, _____ defines the trend of replacing public ownership with private ownership.

33. _____ occurs when government removes legal constraints to allow greater competition in industries that once were regulated.

34. A period of falling prices that erodes values and business confidence is known as _____.

35. Wholesale prices paid by sellers for finished , intermediate, and crude goods are tracked by the indices known as the _____.

36. The widest measure of a nation's economic activity, the _____, counts the dollar value of all the goods and services produced within a nation's borders.

37. A nation's _____ measures the relationship between that nation's output of goods and services and the inputs needed to produce them.

Analysis of Learning Goals

Learning Goal 3.1: Distinguish between microeconomics and macroeconomics.

True or False

1. ___ Macroeconomics deals with large issues that affect a country's overall economy.

2. ___ Microeconomics is concerned with the economic activities of an individual or a firm.

3. ___ Government policy that impacts the overall economy is a good example of a microeconomic issue.

4. ___ While macroeconomics looks at economic policies within individual nations, it has no application in understanding the overall world economy.

Learning Goal 3.2: Explain the factors that drive demand and supply.

Short Answer

1. List and define the factors that the collectively determine demand.

   a.

   b.

   c.

   d.

   e.

   f.

2. List and define the factors that collectively determine supply.

   a.

   b.

Name_____ Instructor_____

Section _____ Date_____

    c.

    d.

Learning Goal 3.3:   Compare the three major types of economic systems.

True or False

1. ___   Socialism is an economic system in which the government owns all the nation's productive capacity.

2. ___   Most modern economies blend free enterprise with some degree of government regulation and are known as mixed market economies.

3. ___   Karl Marx is credited with developing the Communist theory.

4. ___   Under communism, the government owns and operates only the basic industries.

5. ___   Communism and Socialism are both planned economies in which government controls determine economic goals and economic allocations.

Learning Goal 3.4: Describe each of the four different types of market structures in a private enterprise system

Listing. List the four basic types of competition.

1. _____   The industry is made up of many firms of similar size whose products are indistinguishable.

2. _____   Producers are able to differentiate their products.

3. _____   There is only one seller in the industry.

4. _____   Because the industries require large capital investment, there are very few producers.

Learning Goal 3.5: Identify and describe the four stages of the business cycle.

Multiple Choice

1. The stage characterized by low unemployment and strong consumer confidence is
    called:

    a. prosperity.   c. recovery.
    b. recession.   d. depression.

2. A contraction in the gross domestic product (GDP) that lasts six months or more is
    called:

    a. prosperity.   c. recovery.
    b. recession.   d. depression.

3. When an economic slowdown continues in a downward spiral over a long period of
    time, we have:

    a. prosperity.   c. recovery.
    b. recession.   d. depression.

4. After an economic downturn, when consumer spending begins to increase and
    business activity accelerates, the country is in:

    a. prosperity.   c. recovery.
    b. recession.   d. depression

Learning Goal 3.6: Explain how productivity, price-level changes, and employment
levels affect the stability of a nation's economy.

True or False

1. ___ A general decline in the prices of goods and services is known as inflation.

2. ___ The most important measure of a company or nation's efficiency and
        competitiveness is its level of productivity.

3. ___ Unemployment usually declines during a recession.

4. ___ Inflation can result from the shortages created by excess demand and/or the
        increased costs of production

Name_____ Instructor_____

Section _____ Date_____

5. ____ A rise in the cost of materials or labor can produce cost-push inflation.

6. ____ The most widely used measure of inflation in the United States is the Consumer Price Index (CPI).

Learning Goal 3.7: Discuss how monetary policy and fiscal policy are used to manage an economy's performance.

Short Answer

1.   Define monetary policy.

2.   Define fiscal policy.

3.   Give examples of how monetary and fiscal policy can be used to combat inflation and unemployment.

Learning Goal 3.8: Describe the major global economic challenges of the 21st century.

Short Answer

There are five interrelated areas on which American businesses should concentrate to meet the global economic challenges of the 21st century. Briefly list and explain each.

1.

2.

3.

4.

5.

Name_____ Instructor_____

Section _____ Date_____

Self Review

True or False

1. ____ Economics is the study of people and the choices they make using scarce resources.

2. ____ Microeconomics addresses such questions as how to maintain an adequate supply of the resources people want, and whether demand will exceed availability.

3. ____ If consumers' incomes increase more products may be sold, in other words, the demand curve is shifted to the right.

4. ____ If the demand curve shifts to the right and the supply curve remains constant, the equilibrium price will increase.

5. ____ The shift from a manufacturing to a service economy has required workers with different skills, resulting in structural unemployment.

6. ____ A restrictive monetary policy helps reduce inflation.

7. ____ As in any competitive situation, global competition focuses exclusively on keeping costs down.

8. ____ Global competitiveness depends on improving working skills to take full advantage of new technologies that enhance use, management and control of information.

9. ____ Macroeconomics deals with the study of the overall operations of an economy and its various components.

10. ____ Policies to reduce unemployment would be primarily a concern of microeconomics.

11. ____ Generally a decrease in the price of travel will increase the demand for travel.

12. ___ If the price of apples increases, consumers may tend to substitute other fruits for apples.

13. ___ A surplus of a product or service will bring the price of that product or service down.

14. ___ Excess demand for a product tends to generate pressure to push the price back down toward equilibrium.

15. ___ A restrictive monetary policy helps reduce unemployment.

16. ___ When the federal government runs a budget deficit, the national debt is also increased.

17. ___ In monopolistic competition, the industry requires such large capital investment that there are very few producers.

18. ___ The major difference between pure and monopolistic competition is whether or not the producers in the industry can differentiate their products.

19. ___ Privatization occurs when private companies are taken over and run by the government.

20. ___ The U.S. Treasury finances the national debt through the sales of Treasury bills, Treasury notes, and Treasury bonds.

Multiple Choice

1. Which of the following is a macroeconomic issue?

   a. inflation.
   b. the business cycle.
   c. unemployment.
   d. all of the above.

2. The common factor that directly impacts both supply and demand is:

   a. government policy.
   b. advertising.
   c. price.
   d. gross domestic product.

Name _____ Instructor_____

Section _____ Date_____

3. If buyer optimism improves:

    a.   the demand curve shifts to the right.
    b.   the demand curve shifts to the left.
    c.   the supply curve shifts to the right.
    d.   the supply curve shifts to the left.

4. The total dollar value of the goods and services produced in a country during a year is known as:

    a.   the business cycle.   c.   the consumer price index.
    b.   gross domestic product.   d.   all of the above.

5. When the United States government influences the economy through government spending and tax collections, this is referred to as:

    a.   tax policy.   c.   fiscal policy.
    b.   monetary policy.   d.   political maneuvering.

6. During the late fall retailers tend to hire many people, and in January lay-off many of them. This results in:

    a.   structural unemployment.   c.   seasonal unemployment.
    b.   cyclical unemployment.   d.   frictional unemployment.

7. People with the necessary skills who are temporarily out of work and seeking employment are classified as:

    a.   structurally unemployed.   c.   seasonally unemployed.
    b.   cyclically unemployed.   d.   frictionally unemployed.

8. When the economy has contracted for six months or more, the nation is in a(n):

    a.   recession.   c.   inflationary period.
    b.   recovery period.   d.   depression.

9. To be competitive in a global economy the United States should:

   a. concentrate on developing a more highly skilled work force.
   b. be attentive to the aging of the world's population.
   c. concentrate on producing quality products and enhancing customer service.
   e. all of the above.

10. Microeconomics studies the economic actions of:

   a. individuals.   c. individual firms.
   b. families.   d. all of the above.

11. When prices continue to fall, customers and businesses lose confidence and economic activity is reduced. This phenomenon is known as:

   a. propserity.   c. deflation.
   b. inflation.   d. recovery.

Name _____ Instructor_____

Section _____ Date_____

Application Exercises

Ron Schmidt lost his job at the plant after 10 years working as a production employee. He has been trying to find other employment for over a year, but without success. Jobs either pay much less than he was earning, or require skills he doesn't have.

1.   What kind of unemployment is Ron experiencing?

2.   What suggestions can you make to help Ron find new employment?

Short Essay Questions

1.   What is the business cycle? What is meant when we say that the business cycle has been "flattened?"

2. Define communism, socialism, capitalism, and mixed market economy. How do they differ from one another?

CHAPTER 4

Competing in Global Markets

Chapter Summary: Key Concepts

Why Nations Trade

Importing/exporting

Exporting involves selling products and services abroad; importing, purchasing foreign goods and services. This trade is essential because it helps boost economic growth.

International sources of factors of production

Business decisions to operate abroad depend on the availability, price, and quality of labor, natural resources, capital, and entrepreneurship found in a foreign country.

Size of the international marketplace

Most of the world's population lives outside the developed nations, providing a rich source of new markets. As growth rates in developing nations rise, these places will see improved standards of living and will provide even greater opportunities for global business.

Major world markets

While the major U.S. trading partners are Canada and Mexico, the U.S. has other important global partners in all the world's major market regions. Most of the world's most attractive emerging markets are located around the Pacific Rim and in Latin America.

Absolute and comparative advantage

A country has an absolute advantage when it can maintain a monopoly or consistently produce at a lower cost than any competitor. This is very rare today. A comparative advantage occurs when a nation can produce one good more efficiently than can other producers, and then exports what it does best. Each nation exploiting its comparative advantage in the global marketplace leads to higher standards of living everywhere.

Measuring Trade between Nations

Balance of trade	The relationship between a country's imports and exports.
Balance of payments	The flow of money into or out of a country.
Major U.S. exports and imports	The U.S. leads the world in the international trade of goods and services. Strong prosperity and diversity make the U.S. the world's leading importer. While the U.S. is a major importer of goods, it is also a major exporter of technical, business, and financial services.
Exchange rates	The value of one nation's currency relative to the currencies of other countries. These values fluctuate in free floating exchange markets depending on each country's relative trade and investment prospects.

Barriers to International Trade

Social and cultural differences	Differences in language, values, and religious attitudes are challenges that must be recognized and overcome in the global marketplace.
Economic differences	Infrastructures vary widely, and must be considered when doing business in another country. Differing currencies and their relative shifts in value must also be considered.
Political and legal differences	Changing political climates in many parts of the world have changed the market and legal environments in these places. International business requires managers to be aware of three dimensions of law: U.S. law, international regulations, and the laws in the countries where they plan to trade. To regulate international commerce, the U.S. and many other countries have ratified treaties and other agreements.
Types of trade restrictions	Tariffs are taxes or surcharges imposed on imported goods, and may be levied for the purposes of generating revenue for a government or protecting domestic industries. Nontariff barriers include quotas, measures to prevent dumping, the embargo, and exchange controls.

Reducing Barriers to International Trade

Organizations promoting international trade
Organizations that promote international trade include the General Agreement on Tariffs and Trade (GATT), its successor, the World Trade Organization (WTO), the World Bank, and the International Monetary Fund (IMF).

International economic communities
International economic communities such as NAFTA and the European Union have developed. They try to reduce trade barriers and promote regional economic integration.

Going Global

Levels of involvement
Direct and indirect exporting is the simplest and least risky level. Countertrade occurs when payments are made in local products instead of currency. Contractual agreements such as franchising, foreign licensing or subcontracting involve more risk but also more control. Firms can make direct investment in a foreign market through acquisitions, joint ventures, or establishing an overseas division for greater control accompanied by greater risk.

Multinational firms
Firms that operate production and/or marketing facilities on an international level. These firms also integrate capital, technologies, and even ideas from their various global operations.

Sources of export assistance
The U.S. Department of Commerce provides information about federal export programs, access to other trade information, and foreign commercial guides. They can also offer advice and help businesspeople find foreign contacts.

Developing a Strategy for International Business

Global business strategies
Uses a single standardized product or marketing effort to address the same market segments in the firm's domestic and foreign markets.

Multidomestic business strategies
Develops and markets products to serve different needs and tastes of separate national markets.

Business Vocabulary

absolute advantage	global business strategy
balance of payments	importing
balance of trade	infrastructure
comparative advantage	International Monetary Fund (IMF)
countertrade	joint venture
devaluation	maquiladora
dumping	multinational corporation (MNC)
cmbargo	multidomestic business strategy
European Union (EU)	North American Free Trade
exchange control	Agreement (NAFTA)
exchange rate	protective tariffs
exporting	quota
floating exchange rates	revenue tariffs
franchise	subcontracting
foreign licensing agreement	World Bank
General Agreement on Trade	World Trade Organization (WTO)
and Tariffs (GATT)	

Application of Vocabulary

Select the term from the list above that best completes the statements beginning below.
Write that term in the space provided.

1. _____ is selling domestically produced products abroad.

2. Buying foreign goods and raw materials is defined as _____.

3. _____ is the relationship between a country's exports and imports.

4. _____ is the relationship between the flow of money into and out of a country.

5. The reduction in value of a country's currency is called _____.

6. The _____ of a country is based on the rate at which its currency is valued against other currencies.

Name _____ Instructor _____

Section _____ Date _____

7. In rare situations, a country has a monopolistic position in the international market, known as a(n)_____.

8. A country is said to have a (n) _____ when that country can supply a product more efficiently or at a lower cost than other countries can.

9. Today, _____ means that the value of a country's currency responds to the international market's supply and demand for that currency.

10. _____ are taxes on imports designed to raise funds for the government of the importing country.

11. In order to help domestic industries a _____ limits the number of products in certain categories that can be imported.

12. A complete ban on importing certain products is called an _____.

13. Governments that control access to foreign currency exchange in accordance with national policy are exercising _____.

14. A _____ is a contractual agreement in which a wholesaler or retailer gains the right to sell another company's products under that firm's brand name in compliance with that firm's operating requirements.

15. If a country tries to penetrate foreign markets by selling goods or services abroad at a price lower than it charges in its own domestic market, it is engaged in

_____.

16. The _____ is the accord that removes trade barriers among Canada, Mexico, and the United States over a 15 year period.

17. The _____ is involved with making short term loans to countries in order to promote international trade.

18. A contractual agreement in which one firm allows another to produce or sell its product or use its trademark, patent, or manufacturing processes in a specific geographic area in exchange for royalties is a _____.

19. International bartering agreements used to facilitate trade are known as

_____.

20. _____ occurs when a firm hires a local company to produce, distribute, or sell a good or service in a foreign market.

21. A corporation that operates, produces, and/or markets on an international level is known as a _____.

22. Taxes on imports designed to discourage foreign competition with domestic industries are known as _____.

23. The _____ is an international trade accord to reduce tariffs and standardize trading rules worldwide.

24. The _____ makes long-term loans for economic development projects.

25. A firm following a _____ uses a standardized product and marketing strategy worldwide.

26. If a firm relies on market segmentation to identify specific foreign markets, tailoring the marketing mix to match their specific traits, it is using a _____ _____.

27. A country's basic system of communication, transportation, energy and other utility resources is collectively called its _____.

28. A _____ is a cooperative agreement that allows a company to share risks, costs, profits, and management responsibilities with one or more partners in the host country.

29. A(n) _____ is a foreign-owned factory along the U.S.-Mexican border that hires lower-wage workers to produce lot cost product for sale mostly in the United States.

30. The federation of 25 European countries that seeks to protect and promote trade among them is called the _____.

31. The _____ is the institution with 135 member countries that succeeds GATT in monitoring and enforcing trade agreements.

Name _____ Instructor _____

Section _____ Date _____

Analysis of Learning Goals

Learning Goal 4.1: Explain the importance of international business and the main reasons nations trade.

True or False

1. ___ Overall, foreign trade now accounts for less than 10% of U.S. gross domestic product.

2. ___ The U.S. has important trading partners in each of the world's major market regions: North America, Western Europe, the Pacific Rim, and Latin America.

3. ___ Trading with other countries increases a company's dependence on economic conditions in its home market.

4. ___ International trade helps companies spread risk, and provides new sources of both customers and employees.

Learning Goal 4.2: Discuss the relationship of absolute and comparative advantage to international trade.

Multiple Choice

1. If a nation has the ability to produce a product at lower cost and higher efficiency than it can supply other products, that nation has:

   a. an absolute advantage.   d. an excellent work force.
   b. a comparative advantage.   e. luck.
   c. a monopoly.

2. A country that is the sole producer, or can produce an item for less than any other nation, has:

   a. an absolute advantage.   d. a slight advantage
   b. a comparative advantage.   e. luck.
   c. an oligopoly

3.   Specialization of production among nations:

   a.   allows each nation to focus on producing what it does best.
   b.   means consumers have access to the most efficient producers of goods and services they want to buy.
   c.   is the basis of international trade.
   d.   is a major means of raising the standard of living for people throughout the world
   e.   all of the above.

Learning Goal 4.3: Describe how nations measure international trade and the significance of exchange rates.

True or False

1. ___   If imports exceed exports, a country is said to have a favorable balance of trade.

2. ___   An unfavorable balance of trade results in a trade deficit.

3. ___   A strong dollar helps the U.S. create a favorable balance of trade.

4. ___   The value of a nation's currency against other currencies varies with the nation's trade and investment prospects.

5. ___   The overall flow of money into or out of a country comprises that country's balance of trade.

6. ___   All of the world's hard currencies are based on a fixed standard: the price of gold.

Learning Goal 4.4: Identify the major barriers that confront global businesses.

Short Answer

Each of the following represents a potential obstacle to global business. Define and give an example of each.

1.   Social and cultural barriers.

Name _____ Instructor _____

Section _____ Date _____

2. Economic differences.

3. Political and legal obstacles.

4. Tariffs and trade restrictions.

Learning Goal 4.5: Explain how international trade organizations and economic communities reduce barriers to international trade.

True or False

1. ___ Where obstacles to multinational economic integration still exist, the trend is toward greater free trade.

2. ___ The European Union (EU) has the goal of erasing trade barriers throughout Europe.

3. ___ The General Agreement on Trade and Tariffs (GATT) has been succeeded by the World Trade Organization (WTO) and includes 135 countries.

4. ___ NAFTA created a free trade zone between Canada, Mexico, and the U.S.

5. ___ The World Bank is also known as the International Monetary Fund (IMF).

Learning Goal 4.6: Compare the different levels of involvement used by businesses when entering global markets.

True or False

1. ___   A country that produces goods at home and sells them abroad is engaged in exporting.

2. ___   Contracting with a foreign manufacturer to produce a product rather than exporting it is known as foreign licensing.

3. ___   Franchising is an especially appropriate means for selling services abroad.

4. ___   Direct investment occurs when a firm acquires or creates production or marketing facilities abroad.

5. ___   In general, the greater degree of control a company exercises through foreign investment, the less risk the company faces.

Learning Goal 4.7: Distinguish between a global business strategy and a multidomestic business strategy.

True or False

1. ___   A company that produces one standard product to be sold worldwide has adopted a global business strategy.

2. ___   When a unique product and/or marketing strategy is designed for each foreign market, a multidomestic business strategy is in use.

3. ___   A multidomestic business strategy greatly reduces the costs and risks of selling in different markets.

4. ___   If a firm wants to develop product and/or marketing strategies to appeal to buying habits of particular national markets, it is utilizing a global business strategy.

Name _____ Instructor _____

Section _____ Date _____

Self Review

True or False

1. ___ The United States is the world's largest importer.

2. ___ Foreign trade is less critical to the United States than to countries such as Mexico.

3. ___ When a nation's exports exceed its imports, it is said to have a favorable balance of trade.

4. ___ A favorable balance of payments means that there is a net money flow into the nation.

5. ___ Countertrade is often used to enter markets of developing nations who don't otherwise have enough credit or currency to buy the imports it wants.

6. ___ Dumping refers to a practice of countries carrying their waste products out to sea beyond their international boundary and disposing of them in the ocean.

7. ___ An embargo is a tax levied on products imported from abroad.

8. ___ The European Union is a common market.

9. ___ A revenue tariff produces revenue for the government of the importing country.

10. ___ A complete ban on certain products is called a tariff.

11. ___ In a free trade area, the participants have no tariffs or trade restrictions.

12. ___ A joint venture shares the costs, risks, and management of foreign operations with a foreign firm or government.

13. ___ Exchange control is the regulation of foreign trade through a central bank or government agency.

14. ___ If a firm allows a foreign company to produce and distribute its products or use its trademarks or patents, it is engaged in dumping.

15. ___ International tariff levels are regulated by the International Monetary Fund.

16. ___ The International Monetary Fund was established to make long-term loans to countries requiring assistance in conducting trade.

17. ___ Virtually all successful global exporters are large firms.

18. ___ Population growth in developed nations is significantly greater than in developing nations.

19. ___ The number one trading partner of the United States is now China.

20. ___ A country's size, per-capital income, and stage of economic development are among the economic factors to consider when evaluating it as a candidate for an international business venture.

Multiple Choice

1. Which of the following does *NOT* affect the U.S. balance of payments?

   a. tourism
   b. military expenditures abroad
   c. congressional budget actions
   d. foreign investments
   e. exports

2. U.S. firms operating abroad must conform to:

   a. U.S. law.
   b. host country law.
   c. international regulations.
   d. all of the above.

3. As a result of U.S. ability to grow wheat, there is a surplus. What is the most profitable short-term method to handle the surplus?

   a. export the wheat
   b. lower the selling price
   c. store the surplus until there is a domestic shortage
   d. advertise it on television
   e. stop planting wheat

Name _____ Instructor _____

Section _____ Date _____

4. At the end of the year, a country with limited resources determined that the amount of goods it imported was approximately 30 percent more than the amount of domestically produced goods it exported. This country has experienced:

   a. a favorable balance of payments.
   b. a successful attempt at self-sufficiency.
   c. an unfavorable balance of trade.
   d. an absolute advantage.
   e. all of the above.

5. To help reverse an unfavorable balance of payments, a country might:

   a. import more foreign goods.
   b. supply an underdeveloped nation with personnel and equipment to help start a new industry.
   c. start a campaign to encourage foreign tourists.
   d. establish a military base in a friendly foreign country.
   e. encourage its citizens to travel abroad.

6. Business firms that invest in foreign countries may be contributing to their own country's:

   a. unfavorable balance of payments.
   b. ability to import more foreign goods.
   c. employment standards.
   d. favorable balance of trade.

7. Obstacles to international trade that occur due to uncertain transportation, poor communications systems, and unreliable utility systems are examples of:

   a. cultural barriers.   c. tariffs and trade restrictions.
   b. weak infrastructures.   d. political and legal obstacles.

8. The price of imported goods is increased by:

   a. an evaluation of a nation's currency.
   b. a devaluation of a nation's currency.
   c. a revaluation of a nation's currency.
   d. the strengthening of a nation's currency.

9. A floating exchange rate:

    a. depends on the world price of gold.
    b. is currently unpopular with most industrial nations.
    c. automatically leads to devaluation of a nation's currency.
    d. varies according to market conditions.
    e. depends on the level of rainfall.

10. The international business arrangement whereby Saudi Arabia sells oil to Japan in return for fresh water would be an example of :

    a. absolute advantage.   d. countertrade.
    b. exchange rate fluctuation.   e. specialization.
    c. licensing.

11. The lender of last resort for troubled nations is the:

    a. World Bank.   c. NAFTA.
    b. International Monetary Fund (IMF).   d. World Trade Organization (WTO).

12. A tax on imports is a(n):

    a. quota.   c. tariff.
    b. embargo.   d. exchange control.

13. A foreign firm given the right to produce, sell, or utilize a trademark, patent or process in exchange for royalty payments is a(n):

    a. revenue agent.   c. license holder.
    b. joint venture.   d. exporter.

Application Exercise

During a conversation between the director of the international division and the president of a motor manufacturing company, the international director stated that the firm is less and less involved in direct or indirect exporting and more involved in international production. She noted that it may be to the firm's advantage to either enter into a joint venture or set up a foreign licensing agreement with some other countries.

Name _____ Instructor _____

Section _____ Date _____

The president also stated that while she is familiar with direct and indirect exporting, she knows very little about joint ventures or foreign licensing agreements. She wants the director to write up a report explaining each arrangement.

What should be included in the report?

Short Essay Questions

1. The United States has been running a trade deficit for several years. What exactly is a trade deficit, and how does it arise? What steps might the U.S. take to reverse this situation?

2. "If each country were to produce the product(s) in which it enjoys a comparative advantage, the standard of living worldwide would be enhanced." What exactly is a comparative advantage? Is the statement above true or false? Why?

PART I APPENDIX

The Legal Framework for Business

Summary: Key Concepts

Legal System and Administrative Agencies

Law	Standards set by the government and society in the form of legislation or custom.
Judiciary system	The branch of government charged with deciding disputes through the application of laws. Includes federal, state, and local courts.
Administrative agencies	Often created by law, they monitor and enforce the laws. The Security and Exchange Commission (SEC) and the Environmental Protection Agency (EPA) are examples.

Types of Law

Common law	Body of law arising out of judicial decisions.
Statutory law	Written law, including state and federal constitutions and legislation. Also included are treaties and local ordinances.
International law	Numerous regulations govern international commerce, including domestic laws of trading partners, trade agreements such as NAFTA, and rulings of such organizations as the World Trade Organization.
Business law	All law affects business. Laws that directly influence and regulate the management of business activities are included in the narrow definition of business law.

Regulatory Environment for Business

Antitrust and business regulation	The laws detailed in the first table on page 142 are designed to prevent monopolies, ensure fair competition, ban deceptive advertising, and require diligence in tracing funds used in international business transactions.
Business deregulation	The laws shown in the second table on page 142 were passed to replace federal regulation with free market tools in specific industries. Deregulation seeks to enhance efficiency and lower prices to customers.

Laws to Protect Consumers, Employees, Investors and to Regulate Cyberspace and Telecommunications

Consumer protection	The first table on page 143 details major federal legislation that protects consumers in areas such as credit, product safety, environmental protection, and labeling of consumer products. Many states and local governments have also passed specific laws to protect their consumers.
Employee protection	The second table on page 143 details laws passed that insure fair pay, a safe workplace, freedom from workplace discrimination, the ability to take family leave, and assistance to the unemployed.
Investor protection	The first table on page 144 lists three important pieces of legislation. These laws regulate public transactions of securities, and create agencies to oversee securities, accounting, and banking practices.
Cyberspace and telecommunications protection	The second table on page 144 list some of the major laws enacted to regulate cyberspace and telecommunications. Specifically these laws are aimed at reducing fraud and abuse, preventing cyberterrorism, and protecting online privacy.

The Core of Business Law

Contract law

Deals with legally enforceable agreements. Four elements necessary for an enforceable contract are agreement, consideration, legal and serious purpose, and capacity.

Law of agency

Describes a legal relationship in which one party, the principal, appoints another party, the agent, to enter into contracts with third parties. The principal is generally bound by the actions of the agent.

Uniform commercial code

This contains laws that regulate businesses with regard to sales, warranties for sales transactions, and negotiable instruments. Sales law concerns the sale and transfer of goods and services for money or credit. Warranties are express or implied. Negotiable instruments are forms of commercial paper that are transferable among individuals and businesses.

Property law and law of bailment

Property law deals with the rights to own, use, and dispose of tangible, intangible, and real property. The law of bailment governs the surrender of personal property that is to be returned at a later date.

Trademarks, patents, and copyrights

Legal protection given to the owners of these intangible assets.

Law of torts

Refers to civil wrong inflicted on another person or their property. Includes intentional wrongdoing, slander, libel, fraud, and negligence. One especially important area of tort law for business deals with product liability.

Bankruptcy law

Covers the legal nonpayment of financial obligations with the dual purpose of protecting creditors by providing a way to seize and distribute the debtors' assets, and also protecting debtors by allowing them to start fresh as contributors to society. There are laws that govern both personal and business bankruptcies.

Name_____ Instructor_____

Section_____ Date_____

Tax law   Taxes are levied by the federal, state, county, and
                               local governmental units. They generate revenues
                               government uses to buy industry's goods and services,
                               and to perform other government functions.

Business Vocabulary

agency	law
appellate court	negotiable instruments
bankruptcy	patent
breach of contract	product liability
business law	sales law
common law	statutory law
contract	taxes
copyright	tort
damages	trademarks
international law	trial court
judiciary	

Application of Vocabulary

Select the term from the list above that best completes the statements below. Write that term in the space provided.

1. The _____ is an enforceable set of rules and standards governing interpersonal and institutional relationships in an organized society.

2. The body of law arising out of judicial decisions related to the unwritten law the United States inherited from England is known as _____.

3. Written law, including federal and state constitutions, legislative enactments, treaties of the federal government, and ordinances of local governments are called _____
   _____.

4. The _____ is a higher court that can review and correct any lower court error.

Name_____ Instructor_____

Section_____ Date_____

5. A _____ is a legally enforceable agreement between two or more parties regarding a specified act or thing.

6. The court system is that branch of government known as the _____.

7. _____ governs the sales of goods or services for money or credit.

8. _____ are the assessments by which government units raise revenue.

9. When a valid contract has been violated we say there has been a _____ _____.

10. Court awarded financial payments to compensate for a loss and related suffering are known as _____.

11. The legal nonpayment of financial obligations of businesses or individuals is called _____.

12. A _____ protects written material, such as books, designs, photos, computer software, and the like, for the author's lifetime, plus 70 years. In cases where a business is the creator of the asset, protection lasts 95 years.

13. A _____ guarantees an inventor exclusive rights to an invention for 17 years.

14. The numerous regulations that govern international commerce are collectively known as _____.

15. A _____ is any civil wrong inflicted on another person or the person's property.

16. _____ consists of those aspects of law that most directly influence and regulate the management of various types of business activity.

17. Any court of general jurisdiction, such as a circuit court, district court, or superior court is known as a _____.

18. The area of tort law that holds businesses liable for negligence in the design, manufacture, sale, and/or use of products is _____.

19. Legally protected words, symbols, or other designations used to identify a product are known as _____.

20. Checks, drafts, certificates of deposit, notes, or any commercial paper that is transferable among individuals and businesses are called _____ _____.

21. A(n) _____ relationship exists when one party, called a *principal*, appoints another party, called the *agent*, to enter into contracts with third parties on the principal's behalf.

Self Review

True or False

1. ___ Business taxes are the largest single source of revenue for the federal government.

2. ___ Real property refers to any tangible personal property.

3. ___ Intangible property consists of documents or other written instruments.

4. ___ Strict liability is the legal concept that covers injuries caused by products regardless of whether the manufacturer is proven negligent.

5. ___ A company is generally held liable for injuries inflicted by its products if such injuries result from negligence on the part of the producer in the design, manufacturing, sale, or use of the product.

6. ___ Something for which people have the unrestricted right of possession and use is called a warranty.

7. ___ Tort law compensates injured persons who are the victims of noncriminal wrongs.

8. ___ A contract must be for a lawful purpose to be legally enforceable.

9. ___ Businesses can be held liable for the negligence of their employees or other agents under agency law.

10. ___ Common law deals with precedent.

11. ___ Statutory law is law by enactment.

Name_____ Instructor_____

Section_____ Date_____

12. ___ The federal, state, and local government units can all enact laws.

13. ___ A warranty only exists if it is in writing.

14. ___ While businesses can declare bankruptcy, individuals cannot.

15. ___ It is illegal for two government units to both tax the same income.

16. ___ The FTC has broad powers to investigate business practices and to insure fair competition.

17. ___ There are still no federal laws regulating cyberspace.

18. ___ It is now easier than ever for individuals to declare bankruptcy.

Multiple Choice

1. Those aspects of law that most directly influence and regulate the management of various type of business activity are know as:

   a. business law.
   b. criminal law.
   c. international law.
   d. unified law.

2. A body of unwritten legal principles developed from past court cases is called:

   a. statutory law.
   b. common law.
   c. unified law.
   d. civil law.

3. The authority that a court has to hear a particular matter or case is called:

   a. trial coverage.
   b. jurisdiction.
   c. court districts.
   d. priority.

4. All of the following are courts of general jurisdiction *EXCEPT*:

   a. superior courts.
   b. circuit courts.
   c. district courts.
   d. tax courts.

5. A legally enforceable agreement between two or more individuals or businesses is a:

    a. tort.   c. law.
    b. contract.   d. bailment.

6. Something of legal value that each party involved in a contract agrees to exchange is known as:

    a. consideration.   c. contractual capacity.
    b. mutual assent.   d. a gift.

7. The losing party in a trial court has a right to ask a higher court to review the case for errors in the trial court's interpretations. This process is known as:

    a. mediation.   c. appeal.
    b. repeal.   d. reversal.

8. When one party agrees to provide a service for another party, and both parties agree in writing on date, time, and price, they are entered into a:

    a. contract.   c. service agreement.
    b. commercial agreement.   d. tort.

9. All the following are elements of a contract, *EXCEPT*:

    a. agreement.   d. consideration.
    b. capacity.   e. reward.
    c. legal purpose.

10. The legal ability of a person to enter into a contract is called:

    a. the legal value of the exchange.   c. ability of the person.
    b. capacity of the person.   d. legality of the person.

11. In exchange for $1,000 one person asked another person to drive the getaway car after a bank robbery. The second person agreed, but later refused to follow through with it. This would not be a binding contract because it lacked:

    a. consideration.   c. legal purpose.
    b. capacity.   d. mutual assent.

Name _____ Instructor _____

Section _____ Date _____

12. Intangible personal property includes all of the following, *EXCEPT*:

    a. inventory.
    b. copyrights.
    c. patents.
    d. trademarks.
    e. stocks.

13. A body of statutes that replaced several areas of business law formerly covered individually by each state's common law of contracts is known as the:

    a. Uniform Sales Contract.
    b. Unified Contract of Sales.
    c. Universal Commercial Act.
    d. Uniform Commercial Code.
    e. Interstate Contract of Sales.

14. A patent is an exclusive right granted by the federal government to the inventor for:

    a. five years.
    b. seventeen years.
    c. twenty-two years.
    d. the creator's lifetime plus fifty years.
    e. ever.

15. A copyright is an exclusive right granted by the federal government to an individual creator for:

    a. fifty years.
    b. one hundred years.
    c. the creator's lifetime.
    d. the creator's lifetime plus seventy years.
    e. ever.

16. For a company, the copyright for a creation lasts:

    a. 95 years.
    b. fifty years.
    c. forever.
    d. is the same as for individual creators.

17. The procedure by which a negotiable instrument is made transferable by signing the back of the instrument is called:

    a. consideration.
    b. endorsement.
    c. negotiable signature.
    d. agreement.
    e. consent.

18. The body of laws that deals with granting the right of one person to use another person's property is known as the law of:

    a. bailment.
    b. use.
    c. agreement.
    d. consent.
    e. borrowing.

19. The bankruptcy law that pertains to businesses which allows the firm to reorganize and develop a plan of repayment is known as:

    a. Chapter 1.
    b. Chapter 9.
    c. Chapter 11.
    d. Chapter 18.
    e. Chapter 24.

20. Federal regulation of business includes:

    a. antitrust law and protection of competition.
    b. consumer, investor, and employee protection.
    c. deregulation.
    d. regulation of cyberspace.
    e. all of the above.

CHAPTER 5

Options for Organizing Small and Large Businesses

Chapter Summary: Key Concepts

Most Businesses are Small Businesses

Small business

A vital component of the our economy, small business accounts for approximately 90% of U.S. firms. A small business is generally defined as being a minor player in its industry, having relatively few employees, and one that is independently owned, operated, and managed.

Typical Ventures

Small businesses in America operate in nearly all industries, but tend to be concentrated in the retail, construction and services sectors of the economy.

Home-based businesses

There is a growing trend for firms to be operated from the residence of the business owner. This growth in home-based businesses is expected to continue and even accelerate in the first decade of the 21st century.

Contributions of Small Business to the Economy

Importance of small business

Small businesses create more new jobs in the U.S. economy than do larger firms. They create new industries and are important to local economic growth. They offer attractive opportunities to women and minorities, and are key providers of employment to immigrants and former welfare recipients.

Advantages of small business

Small business are key innovative engines in both products and business processes. They excel in providing outstanding customer service, operating at lower cost, and filling isolated market niches.

Unique challenges for small businesses

Small businesses must operate with fewer resources than large ones, can suffer from financial limitations and management inadequacies, and often find that taxes and government regulation impose excessive burdens.

Increasing the Likelihood of Business Success

Business plan   A written document that clearly states the business
                                  objectives, specific plans for their achievement, and the
                                  standards by which the business will measure its
                                  performance.

**Small Business   A federal government agency providing aid, counsel,
Administration (SBA)**   and assistance to small business in areas such as funding,
                                  management, and bidding on government contracts.

Business incubators   Local community agencies have increasingly developed
                                  low-cost, shared business facilities to small, start-up
                                  ventures. They generally offer management support
                                  services, shared clerical staff, and advice from in-house
                                  mentors.

Corporate alliances   Many small businesses have formed alliances with larger
                                  firms to help achieve mutual goals.

Small Business Opportunities for Women and Minorities

**Growing Importance   Small businesses offer attractive opportunities to women
of women and minorities**   and minorities, and an increasing proportion of small
                                 businesses have been started by these segments of our
                                 population.

Women-Owned Businesses   Almost 2 of every 5 U.S. businesses are owned by
                                 women. Women have opened businesses at an increasing
                                 rate, particularly in construction, wholesale trade,
                                 transportation and communications, agribusiness, and
                                 manufacturing industries.

Minority Owned Businesses   In recent years, the growth in the number of businesses
                                 owned by African Americans, Hispanics, and Asian
                                 Americans has far outpaced the growth in the number of
                                 U.S. businesses overall. Immigrants are especially likely
                                 to open small businesses. Hispanics are the nation's
                                 largest group of minority business owners, and even more
                                 growth lies ahead for this group due to NAFTA.

The Franchising Alternative

Franchising
A business arrangement involving a contract between the franchisor and the franchisee. This contract specifies the operational and marketing methods the franchisee is expected to use and the aid the franchisor will offer as a product or service is brought to market.

Benefits to Franchisor
Franchising allows the franchisor to expand the business more rapidly, and assures motivated managers in new business units.

Benefits to Franchisee
Benefits include prior performance record, a tested management program, and business training.

Problems in Franchising
Franchise fees and future payments are costly to franchisees. They may give up some independence under the franchise contract, and the entire franchise can be adversely affected by bad performance at one franchise unit.

Small Business Goes Global

Importance in global commerce
Modern information technology and the expertise of many minority and immigrant business owners have combined to make small business an important component of U.S. international trade. U.S. Exporting is dominated by firms with fewer than 500 employees.

Growth Strategies
Licensing agreements and the reach of the Internet allow small businesses to reach international markets quickly.

Alternatives for Organizing a Business

Sole proprietorship
Ownership (and usually operation) of an organization by a single individual.

Partnership
An association of two or more persons who operate a business as co-owners by voluntary agreement.

Corporation

An association of persons created by statute as a legal entity with authority to act and have liability separate and apart from its owners. It is owned by stockholders, with a board of directors having governing authority.

Organizing and Operating a Corporation

Types of corporations

A firm is considered a domestic corporation in the state where it is incorporated, while foreign corporations are those who do business in one state while being incorporated in another. Alien corporations operate in the U.S. but are incorporated in another country.

Corporate charter

Once a business decides where it wants to incorporate, a corporate charter must be submitted to that state.

Levels of management

Corporations generally have three levels of management: top managers, middle managers, and supervisory managers. Top management is appointed by the Board of Directors, who in turn, are elected by the stockholders.

Employee ownership

The firm is purchased by the employees, thus they are now the owners and employees.

Not-for-profit corporations

These firms pursue objectives other than returning profits to owners. Charitable groups social welfare organizations, and religious congregations are obvious examples. These organizations do not issue or sell stock, and they are exempt from paying income taxes.

When Businesses Join Forces

Mergers

Two or more firms that combine--vertically, horizontally, or from unrelated industries (conglomeration)--to form a new organization for more efficient operation.

Acquisitions

One firm purchases the property and assumes the obligations of another, or when one firm buys a division or subsidiary from another firm.

Name _____ Instructor _____

Section _____ Date _____

Public and Collective Ownership

Public ownership   The ownership and operation of an organization by a
                              government unit or agency.

Cooperatives   Business owners join forces to collectively operate all or
                              part of the functions in their industry.

Business Vocabulary

acquisition
alien corporation
business incubator
business plan
board of directors
closely held corporation
common stockholders
conglomerate merger
cooperative
corporation
corporate charter
domestic corporation
foreign corporation
franchise
franchisee
franchisor
home-based business

horizontal merger
inside director
joint venture
limited liability company (LLC)
merger
outside directors
partnership
preferred stockholders
public ownership
S corporations
set-aside programs
sole proprietorship
small business
Small Business Administration (SBA)
Small Business Investment Company
     (SBIC)
vertical merger

Application of Vocabulary

Select the term from the list above that best completes the statements beginning on the
next page. Write that term in the space provided.

1. A(n) _____ occurs when one company buys the assets and assumes the liabilities of another firm.

2. A contract that establishes a relationship between a supplier and a dealer of a good or service that specifies the methods the dealer can use is known as a(n)_____

3. The purchaser of a franchise is known as the _____.

4. _____ are companies that sell franchises to independent business people.

5. Under the company form known as a(n) _____ , the firm is governed under an operating agreement resembling a partnership, except that each partner's liability for the actions of the other owners is limited.

6. A corporation that operates in the state in which it was chartered is considered a _____ in that state.

7. A(n) _____ is the legal document granted by the state of incorporation that formally establishes a corporation.

8. A(n) _____ is merger between firms whose businesses are unrelated.

9. The _____, operated from the residence of the business owner, is a widely used and low cost option for new firms.

10. The _____ is the principal federal government agency that aids, counsels, and assists small businesses.

11. The true owners of a corporation, who are empowered to elect the board of directors, are known as the _____.

12. In a(n) _____, one firm combines with another firm in the same industry.

13. _____ is generally defined as any firm that is independently owned and operated, that is not dominant in its market, and that meets a variety of size standards for income and number of employees.

14. A(n) _____ is a legal organization whose assets and liabilities are separate from those of its owner(s).

15. A business that is owned by one person is a(n) _____.

Name _____ Instructor _____

Section _____ Date _____

16. A(n) _____ is an organization in which the owners operate collectively.

17. If a corporation is dissolved, the _____ have the first claim to the corporate assets after all debts have been paid.

18. A corporation incorporated in another country that does business in the United States is called a(n) _____.

19. _____ means an organization is owned and operated by a government unit.

20. Two or more persons who operate a business as co-owners form a(n) _____.

21. A(n) _____ is a corporation with relatively few stockholders whose stock is generally unavailable to outsiders.

22. The governing authority of a corporation, elected by the common stockholders, is called the _____.

23. Members of the board of directors who are not employed by the organization are known as _____.

24. _____ can elect to be taxed as partnerships while maintaining the advantages of corporations.

25. When firms at different levels in the production and/or marketing process decide to combine into one company, a _____ has occurred.

26. A member of the board of directors who is also employed by the corporation is called an _____.

27. When two or more firms combine to make one company, a _____ has occurred.

28. The federal government has enacted _____ to ensure that small businesses will be able to get part of the federal government's business by requiring that all or part of certain government contracts be given to small businesses.

29. A(n) _____ is an organization that provides low-cost common facilities and services to small, start-up businesses.

30. A(n) _____ is a federally licensed investment group that makes loans to small firms.

31. A(n) _____ is a written document that provides an orderly statement of a company's goals, the methods by which it intends to achieve those goals, and the standards by which it will measure achievements.

32. A corporation that has been incorporated in a state other than the one in which it is operating is known as a(n) _____.

33. A partnership between companies formed for a specific undertaking is called a(n) _____.

Analysis of Learning Goals

Learning Goal 5.1: Distinguish between small and large businesses, and identify the industries in which most small firms are established.

Multiple Choice

1. The Small Business Administration defines a small business as:

    a. independently owned and managed.
    b. a firm that is not dominant in its industry.
    c. a firm that meets industry-specific size standards for income or number of employees.
    d. all of the above.

2. The federal government agency that is set up to work with small businesses is the:

    a. BBC.   c. FTC.
    b. SBC.   d. SBA.

3. Which of the following industries tends to attract small business?

    a. retailing.   d. construction.
    b. agriculture.   e. all of the above.
    c. services.

Name _____ Instructor_____

Section _____ Date _____

4. Home-based businesses:

    a. are illegal in most states.
    b. don't have to pay income taxes.
    c. are widespread and rapidly growing
    d. account for fewer than 50% of firms with revenues of $25,000 or less.

Learning Goal 5.2: Discuss the economic and social contributions of small business.

True or False

1. ___ It is fair to say that a strong small business sector is the backbone of the private enterprise system.

2. ___ Many of today's large businesses were started by entrepreneurs.

3. ___ In the United States, the number of small businesses is declining.

4. ___ Almost two-thirds of all new jobs are created by small business.

5. ___ More than half of people in the nation's private work force are employed by small business.

6. ___ Small business accounts for barely one-quarter of the nation's private GDP.

7. ___ Small businesses are more likely to hire recent immigrants and former welfare recipients than are larger businesses.

Learning Goal 5.3: Compare the advantages and disadvantages of small business.

Compare and Contrast

Indicate whether each item below is an advantage or disadvantage of small business.

	Advantage	Disadvantage
1. managerial know how	_____	_____
2. innovative behavior	_____	_____
3. lower operating costs and overhead	_____	_____
4. government regulations	_____	_____
5. financing capability	_____	_____
6. ability to fill market niches	_____	_____
7. personalized customer service	_____	_____

Learning Goal 5.4: Describe how the Small Business Administration assists small-business owners.

Short Answer

List and discuss three major areas in which the Small Business Administration offers programs and services.

1.

2.

3.

Name _____ Instructor_____

Section _____ Date _____

Learning Goal 5.5: Explain how franchising can provide opportunities for both franchisors and franchisees.

True or False

1. ___ A franchise is a contract between a manufacturer or supplier and a dealer that specifies the methods to be used in marketing a good or service.

2. ___ A well established franchise is cheaper to open than an independent small business.

3. ___ Many franchisors offer training services for franchisees and their employees.

4. ___ Major advantages of franchises include a tested management system, name recognition, and a proven business model.

5. ___ The buyer of a franchise is known as the franchisor.

6. ___ One franchise unit can suffer from the actions or poor performance of other units of the same franchise.

7. ___ Franchises offer entrepreneurs greater independence and flexibility than other types of small businesses.

Learning Goal 5.6: Summarize the three basic forms of business ownership and the advantages and disadvantages of each form.

Multiple Choice

1. The most widely used form of business ownership is:

   a. general partnership.   c. corporation.
   b. sole proprietorship.   d. limited partnership.

2. Additional capital is most easily obtained if the form of ownership is a:

    a. general partnership.   c. corporation.
    b. sole proprietorship.   d. limited partnership.

3. Limited financial liability is the most important advantage of which form of ownership?

    a. general partnership.   c. corporation.
    b. sole proprietorship.   d. all of the above.

True or False

4. ___ Sole proprietorships give owners ease of formation and dissolution, maximum flexibility, and the owner retains all the after tax profits.

5. ___ Sole proprietorships suffer from financial limitations and unlimited financial liability.

6. ___ Like sole proprietorships, partnerships are easy to form and dissolve.

7. ___ Major advantages that can be achieved through the partnership form of ownership include complimentary management skills and expanded financial capability.

8. ___ Corporations face fewer tax disadvantages and legal restrictions than other forms of business ownership.

Learning Goal 5.7: Identify the levels of corporate management.

True or False

1. ___ Top managers include job titles like CEO, CFO, President, Mayor, or Governor.

2. ___ Top managers are responsible for the day-to-day operational functions of the firm.

3. ___ Managers who directly supervise employees and coordinate day-to-day operations of the firm are known as supervisory managers.

4. ___ The board of directors is elected by the corporation's common stockholders and appoints top management.

Name _____ Instructor _____

Section _____ Date _____

Learning Goal 5.8: Describe recent trends in mergers and acquisitions.

Multiple Choice

1.   When two or more firms combine to form one company, we say that the firms have:

   a.   practiced divestiture.
   b.   been taken private.
   c.   become a cooperative.
   d.   merged.

2.   When one firm purchases the property and assumes the liabilities of another firm, there has been a(n):

   a.   vertical merger.
   b.   horizontal merger.
   c.   acquisition.
   d.   divestiture.

3.   If a sporting goods manufacturer combines with a firm that operates sporting goods retailers, this would be an example of:

   a.   a vertical merger.
   b.   a horizontal merger.
   c.   a conglomerate merger.
   d.   an employee ownership arrangement.

4.   If this sporting goods manufacturer combined with a food company, this would be an example of:

   a.   a vertical merger.
   b.   a horizontal merger.
   c.   a conglomerate merger.
   d.   public ownership.

5.   If this sporting goods manufacturer combines with a manufacturer of tennis nets, this would be an example of:

   a.   a vertical merger.
   b.   a horizontal merger.
   c.   a conglomerate merger.
   d.   a divestiture.

Learning Goal 5.9: Differentiate among private ownership, public ownership, and collective ownership (cooperatives).

Multiple Choice

1. When a group of wheat farmers collectively purchases a grain elevator, this is an example of:

    a. private ownership.
    b. public ownership.
    c. cooperative ownership.
    d. employee ownership.

2. If the city of Los Angeles owns a parking garage on Main Street, the garage is said to be:

    a. privately owned.
    b. publicly owned.
    c. cooperatively owned.
    d. collectively owned.

3. When a firm's workers own most or all of the firm's stock, it is an example of:

    a. public ownership.
    b. employee ownership.
    c. cooperative ownership.
    d. a firm going private.

4. Private organizations who pursue objectives other than returning profits to the owners are known as:

    a. employee-owned firms.
    b. not-for-profit corporations.
    c. cooperatives.
    d. all of the above.

Self Review

True or False

1. ___ Most businesses in the United States are organized as corporations.

2. ___ The quickest and simplest form of business ownership to start is the sole proprietorship.

3. ___ The government usually offers small businesses the option of foregoing the paperwork required of larger businesses.

4. ___ A partnership is defined as an association of two or more persons who are co-owners of a business.

Name _____ Instructor _____

Section _____ Date _____

5. ___ In a partnership, the death of one partner does not affect the business in any way.

6. ___ Many small business owners get added help in lowering costs by involving family members who often contribute without being paid.

7. ___ A Limited Liability Company (LLC) is governed by an operating agreement similar to a partnership agreement with the advantage of limited liability for owners.

8. ___ A franchise owner typically can generate profits faster than an independent business owner can.

9. ___ On average, more than 60% of small businesses dissolve within six years of being formed.

10. ___ The SBA will lend money to anyone with a really good idea.

11. ___ A corporation is a legal entity separate from the owners.

12. ___ A conglomerate merger is a merger of unrelated firms.

13. ___ Poor management is a frequently cited reason for small business failure.

14. ___ An organization that is operated collectively by its owners is a cooperative.

15. ___ The type of stock that entitles owners to voting rights and represents the true ownership of the corporation is referred to as common stock.

16. ___ Fewer than 25% of businesses in the United States qualify as small businesses.

17. ___ A Small Business Investment Company (SBIC) is an investment group that funds small businesses under an SBA license.

18.___ The number of minority- and women-owned businesses is increasing.

19. ___ An important disadvantage of sole proprietorships is lack of continuity.

20. ___ Because of their many disadvantages, sole proprietorships have largely become a thing of the past.

21. ___ Small business plays a key role in international trade, accounting for approximately 25% of U.S. exports.

Multiple Choice

1. One advantage of purchasing a franchise is:

   a. the purchaser is guaranteed success.
   b. the franchisee gets a tested business model.
   c. there is a great deal of operational independence for the franchisee.
   d. it is usually a cheaper way to open a new business than starting from scratch.

2. When managers or a group of stockholders buy up all of a firm's stock the firm then becomes:

   a. a privately owned corporation.
   b. a cooperative.
   c. an LLC.
   d. a joint venture.

3. When two firms in the same industry merge, it is called a(n):

   a. conglomerate merger.
   b. vertical merger.
   c. horizontal merger.
   d. acquisition.

4. A corporation chartered in another nation but operating in the United States is known as a(n):

   a. domestic corporation.
   b. foreign corporation.
   c. alien corporation.
   d. national corporation.

5. Stockholders who have a prior claim to dividends and assets are known as:

   a. creditors.
   b. preferred stockholders.
   c. common stockholders.
   d. partners.

6. The tier of management responsible for coordinating the day-to-day operations of a firm is:

   a. top management.
   b. middle management.
   c. supervisory management.
   d. the board of directors.

Name _____ Instructor_____

Section _____ Date _____

7. The purpose of a business plan should be to:

   a. clarify the entrepreneur's ideas for a business.
   b. create a document that can be shown to potential investors, lenders, or suppliers.
   c. decide upon the business's organization and structure.
   d. spell out marketing and financial plans.
   e. all of the above.

8. If one firm acquires the property and assumes the obligations of another, it is called a(n):

   a. cooperative.   c. acquisition.
   b. merger.   d. joint venture.

9. Employee ownership:

   a. is a situation in which a firm's workers buy shares of stock in the business.
   b. is growing.
   c. means employees will be eligible to earn dividends.
   d. all of the above.

10. When a government agency or unit owns and operates an organization, it is known as:

   a. private ownership.   c. conglomerate ownership.
   b. public ownership.   d. employee ownership.

11. The formal document that must be submitted to the state in order to form a corporation is known as:

   a. a business plan.   c. a corporate charter.
   b. a corporate merger.   d. corporate management.

12. The group who is elected by stockholders and who hires top management is called:

   a. the Board of Directors.   c. supervisory management.
   b. middle management.   d. not-for-profit management.

13. The owners of a corporation are known as the:

    a. Board of Directors.   c. partners.
    b. stockholders.   d. management.

14. To ensure that small businesses receive a reasonable portion of government procurement contracts, certain government contracts (or portions of those contracts) are reserved for small businesses in what are known as:

    a. joint ventures.   c. set-aside programs.
    b. business incubators.   d. corporate assistance programs.

15. Business incubators:
    a. are generally sponsored by local community agencies.
    b. provide shared space and services for new small businesses.
    c. often offer management counseling and in-house mentors.
    d. all of the above.

Application Exercises

Application Exercise I

Daryl Fox is a self-employed real estate agent. For the past ten years, he has been advising shopping center developers on such things as type and size of centers for given locations. During the course of his business, he has become friendly with the Keller Development Company, which is presently organized as a sole proprietorship. Daryl Fox and Chuck Keller, president of the Keller Development Company, are discussing the possibility of going into business together. Daryl's sister, Delores Reyes, is an accountant and has been employed by a large accounting firm for several years. She, too, would like to have her own business rather than work for someone else. The three of them have decided that they collectively have the necessary skills and funds to start a large-scale operation.

1. What legal form of business ownership should you recommend? Why have you selected that form?

Name _____ Instructor _____

Section _____ Date _____

2. To protect Daryl Fox, Chuck Keller, and Delores Reyes, which form would you not recommend? Why did you make this decision?

3. Do you anticipate any problem areas in this arrangement? If yes, what problems?

4. How would this endeavor benefit Mr. Fox? Mr. Keller? Mrs. Reyes?

Application Exercise II

Winning the state lottery netted Albert DeLuca slightly over $100,000. His good friend Carla Hall is a talented jewelry designer, but does not have any money. Carla suggested that the two of them form a partnership, with Albert investing half his winnings and Carla contributing her talents. They decided on a general partnership. About two weeks later Al left for an around-the-world vacation. Carla stayed on to run the business. When All returned home eight months later, he found that both Carla and the $50,000 were gone. The next day the creditors of the business came to Al with bills in excess of $80,000.

1. What is Al's liability?

2. What is Carla's liability?

3. If you met Al when he won the lottery, what advice would you have given him?

Short Essay Questions

1. What are advantages small business brings to the U.S. economy? What disadvantages must successful small businesses overcome?

Name _____ Instructor _____

Section _____ Date _____

2. What is franchising? How important is franchising as a form of small business?
   What are the advantages and disadvantages franchisees can expect?

3. Name and define the three major forms of business ownership, citing their respective
   advantages and disadvantages.

4.   Define and distinguish a merger and an acquisition. What are the major types of mergers? How do mergers and acquisitions figure into the new global marketplace?

CHAPTER 6

Starting Your Own Business: The Entrepreneurship Alternative

Chapter Summary: Key Concepts

What is an Entrepreneur?

Entrepreneur	The person who seeks a profitable opportunity, and takes the necessary risks to set up and operate a business.
Categories of Entrepreneurs	Classic entrepreneurs identify business opportunities and allocate available resources to tap those markets. Intrapreneurs are entrepreneurially oriented people who seek to develop new products, ideas and ventures within large organizations. Change agents are managers who seek to revitalize established firms.

Reasons to Choose Entrepreneurship as a Career Path

Be your own boss	Many people choose entrepreneurship because of the desire to be self-managed and to have the opportunity to pursue their ideas in their own way.
Financial success	Research shows that self-employed Americans are much more likely to become millionaires than those who work for someone else.
Job security	Many people who have lost their jobs or who have difficulty finding a position during an economic downturn decide to create their own job security by starting their own businesses.
Quality of life	Entrepreneurs have more choice over when, where, and how to work. They can often pursue broader social objectives through their own ventures. And many people believe the flexibility of entrepreneurship will allow them to spend more time with family.

Positive Environment for Entrepreneurship	Conditions have never been better for entrepreneurs. Increased opportunities through globalization, better educational opportunities, information technology, and positive demographic and economic trends make entrepreneurship an attractive career option.

Influence of Entrepreneurs on the Economy

Innovation	Entrepreneurs create new products, build new industries and renew old ones. Entrepreneurs account for the vast majority of invention and innovation over the last 60 years.
Job generation	Fast-growing start-ups (_gazelles_) are the principal job creators in the U.S., while also increasing job opportunities in local economies.
Diversity	The number of women- and minority-owned start-ups has grown tremendously in recent years, and the range of businesses they operate defeats the usual stereotypes. Many larger firms, realizing the importance of this diversity to the U.S. economy, have developed diversity programs to encourage small business among under-represented groups in our economy.

Characteristics of Successful Entrepreneurs

Vision	The overall idea for how to make a business idea a success coupled with the passion to pursue it.
High energy level	Entrepreneurs typically work long hours, with little staff. They have to work hard to seize opportunities in a timely manner.
Need to achieve	Entrepreneurs typically have a strong competitive drive and a desire to excel.
Self-confidence and optimism	Entrepreneurs believe in their ability to succeed, and they are able to instill their optimism in others.
Tolerance for failure	Entrepreneurs must be able to view setbacks and failures as learning experiences.

Creativity

Entrepreneurs typically conceive new ideas for goods and services and devise innovative ways to overcome difficult problems and situations.

Tolerance for ambiguity

Since dealing with unexpected events is the norm for most entrepreneurs, they tend to take in stride the uncertainties associated with launching a venture. They stay close to their customers and are able to react and change quickly.

Internal locus of control

Entrepreneurs take personal responsibility for the success or failure of their actions, and tend to believe that they control their own fates.

Starting a New Venture

Ways to enter a new venture

An aspiring entrepreneur can begin with a brand new idea, enter a franchise, or buy an existing business.

Creating a business plan

A good plan helps focus the entrepreneur, and should state company goals, outline sales and marketing strategies, and determine financial needs and sources of funds.

Financing a new enterprise

Entrepreneurs may use debt financing, but borrowed funds must be repaid. They also use equity financing when they invest their own savings, take on partners, or attract other investors such as venture capitalists and angel investors.

Engendering the Entrepreneurial Spirit in Large Organizations.

Intrapreneurship

Large companies try to benefit from the entrepreneurial spirit by taking specific steps to promote innovation within their organizational structures.

Business Vocabulary

angel investors
change agent
classic entrepreneur
debt financing
entrepreneurs
equity financing
gazelles
internal locus of control
intrapreneur
intrapreneurship
need to achieve
seed capital
venture capitalists
vision

Application of Vocabulary

Select the term from the list above that best completes the statements beginning on the following page. Write that term in the space provided.

Name _____ Instructor _____

Section _____ Date _____

1. People who seek profitable opportunities, and who take the necessary risks to set up and operate a business are known as _____.

2. An entrepreneurially oriented person who develops innovations within the context of a large organization is called a(n) _____.

3. _____ are business firms or groups of individual that invest in new and growing firms.

4. _____ is the initial funding needed to launch a new venture.

5. Wealthy individuals who invest directly in a new venture in exchange for an equity stake are called _____.

6. Financing from borrowed funds that entrepreneurs must repay is known as _____ _____.

7. Funds invested in new ventures in exchange for part ownership constitute _____.

8. _____ is the process of promoting innovation within an existing organization's structure.

9. The overall idea that inspires and guides an entrepreneur in the development of a business is called _____.

10. Successful entrepreneurs generally have a high _____, that is, the competitive drive that leads them to identify a goal and dedicate themselves to its attainment.

11. A(n) _____ is a manager who tries to revitalize an established firm to keep it competitive.

12. Successful entrepreneurs tend to have a(n) _____, that is, they take control of and responsibility for their own success or failure.

13. The most common type of entrepreneur, one who identifies a business opportunity and allocates available resources to tap that market, is known as a(n) _____.

14. _____ are fast-growing start-ups that create many new jobs in the economy.

Analysis of Learning Goals

Learning Goal 6.1: Define the term *entrepreneur*, and distinguish among entrepreneurs, small-business owners, and managers.

True or False

1. ___   An entrepreneur is an employee of a large organization.

2. ___   Merely owning a business makes you an entrepreneur.

3. ___   Managers are employees who direct the efforts of others to achieve an organization's goals.

4. ___   All managers are entrepreneurs.

5. ___   An entrepreneur seeks a profitable opportunity, then takes the risks necessary to open and operate a new venture.

Learning Goal 6.2: Identify three different types of entrepreneurs.

Short Answer

Your text identifies classic entrepreneurs, intrapreneurs, and changes agents as the types of entrepreneurs. Briefly describe each.

1. classic entrepreneur.

2. intrapreneur.

3. change agents.

Name _____ Instructor _____

Section _____ Date _____

Learning Goal 6.3: Explain why people choose to become entrepreneurs.

True or False

1. ____   Fewer than 1% of Americans are engaged in starting a new business at any given time.

2. ____   More young people are interested in starting their own businesses than ever before.

3. ____   A major reason many people decide to become entrepreneurs is the opportunity to be your own boss.

4. ____   When larger firms reduce their payrolls through downsizing and layoffs, many people opt to create their own job security by starting their own business.

5. ____   You are guaranteed job security when you start your own business.

6. ____   Entrepreneurs are wealth creators.

Learning Goal 6.4: Discuss conditions that encourage opportunities for entrepreneurs.

True or False

1. ____   There are a growing number of financing options to fund new businesses.

2. ____   Modern entrepreneurs are finding fewer opportunities to market their products in other nations than they had in the past.

3. ____   There are more programs designed to teach entrepreneurship than there were 20 years ago.

4. ____   Information technology has had little to do with the burst in entrepreneurial activity.

5. ____   The growth of entrepreneurship is a worldwide phenomenon.

Learning Goal 6.5: Describe the role of entrepreneurs in the economy.

Multiple Choice

1. Entrepreneurs bring about innovation through:

   a. creating new products.   c. bringing new life to old industries.
   b. building new industries.   d. all of the above.

2. Fast-growing start-up companies that generate lots of new jobs are known as:

   a. gazelles.   c. seed money providers.
   b. venture capitalists.   d. angel investors.

3. The number of women- and minority-owned startups:

   a. has been hindered by lack of concern by large firms.
   b. is declining as these workers find greater opportunities with large companies.
   c. is uneven: many more men than women start new businesses.
   d. has increased dramatically in recent years.

Learning Goal 6.6: Identify personality traits that typically characterize successful entrepreneurs.

Short Answer

List and discuss the eight major traits commonly found among entrepreneurs.

1.

2.

3.

4.

Name _____ Instructor _____

Section _____ Date _____

5.

6.

7.

8

Learning Goal 6.7: Summarize the process of starting a new venture.

True or False

1. ____   The first step in starting a new business is to find the financing.

2. ____   A good business idea is usually something you like to do and are good at doing.

3. ____   Buying a franchise is a less risky way to begin a business than starting a new firm.

4. ____   A good idea for a business should aim to satisfy an unmet need in the marketplace.

5. ____   Most new ventures are formed to solve problems that people have experienced at work or in their personal lives.

6. ____   Equity financing means using borrowed funds to finance a business venture.

Learning Goal 6.8: Explain how organizations promote intrapreneurship.

Short Answer

Your text lists three specific things a large company can do to encourage intrapreneurship. List and discuss each below.

1.

2.

3.

Self Review

True or False

1. ___ An increasing number of small businesses are started by professionals and managers who separated from large corporations when those firms downsized.

2. ___ Today, many online sites exist to aid entrepreneurs in constructing a business plan.

3. ___ Many entrepreneurs start a business because they have created something new and want to make it a market success themselves.

4. ___ The classic entrepreneur is a manager within a large company who develops new ideas.

5. ___ A change agent is also known as a "turnaround entrepreneur" and is someone who seeks to revitalize an established firm.

6. ___ The aging of the population and growth of dual-income families creates opportunities for entrepreneurs to market new goods and services.

7. ___ Entrepreneurial firms find they really can't compete effectively in an economy based on knowledge and information technology.

Name _____   Instructor _____

Section _____   Date _____

8. ___   In recent years, large established companies have created more new jobs in the economy than have entrepreneurial start-ups.

9. ___   Rapid growth of new businesses is expected to be a significant source of new jobs in the future.

10. ___   Children of small business owners are less likely than others to start their own businesses.

11. ___   Once you have a great idea for a new product, it is generally unnecessary to determine if there is a need or desire for that product in the marketplace.

12. ___   Entrepreneurs tend to be people who are easily discouraged when things don't go as planned.

13. ___   Large firms can encourage intrapreneurship by using dedicated programs such as skunkworks.

14. ___   Once your new business is off the ground, you can expect to work fewer hours than you would at a regular job.

15. ___   Using credit cards for startup capital may be an option if the company is expected to grow quickly and the debt can be repaid in a short time.

Multiple Choice

1.   It is suggested that entrepreneurs are a "different breed." Which of the following is a characteristic of an entrepreneur?

   a.   a tendency to avoid risks.
   b.   a higher than average need for achievement.
   c.   a low tolerance for ambiguity and failure.
   d.   reliance on the way things have always been done in the past.

2.   Someone who uses entrepreneurial talent while working for large firm is called a(n):

   a.   entrepreneur.   c.   intrapreneur.
   b.   angel investor.   d.   venture capitalist.

3. When trying to find an idea for a new business, it is may be wise to:

    a. list your interests, abilities, values and goals.
    b. consider the job experience you've already had.
    c. think about how to solve problems people have experienced at work or in their personal lives.
    d. look for ways to improve on existing goods and services.
    e. all of the above.

4. When an entrepreneur experiences failure:

    a. the entrepreneur should feel ashamed.
    b. the entrepreneur should treat the failure as a learning experience.
    c. using fraud to cover up the failure might be the best idea.
    d. all of the above.

5. Companies that want to enhance intrapreneurship should:

    a. discourage employees from developing new product ideas on their own.
    b. quickly move proposals for new ventures through the approval process at the firm.
    c. remind employees that it is managers who identify new business ideas.
    d. keep goals relating to new ventures secret until the top management has approved specific ideas.

6. Popular methods for entering new ventures include:

    a. starting a business from scratch, based upon an original idea.
    b. buying an existing business that has potential to be rejuvenated.
    c. buying a franchise.
    d. all of the above.

7. When entrepreneurs borrow money to finance a business venture, they are using:

    a. equity financing.   c. money from venture capitalists.
    b. debt financing.   d. money from angel investors.

8. Sources of equity financing for new ventures include:

    a. family and friends.   d. private investors.
    b. venture capital firms.   e. all of the above.
    c. business partners.

Name _____ Instructor _____

Section _____ Date _____

9. Aspiring entrepreneurs can find information by:

   a. subscribing to magazines and reading books.
   b. using the Internet.
   c. contacting trade associations for the industry in which they have interest.
   d. all of the above.

10. In the U.S., which age group starts the most new businesses?

   a. Between 25 and 34.   c. Between 45 and 54.
   b. Between 35 and 44.   d. People over 55.

Application Exercise

Bill Wong, an insurance company employee, is thinking about changing careers. He is tired of working for others, and would like to start his own business. He thinks he might like to operate a restaurant, and has found one for sale. He is also looking into the possibility of purchasing a fast-food franchise. He has discussed his ideas with his banker and his lawyer, and understands the legal and financial ramifications of each option. Still, he senses he does not know all that he should.

1. What additional information should Bill seek before he makes his decision?

2. What sources of information might Bill consult?

3. What one bit of practical advice would you give him?

Short Essay Questions

1. "The entrepreneurial spirit is thriving in the United States today." Is this statement true or false? Why?

2. What are the most common reasons people give for wanting to start a new firm?

3. What key contributions does entrepreneurship bring to the U.S. economy?

CHAPTER 7

Electronic Commerce: The Internet and Online Business

Chapter Summary: Key Concepts

The Internet: A Vital Key to Business Success

Internet (Net)	Worldwide network of interconnected computers. This global network allows computer users anywhere to send and receive data, sound, and video content.
World Wide Web (Web)	The interlinked collection of Web sites within the Internet. Each site is made of electronic documents or web pages that allow users to access text, graphics, audio and video elements.
Access to the Internet	Internet Service Providers (ISP's) provide individual users access to the Internet, usually by phone or wireless connections. Once connected, the user has point-and-click access to Web sites all over the world.
Who's on the Net	Over 50 percent of Americans are already online, and women make up more than half of U.S. users. Worldwide, the U.S. represents 40 percent of Net users. The average age of users is rising, and Net users tend to be more affluent and to attain higher levels of education than the general population.
The Net's four functions	The Net is used by individuals and businesses to communicate, access information, enjoy entertainment, and conduct transactions online.

The Scope of Electronic Commerce

Electronic commerce

Process of marketing goods and services through computer-based exchanges of data. Also called e-commerce, it has improved business efficiency by minimizing paperwork, simplifying ordering and payment procedures, and providing for online customer service.

B2B e-commerce

Business-to-business e-commerce uses the Internet for business transactions between organizations. It includes the use of EDI (electronic data interchange), extranets, electronic exchanges, and private exchanges.

B2C e-commerce

Business-to-consumer e-commerce, including e-tailing and electronic storefronts. Consumers can learn about products and services, place and tract orders online, and even pay for their purchases electronically.

E-commerce challenges

Security, privacy concerns, system overload, and Internet crime are all issues that must be addressed by firms wanting to engage in e-commerce. They must also develop and maintain user friendly Web sites, manage delivery and return of merchandise, and protect intellectual property and proprietary data online.

Managing a Web Site

Developing successful Web sites

First firms must clarify the goals they aim to achieve. Sites can be used to provide product information only, or to handle orders, payments and inventory tracking online. Selecting a domain name and developing content are followed by placing the site on a server, and registering the site with the major search engines.

Name _____ Instructor _____

Section _____ Date _____

Measuring Web site effectiveness

Measures of effectiveness depend on the purpose of the site. Increased brand awareness and brand loyalty, increased productivity and profitability of online transactions, click-through rates, and conversion rates are common measures of success.

The Global Environment of E-Commerce

E-commerce and global business

Even small firms can sell products and find new suppliers in global markets using Web sites and electronic commerce. The Internet removes limitations of time and space so people in different places and time zones can do business more easily.

Challenges for global e-commerce

While more than half of Internet users use English, providing content in more than one language may be crucial to the site's global success. Global e-commerce often heightens competition, allowing rivals from anywhere in the world to compete in local markets.

Business Vocabulary

business-to-business e-commerce
  (B2B)
business-to-consumer e-commerce
  (B2C)
Children's Online Privacy
  Protection Act (COPPA)
click-through rates
client
conversion rate
domain name
digital subscriber line
  (DSL)
electronic cash
electronic commerce
  (e-commerce)
electronic data interchange
  (EDI)
electronic exchanges
electronic shopping cart

electronic signatures
electronic storefronts
electronic wallets
encryption
extranet
firewall
instant messaging
Internet (Net)
Internet Service Provider (ISP)
newsgroup
online communities
portal
private exchange
server
smart cards
Web host
Web sites
World Wide Web (Web)

Application of Vocabulary

Select the term from the list above that best completes the statements below. Write that
term in the space provided.

1. The _____ is a global network of interconnected computers that allows users
    anywhere to send and receive data, sound, and video content.

2. The collection of resources or sites on the Internet that offers easy access to data and
    multimedia resources is known as the _____.

3. A(n) _____ is an integrated document made up of electronic pages, and
    often also offers hypertext links to other documents.

4. A(n) _____ is a Web site address.

5. A(n) _____ is an organization that provides
    access to the Internet.

Name _____ Instructor _____

Section _____ Date _____

6. A(n) _____ is a broadband technology that offers much higher frequency and faster speeds for data transmission over telephone lines.

7. A(n) _____ is a special computer that holds information that is provided to users on request.

8. Any computer or device that contacts a server requesting information or processing of data is called a(n) _____.

9. _____ is an application that allows e-mail senders to communicate with one another in real time.

10. _____ are groups of people who share information online through chat rooms.

11. If you are seeking information on a selected topic, you might see if there is a special online _____ dealing with that topic.

12. A site that offers links to search engines and other online research and information is called a web _____.

13. _____ makes it possible to market goods and services over the Internet.

14. When two organizations conduct business transactions over the Internet, they are engaged in _____.

15. Web-based marketplaces that cater to a specific industry's needs by allowing buyers and sellers to shop and conduct business are known as _____.

16. External customers or suppliers can access a firm's _____ through the Web, making secure electronic commerce possible.

17. Participants in a(n) _____ can collaborate on product ideas, production scheduling, distribution, order tracking, and any other business functions they want to conduct online.

18. _____ involves selling directly to consumers over the Internet.

19. Regular retailers who want to do business over the Internet can create _____ where they offer items for sale to consumers.

20. Visitors to online retailers click on items they want to buy, thereby adding them to a(n) _____.

21. _____ is the encoding of data for security purposes.

22. Shoppers on the Internet who want to pay for purchases with _____ can register with their banks and pay for their purchases using the Secure Internet Transaction (SET) system.

23. _____ are computer data files at e-commerce checkout counters that contain the data needed to complete a transaction so buyers won't have to re-enter their data each time they make a purchase.

24. Plastic cards that store e-cash or other encrypted information on embedded computer chips are called _____.

25. _____ can be used to enter into legal contracts online.

26. Under the _____, Web sites targeting children younger than 13 years of age must obtain verifiable parental consent before collecting or dispensing data on who the youngster is.

27. A(n) _____ is an electronic barrier that limits access into and out of an organization's network.

28. _____ is the computer-to-computer exchange of quotes, invoices, orders, and other business documents.

29. After developing a Web site, one needs to pay a monthly fee to the _____, an organization who makes that site available to Internet users through its server.

30. _____ measure the percentage of people presented with a banner ad on a Web site who click on it.

31. The _____ measures the percentage of Web site visitors who make purchases.

Name _____ Instructor _____

Section _____ Date _____

Analysis of Learning Goals

Learning Goal 7.1: Discuss how the Internet provides new routes to business success.

Multiple Choice

1. The Internet:

    a. is a computer network within one organization.
    b. is an organization's computer network with access limited to specific customers.
    c. is a global network of interconnected computers.
    d. is a good way to bypass the information superhighway.

2. The Internet:

    a. is only available during normal working hours in North America.
    b. removes limitations of time and space so that transactions can occur 24 hours a day between people in different countries.
    c. is fun to play with but cannot be used for business operations.
    d. requires each user to have a network.

3. The Internet provides profit opportunities for businesses:

    a. who provide equipment, access and content to the Internet .
    b. who use its resources in their business operations.
    c. by reducing the costs of collecting competitive intelligence and marketing research.
    d. all of the above.

4. Businesses can showcase, sell products, and provide customer service and technical support by developing:

    a. Web sites   c. ISP.
    b. DSL.   d. web browsers.

Learning Goal 7.2: Describe the increasing diversity of Internet users.

True or False

1. ___ Very few women use the Internet.

2. ___ Although the Internet originated in the U.S., more than half of Internet users now live in other countries.

3. ___ The average age of Internet users is declining.

4. ___ Net users tend to be more affluent and to attain higher levels of education than the general population.

5. ___ Today, more than half of Americans use the Internet.

Learning Goal 7.3: Summarize the Internet's four functions and provide examples of each.

Short Answer

Define and give examples for each of the following functions:

1. Communication.

2. Information Services.

3. Net Entertainment.

4. E-commerce.

Name _____ Instructor _____

Section _____ Date _____

Learning Goal 7.4: List the major forms of business-to-business (B2B) and business-to-consumer (B2C) e-commerce.

True or False

1. ____ So far, retail transactions are a more important aspect of e-commerce than are business-to-business transactions.

2. ____ Businesses use electronic data exchange (EDI), electronic and private exchanges, and extranets to process transactions with other businesses.

3. ____ Businesses can now handle ordering, invoicing, and payment processes over the Internet.

4. ____ Business processes have been enhanced by the Internet, but providing product information and responsive customer service has not.

5. ____ An extranet designed to permit collaboration between two organizations is a called a private exchange.

Multiple Choice

6. Consumers can conduct which of the following transactions over the Internet?

   a. retail buying.
   b. banking and investment.
   c. travel arrangements.
   d. all of the above.

7. A computer data file at an e-commerce site's checkout counter that contains customer identification, address, and payment information is called:

   a. electronic cash.
   b. a smart card.
   c. an electronic wallet.
   d. all of the above.

8. Plastic cards that store encrypted information on embedded computer chips are known as:

   a. electronic cash.
   b. smart cards.
   c. electronic wallets.
   d. online cash transfers.

Learning Goal 7.5: Describe some challenges associated with Internet selling.

True or False

1. ___ Online security for payment systems and confidentiality of data is a major obstacle to consumer-oriented Internet commerce.

2. ___ Research indicates that Internet users' show little concern about protecting their privacy online.

3. ___ There are no special legal restrictions for Web sites targeting children under age 13.

4. ___ Businesses face challenges in protecting their intellectual property and proprietary data online.

5. ___ Online auctions and investment offers are the least common sources of Internet fraud.

Learning Goal 7.6: Outline how companies develop and manage successful Web sites.

True or False

1. ___ The first step in developing a Web site is to clarify what objective the site will be used to achieve.

2. ___ Sites should download easily and allow easy navigation.

3. ___ Click-through rates are steadily increasing.

4. ___ When it comes to customer communications and service, Web sites generally do more harm than good.

5. ___ Companies are generally better off designing and operating their own Web sites rather than outsourcing those responsibilities.

6. ___ It is easy to measure how well a Web site accomplishes its objectives.

Name _____ Instructor _____

Section _____ Date _____

Learning Goal 7.7: Explain how global opportunities result from e-commerce.

Short Answer

1. How can technology help small companies compete globally?

2. How can technology help larger organizations compete globally?

Self Review

True or False

1. ___ Electronic commerce is the process of marketing goods and services through computer-based exchanges of data.

2. ___ Internet retailing has not been affected by channel conflicts or reliability problems.

3. ___ While many companies have privacy policies, consumers have no assurances these policies will remain in place if a company is sold or goes out of business.

4. ___ Most Web sites are operated by very large businesses.

5. ___ Employees' online behavior or e-mail messages at work are considered private communication, and cannot legally be monitored by employers.

6. ___ Businesspeople can learn about competitors' performance, financial condition, and product offerings using the Internet.

7. ___ Women now represent over 40% of Internet users worldwide.

8. ___ Most electronic commerce occurs between businesses and consumers.

9. ___ Direct distribution using the Internet can cause significant conflict between companies and their marketing intermediaries.

10. ___ Firms can generate profits on the Internet by selling merchandise online, charging user fees, and selling advertising space on their Web sites.

11. ___ Electronic exchanges make it possible for retailers and their suppliers to manage purchases, inventory control, and operations more efficiently.

12. ___ A private exchange is less collaborative than a typical extranet.

13. ___ Online merchants have found that prominently displaying their privacy policy on their Web sites is an effective way to build customers' trust

14. ___ The click-through rate measures the percentage of Web site visitors who make purchases.

15. ___ B2B is Internet commerce between businesses and consumers.

16. ___ There have been no important applications of e-commerce in the not-for-profit sector of the economy.

17. ___ The term "e-tailing" refers to B2C retail sales online.

Multiple Choice

1. Business uses of the Internet include:

   a. gathering information about competitors or industry trends.
   b. promoting products or services through a Web site or banner ad on placed on someone else's Web site.
   c. gathering information about customers who visit a firm's Web site.
   d. all of the above

2. A Web site address is known as a(n):

   a. domain name.   c. encryption.
   b. Web browser.   d. portal.

3. A business like American Online that provides Internet access to customers through its own series of local networks is:

   a. a private network.   c. an Internet Service Provider (ISP).
   b. a private exchange.   d. a Web Browser.

Name _____ Instructor _____

Section _____ Date _____

4. Portals:

    a.   are Web sites designed to be a user's starting place when entering the Web.
    b.   offer links to search engines, news sources, e-mail and chat rooms.
    c.   allow users to bookmark favorite sites in order to click to them directly in the future.
    d.   all of the above.

5. When gathering information from the Web:

    a.   reliability of information is guaranteed.
    b.   it is generally a good idea to check more than once source before acting on the information you obtain.
    c.   information gathered from chat-rooms and via e-mail is as reliable as information provided by a reputable publication.
    d.   you can rest assured since government screens all data to be sure it is accurate.

6. The most successful online retailers:

    a.   have electronic storefronts but no catalogue or traditional retail experience.
    b.   add electronic storefronts to catalogue or traditional retail offerings.
    c.   refuse to accept electronic wallets.
    d.   avoid encryption security protections.

7. The Children's Online Privacy Protection Act (COPPA):

    a.   regulates Web sites targeting children younger than 10 years of age.
    b.   requires Web sites targeting children younger than 13 years of age to obtain "verifiable parental consent" before collecting identifying data.
    c.   allows any Web site to collect names and e-mail addresses of children.
    d.   all of the above.

8. Combinations of hardware and software that keep unauthorized Net users from accessing private corporate data are called:

    a.   intranets.   c.   extranets.
    b.   firewalls.   d.   smart cards.

9. B2B transactions can be conducted using:

    a. a business's own Web site.   c. electronic exchanges.
    b. extranets and private exchanges. d. all of the above.

10. Some Web sites use highlighted terms to allow users to travel immediately to related sites. These are known as:

    a. encryption devices.   c. firewalls.
    b. hyperlinks.   d. online shopping carts.

11. Traffic jams on the Internet:

    a. can be caused by hackers.
    b. can be caused by too many people trying to access a site at the same time.
    c. can cause delays and entire system outages.
    d. all of the above

Application Exercises

Malcolm McDonald makes custom surfboards by hand. He has built a small business out of his garage, and would like to make this his career. He is wondering about what uses he might make of a Web site, and comes to you for some suggestions. Can you give Malcolm five concrete ideas on how to make a Web site work for him?

1.

2.

3.

Name _____ Instructor _____

Section _____ Date _____

4.

5.

Short Essay Questions

1. "The Internet is just a fad, and will likely fade away." Is this statement true or false?
    Why?

2.   What is B2B? Why has B2B enjoyed such phenomenal growth?

3.   What key questions should a business answer as it develops a Web site?

CHAPTER 8

Management, Leadership and the Internal Organization

Chapter Summary: Key Concepts

What is Management?

Management

The achievement of organizational objectives through the use of people and other resources. The skills and principles of management apply in both profit and not-for profit organizations.

The management hierarchy

The management hierarchy has three levels: top, middle, and supervisory management. Top management sets the long term direction, vision, and values of the organization. Middle managers focus on specific operations to implement long term plans. Supervisory managers are responsible for assigning workers to specific jobs and evaluating performance.

Skills needed for managerial success

Successful managers should possess technical, human, and conceptual skills. Technical skills include the ability to understand and use the knowledge and tools of a specific discipline or activity. Human skills are the interpersonal skills managers need to motivate and lead employees to accomplish identified objectives. Conceptual skills, needed especially by top managers, involve the ability to see the big picture by acquiring, analyzing, and interpreting information.

Managerial functions

Managers in any organization must perform the essential functions of planning, organizing, directing, and controlling. Planning is the process of anticipating future events and conditions and determining courses of action for achieving organizational objectives. Organizing is the way in which managers blend human and material resources through a formal structure of tasks and authority. Guiding and motivating employees is called directing. The control function of management evaluates the organization's performance to see if it is accomplishing its objectives.

Setting a Vision and Ethical Standards for the Firm

Vision

A perception of marketplace needs and the methods by which an organization can satisfy them. It must be both focused and flexible enough to adapt to the changing business environment.

Ethical standards

These values are set by top managers, who must focus on the organization's long term success, not merely short term profits or personal gain.

Importance of Planning

Types of planning

Four types of plans used by contemporary organizations are strategic, tactical, operational, and contingency plans. Strategic plans set primary objectives and how to achieve them. Tactical and operation plans provide increasingly specific and detailed plans. Contingency planning allows a firm to manage business continuation and public communication in any crisis.

Planning at different organizational levels

Top managers specialize in long term plans. Middle managers focus on shorter term plans, and develop the organization's policies and procedures. Supervisory managers set daily and weekly plans, rules, and specific activities for each department. Contingency planning is led by top management, but all levels of management participate.

The Strategic Planning Process

Defining the organization's mission

The mission statement is a written explanation of an organization's intentions and aims.

Assessing your competitive position

The firm must evaluate its current position in the marketplace. SWOT analysis is often used in this phase of strategic planning.

Establishing objectives for the organization	Objectives are the specific guideposts used to define and evaluate the organization's performance in such areas as profitability, customer service, employee satisfaction, public relations, and ethical conduct.
Creating strategies for competitive differentiation	Organizations can combine product innovation, technology, and employee motivation to achieve the unique blend that puts it ahead of its competitors.
Implementing, monitoring, and adapting strategic plans	First, managers put the plan into action, and identify the specific methods and resources to be used. Next, managers must monitor feedback about performance, and adapt the plans when performance fails to match expectations or when business conditions change.

Managers as Decision Makers

Programmed and nonprogrammed decisions	For programmed decisions, organizations develop rules, policies, and detailed procedures managers can use to achieve consistent, quick, and inexpensive solutions to common problems. Nonprogrammed decisions involve complex and unique problems or opportunities with important consequences for the organization.
How managers make decisions	Managers take the following steps: they first recognize and define a problem. They next propose alternative solutions. They then determine and implement the correct solution. Finally, they follow up to see if the solution has been effective.

Managers as Leaders

Leadership	Inspiring others to achieve organizational goals.
Leadership styles	Leaders may utilize autocratic, democratic or free-rein styles, adjusting their style to the culture of the organization and to the situation at hand.
Corporate culture	The organization's system of principles, beliefs, and values is generally shaped by the organization's leaders. In a strong culture everyone knows and supports the same objectives.

Organizational Structures

Organization

Defined as a structured grouping of people working together to achieve common objectives, all organizations feature three key elements: human interaction, goal-directed activities, and structure.

Departmentalization

The subdivision of work activities into units within the organization. Five major methods subdivide work by product, geographic area, customer, function, and process.

Delegating work assignments

When managers give work to subordinates, they must consider the task or obligation the subordinate will be undertaking, the authority/power needed to do the job, and how the worker's performance will be evaluated. Authority and responsibility tend to be delegated downward in organizations, while accountability moves upward. Managers are always finally accountable for the work they have delegated to others, so it is important to delegate effectively.

Types of organization structures

There are four basic structural forms: line, line-and-staff, committee, and matrix. The oldest and simplest is the line organization, with its clear chain of command. In the line-and-staff organization, staff departments are developed to support and advise the line. Sometimes the line-and-staff structure puts authority and responsibility jointly in the hands of a group of people, utilizing the committee organization. Finally, the matrix (or project management structure) assigns employees to special projects while retaining their ties to the line-and-staff structure. This structure allows quick adaptation by focusing resources into teams who tackle major problems or projects.

Name _____ Instructor _____

Section _____ Date _____

Business Vocabulary

autocratic leadership
centralization
chain of command
competitive differentiation
committee organization
conceptual skills
contingency planning
controlling
corporate culture
decentralization
decision making
delegation
democratic leadership
departmentalization
directing
empowerment
free-rein leadership
human skills
leadership
line manager
line organization
line-and-staff organization

management
matrix structure
middle management
mission statement
nonprogrammed decision
objectives
operational plans
organization
organization chart
organizing
planning
programmed decision
span of management
staff managers
strategic planning
supervisory management
SWOT analysis
tactical planning
technical skills
top management
vision

Application of Vocabulary

Select the term from the list on page two that best completes the statements below. Write that term in the space provided.

1. _____ is the achievement of organizational objectives through people and other resources.

2. The blending of human and material resources into a formal structure of tasks and authority is achieved by the management function of _____.

3. _____ is the management function of guiding and motivating employees to accomplish the organization's objectives

4. _____ is the management function of evaluating an organization's performance to determine if it is meeting its objectives.

5. _____ is the perception of marketplace needs and methods by which an organization can satisfy them.

6. The management function concerned with anticipating the future and determining the best courses of action to achieve organizational objectives is _____,

7. The written statement of an organization's overall intentions and aims is called a _____.

8. A _____ is an organized method of assessing an organization's internal strengths and weaknesses, and external opportunities and threats.

9. _____ specify end goals for an organization and serve as standards for evaluation of performance in such areas as profitability, customer service, employee satisfaction, and social responsibility.

10. _____ is the most far reaching level of planning, and is the process of determining the primary objectives of the organization, adopting courses of action, and allocating the resources necessary to achieve those objectives.

11. Planning and allocating resources for current and near-term activities required to implement overall strategies is achieved through _____.

12. _____ use standards or schedules for implementing tactical plans.

13. _____ is the ability to direct and inspire people to attain organizational goals.

14. When organizations try to anticipate and meet emergencies, enabling them to resume operations as quickly and smoothly as possible, they are engaged in _____.

15. _____ occurs when work activities are subdivided into units within the organization on the basis of product, process, geography, function or customer.

Name _____ Instructor _____

Section _____ Date _____

16. A _____ is the unique combination of a company's abilities and approaches that makes it more successful than its competitors.

17. _____ is the act of assigning work activities to subordinates.

18. The _____ process involves recognizing and identifying a problem, developing and evaluating alternatives, selecting and implementing an alternative, and doing a follow up.

19. _____ include a manager's ability to use the techniques, knowledge, and tools of a specific discipline or department.

20. A manager's ability to work with and through people requires _____ _____.

21. _____ involve the ability to see the organization as a unified whole and understand how each part interacts with others.

22. A(n) _____ uses policies, procedures and rules to implement a previously determined response in a frequently occurring situation.

23. When a manager must develop a response to a new or unique situation with important consequences for the organization, that manager is making a

_____.

24. When a manager makes decisions without consulting others, the _____ _____ style is in use.

25. Managers who involve subordinates in decision making are using the _____ _____ style of leadership.

26. The _____ style of leadership means that managers allow subordinates to make most decisions.

27. _____ means that managers lead employees by sharing power, responsibility, and decision making with them.

28. The _____ is the number of employees one manager supervises.

29. A(n) _____ is a structured grouping of people working together to achieve common objectives.

30. A(n) _____ is an organization member with authority to direct subordinates in the functions required to produce and market goods and services.

31. _____ provide information, advice, or technical assistance to aid line managers.

32. Retaining decision making at top management levels is known as _____.

33. When decision making authority is pushed down to lower organization levels, _____ is in use.

34. A(n) _____ is a graphic outline of authority and responsibility relationships.

35. _____ is the highest level of the management hierarchy, made up of executives who develop long-range plans and interact with the public and outside entities.

36. _____ is the level of management responsible for the details of assigning workers to specific jobs and evaluating performance.

37. _____ is the level of management responsible for developing the plans and procedures to implement the general plans of top management.

38. The _____ is the set of relationships in an organization that indicates who gives direction to whom and who reports to whom.

39. The oldest and simplest organization form, in which there is a clear flow of authority from the chief executive to the subordinates, is the _____.

40. The most common modern organization form, that combines a line organization with staff departments, is the _____.

Name _____ Instructor _____

Section _____ Date _____

41. An organization structure in which authority and responsibility are jointly held by a group of individuals is the _____.

42. In a _____, specialists from different functional areas of the organization are brought together to work on specific projects.

43. The value system of an organization is called its _____.

Analysis of Learning Goals

Learning Goal 8.1: Define *management* and the three types of skills necessary for managerial success.

True or False

1. ____ Management is defined as the process of achieving organizational objectives through people and other resources.

2. ____ The highest level of management includes CEO's and is called middle management.

3. ____ The lowest level of management is supervisory management, whose job it is to direct the day to day operational activities of employees.

4. ____ Today, the essential role of a manager is simply being the boss.

Short Answer

List and define each of the three skills successful managers must have.

5.

6.

7.

Learning Goal 8.2: Explain the role of vision and ethical standards in business success.

True or False

1. ___ Vision is a clear perception of marketplace needs and the methods a company will use to meet those needs.

2. ___ The firm's mission statement rarely relies on the original vision for the firm.

3. ___ While new companies need to develop a vision, large established companies do not.

4. ___ Vision must be focused and yet flexible enough to adapt to changes in the business environment.

5. ___ Setting high ethical standards affects the welfare of everyone with a stake: employees, customers, investors and society in general. However, it has little to do with building a firm's lasting success .

Learning Goal 8.3: Summarize the major benefits of planning and distinguish among strategic planning, tactical planning, and operational planning.

Multiple Choice

1. Through realistic assessments of current and future conditions, planning helps a company to:

   a. turn vision into action.   c. avoid costly mistakes.
   b. take advantage of opportunities.   d. all of the above.

2. The most far-reaching plans that determine the long-range focus and activities of the organization are:

   a. strategic plans.   c. operational
   b. tactical plans.   d. contingency plans.

Name _____ Instructor _____

Section _____ Date _____

3. Plans that set standards and work targets for functional areas such as production, human resources, and marketing are known as:

    a. strategic plans.   c. operational plans
    b. tactical plans.   d. contingency plans.

4. The current and short-range activities needed to implement strategies are articulated in:

    a. strategic plans.   c. operational plans
    b. tactical plans.   d. contingency plans.

5. The type of plans that establish overall objectives and position the organization within its environment are:

    a. strategic plans.   c. operational
    b. tactical plans.   d. contingency plans.

Learning Goal 8.4: Describe the strategic planning process.

Short Answer

Define and explain the six steps in the strategic planning process.

1.

2.

3.

4

5

6

Learning Goal 8.5: Distinguish the major types of business decisions and list the steps in the decision-making process.

Short Answer

1. Define and contrast programmed and nonprogrammed decisions.

2. What are the five steps in the decision making process?

    a.

    b.

    c.

    d.

    e.

Name _____ Instructor _____

Section _____ Date _____

Learning Goal 8.6: Define *leadership* and compare different leadership styles.

True or False

1. ___   Leadership can be defined as the ability to direct or inspire others to perform the activities needed to reach an organization's objectives.

2. ___   Experts agree that one leadership style works best regardless of the circumstances at hand.

3. ___   Free rein leadership means that managers have lost control of their subordinates and operations will suffer.

4. ___   When a manager actively involves subordinates in decision making, that manager is utilizing the democratic leadership style.

5. ___   The current trend in management is toward more autocratic leadership styles.

Learning Goal 8.7: Discuss the meaning and importance of corporate culture.

True or False

1. ___   Corporate culture refers to the system of principles, beliefs and values prevalent in an organization.

2. ___   Cultures arise spontaneously, and leaders typically have very little influence on an organization's culture.

3. ___   The best leadership style to adopt depends in large measure on the culture of the organization.

4. ___   One generation of employees passes on a corporate culture to newer employees, often as part of the formal training process.

5. ___   An organization's culture can really have very little impact on creating a competitive differentiation for that firm.

Learning Goal 8.8: Explain the five major forms of departmentalization and the four major types of organization structures.

Short Answer

1. What is departmentalization?

2. Name and define the five major ways firms departmentalize.

   a.

   b.

   c.

   d.

   e.

3. Define the line organization:

   a. What are the advantages of the line organization?

   b. What are the weaknesses of the line organization?

Name _____ Instructor _____

Section _____ Date _____

4. What is the line-and-staff organization? Distinguish line managers from staff managers:

    a. What are the advantages enjoyed by this organization form?

    b. What disadvantages can occur in this organization form?

5. Define the committee organization form:

    a. What are its advantages?

    b. What weaknesses can this form exhibit?

6. What is the matrix organization form? How does it arise, and why?

    a. What are the advantages to be gained in the matrix organization form?

    b. What disadvantages may arise in the matrix organization?

Self Review

True or False

1. ___ Management principles apply to all organizations, whether they operate in the profit or not-for-profit sector, and whether they are producers of products or services.

2. ___ Organizing is the management function of motivating and leading employees.

3. ___ An organization's planning process should reflect the competitive differentiation the firm hopes to achieve.

4. ___ The interpersonal skills known as human skills have grown in importance with increased diversity and globalization in the modern business environment.

5. ___ An organization chart is a picture that shows the organization's structure.

6. ___ Empowering employees increases the centralization of an organization.

7. ___ Middle managers generally focus on long-term planning.

8. ___ Ethical standards and the vision of the top management have no bearing on one another.

9. ___ An organization's structure groups people and activities to permit greater and more efficient attainment of organizational objectives.

10. ___ The line-and-staff organization is the oldest and simplest organization structure.

11. ___ As organizations grow larger, the need for organization structure diminishes.

12. ___ A line organization makes maximum use of staff specialists.

13. ___ The committee organization form is often used in conjunction with the line-and-staff organization.

14. ___ The organization structure that uses the team approach to allow large, multi-product firms to focus organizational resources on specific problems or projects is the matrix organization.

15. ___ The line organization is based on authority being passed down the chain of command.

Name _____ Instructor _____

Section _____ Date _____

16. ___ Organizations generally fix on one method of departmentalization and use it at all levels of the firm.

17. ___ Empowerment will thrive in a firm where autocratic leadership styles are common.

18. ___ Both the decision making process and the organizing process require a follow up to be sure the process has produced effective results.

19. ___ A mission statement makes explicit a firm's purpose and aims.

20. ___ Objectives set standards that serve as guideposts in reaching and evaluating an organization's goals.

21. ___ SWOT analysis should help a company recognize constraints, such as when promising opportunities are hampered by financial limitations or other weaknesses.

Multiple Choice

1. The process of anticipating future events and conditions and determining the courses of action for achieving organizational objectives is:

   a. planning.   c. directing.
   b. organizing.   d. controlling.

2. Knowing a computer program or how to maintain a machine are examples of:

   a. technical skills.
   b. human skills.
   c. conceptual skills.

3. Inspiring trust, being a good communicator, and showing empathy with others are examples of:

   a. technical skills.
   b. human skills.
   c. conceptual skills.

4. In order to do the long-range planning that involves the entire organization, top managers need to have developed:

    a. technical skills.
    b. human skills.
    c. conceptual skills.

5. Which of the following is a major advantage of a line organization?

    a. the managers become knowledgeable in several areas.
    b. the chain of command is clear.
    c. the paperwork required of top executives is simple.
    d. morale is improved through participative decision making.

6. Which of the following is an advantage of a committee organization?

    a. it provides for quick decision making.
    b. decisions may be made primarily to achieve a compromise.
    c. workers have more than one supervisor.
    d. willingness to carry through with committee decisions is improved.

7. Which of the following is an advantage of a matrix organization?

    a. flexibility.
    b. employees may have to answer to more than one supervisor.
    c. potential conflicts are minimized.
    d. it is simple to understand.

8. Which of the following is generally considered a line function?

    a. legal.
    b. production.
    c. personnel.
    d. market research.
    e. auditing.

9. Staff managers:

    a. have authority to give orders to line managers.
    b. advise line managers.
    c. are empowered to make decisions about line department operations.
    d. all of the above.

Name _____ Instructor _____

Section _____ Date _____

10. The obligation to perform an assigned task is known as:

    a. responsibility.   d. power.
    b. authority.   e. delegation.
    c. accountability.

11. When employees take on a new responsibility:

    a. they agree to be obligated to complete the task.
    b. they need adequate authority to complete the task.
    c. they are held accountable for the results, as are their supervisors.
    d. all of the above.

12. A manager's span of control is also known as the:

    a. span of management.   c. glass ceiling.
    b. chain of command.   d. corporate culture.

13. SWOT analysis requires management to consider:

    a. internal strengths and weaknesses, external opportunities and threats.
    b. suppliers, workers, other competitors, and time.
    c. strategic planning, working plans, operational plans, and time frames.
    d. sales, workforce, organization structure, and technologies.

14. When a firm's strengths and opportunities mesh, it has:

    a. a problem in the marketplace.
    b. leverage in the marketplace.
    c. vulnerability in the marketplace.
    d. a constraint it must overcome.

Application Exercises

1. Ten years ago, Elaine Bier started a piano tuning and maintenance service. As the business warranted, she added technical and managerial, sales, and clerical personnel. Her customers sign a multi-year agreement. The company employs 20 highly skilled technical people throughout five eastern states. The Baltimore office has two full-time clerical employees. There is one field salesperson and two field troubleshooters. Elaine and Joe Arcelia, her right-hand-man, keep the business going. While the business has continued to grow and profits are excellent, Elaine and Joe are spending too much time overseeing day-to-day problems and activities. At their quarterly meeting with their attorney, they discussed their current situation. The attorney suggested that this "group" should get organized. Elaine and Joe agreed.

    a. What factors should they consider in devising an organizational structure?

    b. What form of organization would you suggest? Why?

2. Paul McKinley has just returned from a management trainee job interview. He explains that he thought he answered most of the questions well, except the one about his personal leadership style. Paul said that the interviewer asked him to analyze what type of leader he sees himself as. Paul explained that although he has given a great deal of thought to the type of leader he would prefer to work with, he has given little thought to his own leadership style.

    a. What suggestions would you give to Paul to help him determine his leadership style?

    b. In the event that Paul has another interview, what answer should Paul give if asked this question again?

Name _____ Instructor _____

Section _____ Date _____

Short Essay Questions

1. What is planning? Name and define the four types of plans.

2. What is delegation? How does it help a manager? an employee? What four basic issues must be addressed for effective delegation to take place?

3. What is corporate culture? What is leadership? How are they related?

CHAPTER 9

Human Resource Management, Motivation and Labor-Management Relations

Chapter Summary: Key Concepts

Human Resource Management is Vital to All Organizations

Core human resource management responsibilities	The core responsibilities include planning for staffing needs, recruiting and selecting employees, training and evaluating performance, managing compensation and benefits, and handling employee separations.
Human resource management objectives	Objectives include providing qualified, well-trained employees for the organization, maximizing employee effectiveness in the organization, and satisfying individual employee needs through monetary compensation, benefits, opportunities to advance, and job satisfaction.
Human resource planning	Human resource managers formulate both long- and short-term plans to provide the right number of qualified employees. Staffing plans are adjusted according to the organization's strategies and in response to changing business conditions.

Recruitment and Selection

Finding qualified candidates	In order to find qualified employees, organizations must recruit applicants. They can look inside the organization, or use external sources such as advertising, state and private employment agencies, job fairs, job banks, college recruiting offices and the Internet. Employee referrals can also be an effective source of external candidates.
Selecting and hiring employees	Employee selection often involves, employment skills testing, interviews, background checks, and medical exams. Poor hiring decisions are extremely costly to organizations, so a careful hiring process is important.

Orientation, Training, and Evaluation

Orientation   Newly hired employees should get an orientation regarding company policies and culture, employee rights and benefits, and other initial information that will help a new employee get off to a good start.

Training programs   Many employers provide initial and on-going training. On-the-job training, coaching, classroom, and computer-based training are common methods. Organizations also pay special attention to preparing employees who will work abroad, and to management development programs.

Performance appraisals The evaluation of an employee's job performance by comparing actual results with desired outcomes.

Compensation

Compensation methods   Pay, in the form of wages, salary, and/or incentive pay, is a major cost for every organization. Compensation is generally based on what competitors are paying , government requirements, the cost of living in that area, the firm's ability to pay, and worker productivity.

Employee benefits   Common benefits include retirement plans, health and disability insurance, sick leave, paid vacation, child and elder care, and even tuition reimbursement. Governments also require contributions from employers for programs such as Medicare, Social Security, unemployment insurance, and workers' compensation.

Flexible benefits   Our increasingly diverse workforce calls for benefit programs that can be tailored to meet the varying needs of employees. Cafeteria-style benefit plans and paid time off programs are examples of how modern firms provide flexibility in their benefit programs.

Flexible work   Firms are also using work schedules that can be varied to meet the needs of our diverse workforce. Some common methods are flextime, the compressed workweek, job sharing programs, and telecommuting.

Employee Separation

Employee termination   Employees voluntarily terminate employment when they move to another job or city, retire, or decide to pursue other interests. Employers terminate employees either due to the need to reduce the workforce, or for cause. Organizations face increased legal pressure regarding terminations, and must clarify when they adhere to the principle of "employment at will."

Downsizing   Downsizing eliminates jobs in a firm to increase efficiency. Downsizing programs include offering early retirement plans, voluntary severance programs, opportunities for internal reassignment, and aid finding new jobs outside the firm.

Outsourcing   Outsourcing relies on outside specialists to perform functions previously performed by the company's own employees. It allows a firm to continue doing what it does best, while hiring other companies who specialize in providing cost effective services and other resources.

Using contingent workers   Contingent workers are employees who work part-time, temporarily, or only the time needed to fulfill a specific contract. Many firms supplement full-time employees in this way, adding flexibility and the ability to acquire specialists as needed.

Motivating Employees

Morale   The mental attitude of employees toward their employer and jobs. High morale is a sign of a well-managed organization. High employee absenteeism, high employee turnover, and strikes are all signs of low morale.

Maslow's hierarchy of needs   Human needs that motivate behavior identified by Abraham Maslow, including physiological, safety and security, social, esteem and self-actualization needs.

Job design and motivation   Job enlargement, job enrichment, and other job design activities seek to make jobs more interesting and to retain talented workers.

Manager's attitudes and motivation	Theory X assumes that employees dislike work and try to avoid it. Management attitudes increasingly rely on Theory Y, and focus on motivating by giving employees the opportunity to meet their higher order needs in the workplace.

Union-Management Relations

Development of labor unions	Labor unions are groups of workers who have banded together to achieve common goals in the areas of wages, hours, working conditions, job security, etc. Seventeen percent of full-time workers in the U.S. belong to labor unions.
Labor legislation	Key pieces of legislation include the Norris-La Guardia Act, the Wagner Act, the Fair Labor Standards Act, The Taft-Hartley Act, the Landrum-Griffin Act, and the Plant Closing Notification Act.
The collective bargaining process	Labor unions negotiate with management to produce collective bargaining agreements that govern issues like compensation, job security, and working conditions.
Settling union-management disputes	In an effort to avoid costly and lengthy legal battles, impartial third parties are often called upon to help settle labor disputes. Mediators are empowered to suggest solutions, while arbitrators can impose legally binding solutions. These methods are increasingly used to help finalize labor contracts, to settle disputes that arise in the interpretation of contracts, and by nonunionized firms to solve employee grievances.
Competitive tactics of unions and management	The main tactics unions can use to gain power in negotiations are threatened or actual strikes, picketing, and boycotts. The main tactics management can use to gain power in negotiations include lockouts, use of strikebreakers, injunctions, and employers' associations.
Employee-management relations in non-union organizations	At non-union companies, management often chooses to offer compensation and benefits comparable to those of unionized firms in the area. These companies also devise methods to handle grievances fairly and to address worker concerns regarding job security.

Name _____ Instructor _____

Section _____ Date _____

Business Vocabulary

alternative dispute resolution (ADR)
   programs
arbitration
boycott
collective bargaining
contingent workers
compressed workweek
downsizing
employee benefits
employers' associations
employment at will
exit interview
flexible benefit plan
flexible work plan
flextime
grievance
human resource management
injunction
job enlargement
job enrichment
job sharing
labor union
lockout

management development programs
mediation
morale
motive
need
on-the-job training
outsourcing
paid time off (PTO)
performance appraisal
picketing
professional employer
   organization (PEO)
salaries
strike
strikebreakers
telecommuters
Theory X
Theory Y
Theory Z
Wages
360-degree performance
   review

Application of Vocabulary

Select the term from the list above that best completes the statements below. Write that term in the space provided.

1. _____ includes
   acquiring, compensating, appraising, and motivating qualified employees to perform
   the necessary activities of an organization and developing an organizational climate
   conducive to maximum efficiency and worker satisfaction.

2. The lack of something people find useful, key to understanding human motivation, is
   called a _____.

3. A _____ is the inner state that directs individuals toward the goal of satisfying a felt need.

4. _____ is the name we give the mental attitude employees have toward their employer and job.

5. _____ is the practice that allows the employment relationship to begin or end at any time at the discretion of either the employer or the employee for any reason.

6. _____ is a job design change that expands the employee's responsibilities by increasing the number and variety of tasks they entail.

7. The managerial assumption that workers dislike work and therefore must be controlled, coerced, or threatened to perform well is known as _____.

8. _____ is the set of managerial assumptions that workers like work, and will, under proper conditions,. seek and accept responsibility while meeting their higher level needs at work.

9. _____ is the management approach emphasizing employee participation as the key to increased productivity and improved quality of work life.

10. Employee rewards such as pension plans, insurance, sick-leave pay, and other things given at full or partial expense to the company are collectively known as _____.

11. _____ means redesigning work to give employees more authority in planning their tasks, deciding how they are to be done, and allowing them to learn related skills or to trade jobs.

12. _____ involves preparing employees for job tasks by allowing them to perform those tasks under the guidance of an experienced employee.

13. Training programs designed to improve the skills and broaden the knowledge of current and potential managers are called _____.

14. A method of allocating a given dollar amount for benefits to each employee and letting the individual select those benefits that best serve their needs is known as a _____.

Name _____ Instructor _____

Section _____ Date _____

15. A(n) _____ involves defining acceptable employee performance levels and evaluating how well employees have achieved them.

16. People who work from home using telephones, e-mail, computers, and fax machines are called _____.

17. _____ is a work scheduling system that allows employees to set their own work hours within parameters specified by the firm.

18. _____ is the streamlining of the management hierarchy and work force in an effort to reduce costs and make the firm more efficient.

19. A _____ program allows two or more employees to divide the tasks of one job.

20. Some firms ask employes who leave voluntarily to participate in an _____ to find out why they decided to leave.

21. _____ occurs when firms hire outside firms or consultants to perform functions previously performed by the company's own employees.

22. The _____ is a scheduling option that allows employees to work the regular number of required hours in fewer than the typical 5 days.

23. A(n) _____ allows employees to adjust their working hours and places of work to accommodate their personal lives.

24. A(n) _____ works in partnerships with small and mid-sized employers to handle a firm's human resource activities such as hiring and training, payroll and benefits, and compliance with labor laws.

25. A performance appraisal that gathers feedback from a panel consisting of co-workers, supervisors, managers, and sometimes even customers, is called a(n) _____.

26. _____ are employees who work part-time, temporarily, or only to fulfill a specific contract.

27. Compensation plans calculated on a weekly, monthly, or annual basis are called _____.

28. _____ represent compensation based on an hourly pay rate or the amount of output produced.

29. A _____ is a group of workers who have banded together to achieve common goals in the key areas of wages, hours, and working conditions.

30. A _____ is a "weapon" used by management to bring pressure on union members by closing the firm.

31. A _____ attempts to prevent people from purchasing goods or services from a firm that is engaged in a labor dispute.

32. A _____ is a complaint that management is violating some provision of the union contract.

33. A(n) _____ is a court order prohibiting some practice.

34. _____ is the use of an impartial third party whose decision is legally binding to settle a union-management dispute.

35. _____ are cooperative efforts by employers to present a united front in dealing with labor unions.

36. During a strike, management may attempt to hire nonunion workers, or _____, to replace the striking workers.

37. Allowing elected representatives to negotiate on behalf of workers was legalized by the Wagner Act, and is known as _____.

38. _____ is the process of settling union-management disputes through recommendations of an impartial third party.

39. A _____ is the most powerful union tool and involves a temporary work stoppage by employees until a dispute has been settled or a contract signed.

40. Workers who march at a plant entrance to protest some management practice are engaged in _____.

Name _____ Instructor_____

Section _____ Date _____

41. An increasing number of nonunion employers have instituted _____
_____ that include open-door policies, employee hot
lines, peer review councils, mediation and arbitration.

42. A formal complaint filed by an employee or a union that management is violating
some provision of a union contract is called a(n) _____.

43. When employers put holiday, vacation and sick days into one account and give
workers flexibility in taking their days off, a _____
program is in use.

Analysis of Learning Goals

Learning Goal 9.1: Explain the importance of human resource management, the
responsibilities of human resource managers, and the role of human resource planning in
an organization's competitive strategy.

True or False

1. ___ As technology has advanced, the need for human resource management has
declined.

2. ___ Human resource management includes finding, training, motivating,
compensating, and appraising enough qualified employees to accomplish
organizational objectives.

3. ___ Managers outside the human resources department rarely have human resource
management responsibilities.

4. ___ Developing an organizational climate that improves employee motivation,
satisfaction, and efficiency is a key focus of human resource management.

5. ___ A growing number of small firms outsource their human resource management
activities to professional employer organizations (PEOs).

6. ___ Human resource planning is designed to provide the right number of properly
skilled employees.

7. ___ Human resource planning really has little to do with motivating workers.

8. ___ Today, there is a shortage of qualified job candidates.

Learning Goal 9.2: Describe how recruitment, selection, orientation, training, and evaluation contribute to placing the right person in a job.

Short Answer

1. What is the recruitment process? Where do employers look for potential employees?

2. What are the steps in the typical selection process? At what stage of this process may candidates be rejected?

3. Why do human resource managers need to be aware of employment law?

4. What sorts of employee training do organizations utilize?

5. What is a performance appraisal? To what uses are these appraisals applied?

Name _____ Instructor _____

Section _____ Date _____

Learning Goal 9.3: Outline the methods employers use to compensate employees through pay systems and benefit programs.

Multiple Choice

1. Payment to workers calculated on a weekly, monthly or annual basis is known as:

    a. wages.
    b. salary.

    c. benefits.
    d. incentive compensation.

2. Compensation programs such as profit sharing, gain sharing, pay for knowledge, bonuses and stock options are known as:

    a. wages.
    b. salary.

    c. incentive compensation programs.
    d. employee benefit programs.

3. A satisfactory compensation program should:

    a. attract well qualified applicants.
    b. keep workers satisfied in their jobs.
    c. inspire workers to be productive.
    d. all of the above.

4. The compensation policy of most employers is based upon:

    a. compensation offered by competitors for labor in the same area.
    b. government legislation and the cost of living.
    c. the company's ability to pay and worker productivity.
    d. all of the above.

5. Benefit programs:

    a. include benefits required by law such as social security.
    b. include pension plans, insurances, paid vacation, sick leave, and family leave.
    c. account for 28% of a typical employee's earnings.
    d. all of the above.

6.   Companies increasing adopt flexible benefit plans, often called:

    a.   compressed workweeks.   c.   cafeteria benefit plans.
    b.   work/life trends.   d.   employment at will.

Learning Goal 9.4: Discuss employee separation and the impact of downsizing and outsourcing.

Compare and Contrast: Which of the following applies to downsizing? to outsourcing?

	Downsizing	Outsourcing
1. reduces the number of workers in an organization	_____	_____
2. relies on outside specialists to do work formerly done by employees	_____	_____
3. adds flexibility	_____	_____
4. reduces costs	_____	_____
5 streamlines the organization's structure	_____	_____
6 means wider job responsibilities for remaining workers	_____	_____
7 allows a company to focus on activities it does best	_____	_____
8. is a prevailing modern trend	_____	_____

Name _____ Instructor _____

Section _____ Date _____

Learning Goal 9.5:   Explain how Maslow's hierarchy of needs theory, job design, and managers' attitudes relate to employee motivation.

Short Answer

1.   Maslow's hierarchy of needs is based on three assumptions. What are they?

   a.

   b.

   c.

2.   Maslow identified five needs in his analysis of motivation. List and define each.

   a.

   b.

   c.

   d.

   e.

True or False

3. ___ Learning new skills, rotating jobs with others, and having more authority to plan and execute one's own job are all examples of job enrichment.

4. ___ While job enrichment can make for greater job satisfaction, there is no evidence that it leads to greater productivity or organizational success.

5. ___ Job enlargement expands the number and variety of tasks in a worker's assignment.

Multiple Choice

6. A manager who thinks that workers are lazy, dislike work, and need constant and close supervision is characterized as:

    a. Theory X.
    b. Theory Y.
    c. Theory Z.

7. Managers who realize that workers want to meet their higher level needs at work are characterized as:

    a. Theory X.
    b. Theory Y.
    c. Theory Z.

8. Theory Z organizations:

    a. blend the best of American and Japanese management practices.
    b. rely on worker empowerment and participative management styles.
    c. may not evaluate and promote workers as frequently as more traditional organizations.
    d. all of the above.

9. The trends of downsizing organizations and empowering work teams favors the use of:

    a. Theory X.
    b. Theory Y.
    c. Theory Z.

Name _____ Instructor _____

Section _____ Date _____

Learning Goal 9.6: Summarize the role of labor unions and list their primary goals.

True or False

1. ___   A labor union is a group of workers who use collective strength to achieve common goals in the areas of compensation, job security, and work conditions.

2. ___   Contract negotiations almost always involve strikes.

3. ___   Today, more than 50% of American workers belong to unions.

4. ___   Union contracts focus exclusively on workers' wages and seniority.

5. ___   Union contracts generally cover a two to three year period.

Learning Goal 9.7: Outline the tactics of labor and management in conflicts between them.

Multiple Choice

1.   All of the following are methods of settling labor-management disputes except:

     a.   collective bargaining.   c.   voluntary arbitration.
     b.   lockouts.   d.   mediation.

2.   Which of the following are weapons management can use against organized labor?

     a.   hiring of strikebreakers   d.   employers' associations
     b.   injunctions   e.   all of the above
     c.   lockouts

3.   Which of the following are weapons unions can use against management?

     a.   threat of strike   d.   picketing
     b.   a walkout or strike   e.   all of the above
     c.   boycotts

4. Which of the following statements is *NOT* descriptive of strikes?

   a. Striking workers often picket the company during the strike.
   b. Strikes can cost employers in lost business while also hurting customers and/or suppliers.
   c. Striking workers are still paid by the company while they are on strike.
   d. Under the Taft-Hartley Act, unions must give 60 days' notice of an intended strike.

Learning Goal 9.8: Describe employee-management relations in nonunion organizations.

Short Answer

1. Alternative dispute resolution (ADR) programs include the following strategies. Define and explain each.

   a. open-door policies.

   b. employee hotlines.

   c. peer review boards.

   d. mediation and arbitration.

Name _____ Instructor _____

Section _____ Date _____

2. Discuss some of the methods used to preserve job security in nonunion firms.

Self Review

True or False

1. ___   According to Theory X, most people welcome increased responsibility.

2. ___   Telework is expected to accelerate as firms increasingly use the Internet.

3. ___   Employment at will means that employers must have a good reason to fire an employee or face a suit.

4. ___   Theory Y is associated with the idea that people are self-motivated.

5. ___   Theory Y advocates are more likely to delegate authority that Theory X advocates.

6. ___   Employment skills tests are often used as a screening device.

7. ___   Hiring from within contributes to employee morale.

8. ___   In a Paid-time-off program, each worker must carefully distinguish when they are using a sick day from when they are using a vacation day.

9. ___   The recruitment and selection process includes finding and evaluating job applicants.

10. ___   Once hired, the first thing an applicant should receive is training.

11. ___ Employee training should be viewed as an ongoing process throughout a worker's tenure with the company.

12. ___ While operating workers require training, few organizations have programs aimed at developing the skills of managers.

13. ___ Performance appraisals are used to make objective decisions about compensation, promotions, additional training needs, transfers, and terminations.

14. ___ Job enrichment, by focusing on motivational aspects of a job, often improves employee morale.

15. ___ Fringe benefits account for less than 10% of the typical employee's compensation.

16. ___ Mediation differs from arbitration in that a mediator's decision is legally binding.

17. ___ Ninety-five percent of all union-management negotiations result in a signed agreement without a work stoppage.

18. ___ Recently, union efforts to recruit new members have been most successful among service and government workers.

Multiple Choice

1. The mental attitude people have toward their employment is known as:

   a. perception.
   b. Theory X.
   c. morale.
   d. maintenance factors.

2. According to Maslow:

   a. a fully satisfied need is the best motivator.
   b. needs arise in a hierarchy.
   c. self-actualization needs are the most fundamental and arise first.
   d. all of the above.

3. Actions taken to avoid danger and the unexpected generally represent responses to:

   a. physiological needs.
   b. safety needs.
   c. social needs.
   d. esteem needs.
   e. self-actualization needs

Name _____ Instructor _____

Section _____ Date _____

4. Gaining respect from others or recognition for a job well done helps to satisfy:

    a.   physiological needs.   d.   esteem needs.
    b.   safety needs.   e.   self-actualization needs
    c.   social needs.

5. The desire to have friends, family, and to be accepted are motivated by:

    a.   physiological needs.   d.   esteem needs.
    b.   safety needs.   e.   self-actualization needs.
    c.   social needs.

6. An organization that offers workers challenging and creative work assignments is appealing to employees':

    a.   physiological needs.   d.   esteem needs.
    b.   safety needs.   e.   self-actualization needs.
    c.   social needs.

7. When organizations downsize:

    a.   they hope to reduce costs and improve performance by streamlining the organization's structure.
    b.   they always utilize layoffs.
    c.   trust and loyalty of remaining employees is automatically enhanced.
    d.   it means that they can avoid outsourcing.

8. Outsourcing:

    a.   relies on outside specialists to perform functions previously performed by the company's own employees.
    b.   adds flexibility while reducing costs.
    c.   allows a company to focus on what it does best.
    d.   all of the above.

9. The 1932 act that reduced management's ability to obtain injunctions halting union activities is the:

    a. Fair Labor Standards Act.   d. Taft-Hartley Act.
    b. Norris-La Guardia Act.   e. Landrum-Griffin Act.
    c. Wagner Act.

10. The 1935 act that established the National Labor Relations Board (NLRB),legalized collective bargaining and ordered employers to bargain with their workers' elected agent is the:

    a. Fair Labor Standards Act.   d. Taft- Hartley Act.
    b. Norris-La Guardia Act.   e. Landrum-Griffin Act.
    c. Wagner Act.

11. The 1938 act that set a federal minimum wage and maximum basic working hours, outlawed child labor, and provided for overtime pay is the:

    a. Fair Labor Standards Act.   d. Taft-Hartley Act.
    b. Norris-La Guardia Act.   e. Landrum-Griffin Act.
    c. Wagner Act.

12. The 1947 act that was designed to curb unfair labor practices and to balance the power of unions and management by prohibiting closed shops, featherbedding, discriminatory activities of unions, and secondary boycotts is the:

    a. Fair Labor Standards Act.   d. Taft-Hartley Act.
    b. Norris-La Guardia Act.   e. Landrum-Griffin Act.
    c. Wagner Act.

13. The 1959 legislation known as the Labor-Management Reporting and Disclosure Act and was passed to promote honesty and democracy in running a union's internal affairs. It is also known as the:

    a. Fair Labor Standards Act.   d. Taft-Hartley Act.
    b. Norris-La Guardia Act.   e. Landrum-Griffin Act.
    c. Wagner Act.

Name _____ Instructor _____

Section _____ Date _____

14. The 1988 Plant-Closing Notification Act:

   a.   applies to firms with more than 100 employees.
   b.   requires management to give workers and local elected officials 60 days
        notice of a shutdown or mass layoff.
   c.   created the Worker Readjustment Program to assist displaced workers.
   d.   all of the above.

Application Exercises

Anita Martinez operates her own business-services consulting company. She has hired several employees in the past, some of whom have worked out well, but many of whom have stayed only a short time before quitting or being fired for failure to perform as she had hoped. She is currently in need of an additional employee and wonders what she might do to enhance her chances of finding the right candidate for the job. Anita has come to you and asked your help in setting up a procedure for selecting suitable candidates.

1.   What suggestions can you make to help her find the right employee?

2.   Once Anita has hired a new employee, what steps can she take to help ensure employee satisfaction?

Short Essay Questions

1. What is human resource management? What activities are involved, and how important are they in achieving organizational objectives?

2. What is motivation, and how can motivation theory be applied in the workplace? Your answer should include Maslow's hierarchy of needs, and an analysis of Theory X, Theory Y and Theory Z. What essential lessons do these theories give us as we try to improve worker motivation?

CHAPTER 10

Improving Performance through Empowerment, Teamwork and Communication

Chapter Summary: Key Concepts

Empowering Employees

Empowerment

Giving employees authority and responsibility to make decisions about their work without traditional approval and control.

Sharing information

Companies share information about financial performance, profitability, and trends in the business environment. Information technology has contributed greatly to this means of empowerment by making it easier for employees to access the information they need to make good decisions on their own.

Sharing decision making authority

Empowerment can mean employees share authority and responsibility for things like purchasing, hiring decisions, scheduling, overseeing special programs and other activities once left to management.

Linking rewards to company performance

Incentive pay plans like pay for knowledge and gain sharing give employees a sense of ownership. Employee stock ownership plans and stock option plans are also means of making employees owners with a stake in the firm's performance.

Teamwork

What is a team?

A team is a group of people with complementary skills who are committed to a common purpose, approach, and set of performance goals. They hold themselves mutually responsible and accountable for accomplishing their objectives. Work teams are relatively permanent groups who perform the day to day work of the organization. Problem solving teams are temporarily formed to address a specific issue.

Team characteristics

Teams can be very large, but tend to be most effective when they have 5-12 members. Team members perform both task specialist roles and socio-emotional roles. Teams whose members have diverse backgrounds provide a broader perspective, and are especially good at finding creative solutions.

Stages of team development

The five stages of team development are forming, storming, norming, performing, and adjourning.

Team cohesiveness and norms

Teams tend to be most productive when they are highly cohesive and share common values, or team norms.

Team conflict

There are many potential sources of team conflict, including scarce resources, unclear roles, poor communication, and personality clashes.

Styles of conflict resolution

The styles of team conflict resolution span a continuum, from cooperative to assertive styles, and the right style will depend on the situation at hand.

The Importance of Effective Communication

Communication process

Six elements are involved: sender, message, channel, audience, feedback, and context.

Basic forms of communication

Communication can be oral or written, formal or informal, verbal and/or nonverbal.

Communication Within the Organization

Internal communication   Messages sent through channels within the organization. Senders and receivers work for the firm.

Communication in teams   Team members can use a centralized communication network, where team members exchange messages through a single person to solve problems or make decisions. Or they can adopt a decentralized communication network, where members communicate freely and reach decisions together.

Communication Outside the Organization

External communication   The exchange of meaningful information through messages transmitted between an organization and its major audiences, such as customers, suppliers, other firms, the general public, and government officials.

International business communication   Communication can be especially important and challenging in the international business arena. Low-context cultures use the "get down to business" style, rely on explicit written and verbal messages, and are common in Europe and the U.S. In contrast, in high-context cultures, such as Japan, Latin America, and India, businesspeople prefer to become well acquainted before discussing business details.

Name _____ Instructor _____

Section _____ Date _____

Business Vocabulary

centralized communication
  network
communication
conflict
decentralized communication
  network
employee stock ownership
  plan (ESOP)
empowerment
external communication
formal communication channel
grapevine
high-context culture
informal communication channel

internal communication
listening
low-context culture
nonverbal communication
problem-solving teams
socio-emotional role
stock options
task-specialist role
team
team cohesiveness
team norm
teamwork
work team

Application of Vocabulary

Select the term from the list above that best completes the statements below. Write that term in the space provided.

1. A small number of people with complementary skills who are committed to a common purpose, approach, and set of performance standards is known as a(n) _____.

2. _____ is the extent to which team members are attracted to the team and motivated to remain part of it.

3. Temporary combinations of workers who gather to solve a specific problem and then disband are known as _____.

4. Teams can experience _____, where there is an antagonistic interaction between parties.

5. A small number of people with complimentary skills who perform the day-to-day work of the organization make up a(n) _____.

Name _____ Instructor _____

Section _____ Date _____

6. People who devote their time and energy to helping the team accomplish its work goals have fulfilled a(n) _____.

7. Those who devote their time and energy to providing support for team members' emotional needs and social unity are performing the _____ _____.

8. _____ involves the meaningful exchange of information through messages.

9. Good communication depends a great deal on good _____, the skill of receiving a message and interpreting its meaning accurately.

10. When communication flows through the chain of command, the _____ _____ is in use.

11. When communication occurs outside formally authorized channels without regard for the organization's hierarchy of authority, it makes use of the _____ _____.

12. Actions and behaviors also communicate meaning, and are collectively known as _____.

13. The communication that takes place within an organization is known as _____ _____.

14. The unofficial internal channel of communication in an organization, which is both fast and surprisingly reliable, is known as the _____.

15. When a single person serves as the means by which other team members communicate, a(n) _____ is in use.

16. The meaningful exchange of information between an organization and its major audiences is known as _____.

17. When team members communicate freely among themselves and reach decisions together they are making use of a(n) _____.

18. Companies granting _____ give employees the opportunity to buy shares of its stock at a set price during a given period of time.

19. A _____ is a standard of conduct that is shared by team members and guides their behavior.

20. A _____ is one in which communication depends as much on everything that surrounds the message as it does on the content of the message itself.

21. In a _____, communication relies on explicit and written messages.

22. _____ gives employees authority and responsibility to make decisions about their work without traditional managerial approval and control.

23. Linking employee rewards to company performance through the use of a(n) _____ gives employees ownership stakes in the company, leading to potential profits when the value of their firm increases.

24. Emphasis on _____, the practice of organizing groups of people to work together to achieve a common objective, is a growing trend in business.

Analysis of Learning Goals

Learning Goal 10.1: Describe why and how organizations empower employees.

Multiple Choice

1. Modern organizations enhance performance through employee involvement using:

   a. employee empowerment.
   b. information sharing.
   c. teamwork.
   d. all of the above.

Name _____ Instructor _____

Section _____ Date _____

2.   By utilizing teamwork:

    a.   a firm's response time and flexibility in meeting customer needs can be improved.
    b.   people work independently rather than collectively.
    c.   employees generally experience lower levels of performance.
    d.   everyone follows the creative lead of a single person.

3.   Employers that empower workers:

    a.   should avoid incentive pay programs.
    b.   needn't give employees the respect that would be given to a partner.
    c.   should link employee rewards to company performance.
    d.   all of the above.

4.   An employee stock ownership plan (ESOP):

    a.   means workers work harder and smarter because they are part owners.
    b.   requires employers to share financial information about company assets, performance and executive salaries with employees.
    c.   holds shares of the company's stock paid for by the employer in a trust fund for the employees.
    d.   all of the above.

Learning Goal 10.2: Distinguish between the two major types of teams in the workplace.

True or False

1. ___   Work teams are permanent small groups of people with complimentary skills who handle the ongoing, day-to-day operations of the organization.

2. ___   Problem-solving teams are temporarily assembled to solve specific problems and then disbanded.

3. ___   Team members hold themselves mutually accountable to achieve common performance goals.

4. ___ A cross functional team blends people from different areas of the organization to solve a problem or take advantage of a new business opportunity.

Learning Goal 10.3: Identify the characteristics of an effective team and the roles played by team members.

Multiple Choice

1. Effective teams:

    a. generally have 30 or more members.
    b. typically have between 5 and 12 members.
    c. work best if team member roles are ambiguous.
    d. are more innovative if everyone has a common background.

2. Effective teams require their members to fill all of the following roles, *EXCEPT*:

    a. task specialist roles.   c. dual roles.
    b. socio-emotional roles.   d. non-participative roles.

3. Diverse teams:

    a. allow a broader perspective in finding creative solutions.
    b. are more innovative than homogeneous teams.
    c. require special attention to the socio-emotional roles so everyone feels at home.
    d. all of the above

4. Teamwork:

    a. has no bearing on employee empowerment.
    b. empowers employees while insuring controls through mutual responsibility and accountability.
    c. works best when there is a high degree of team conflict.
    d. works best when there is a low degree of team diversity.

Name _____ Instructor _____

Section _____ Date _____

Learning Goal 10.4: Summarize the stages of team development.

Short Answer

There are five stages of group development. Name and discuss each stage.

1.

2.

3.

4.

5.

Learning Goal 10.5: Relate team cohesiveness and norms to effective team performance.

True or False

1. ___ Productivity is enhanced when team cohesiveness is low.

2. ___ Team cohesiveness is high when members are attracted to the team and motivated to remain in it.

3. ___ Team cohesiveness is improved when members interact frequently and enjoy being together.

4. ___ Team norms are shared values and expectations of team members.

5. ___ Team norms are generally formal, written guidelines.

Learning Goal 10.6: Describe the factors that can cause conflict in teams and how conflict can be resolved.

Short Answer

1. What are the key factors that can cause conflict within a team?

2. Your text gives five conflict resolutions styles. List and define each.

    a.

    b.

    c.

    d.

    e.

Name _____ Instructor _____

Section _____ Date _____

Learning Goal 10.7: Explain the importance of effective communication skills in business.

True or False

1. ___ Most managers spend 80% of their time in direct communication with others.

2. ___ People with reasonably good English skills need not solicit feedback to ensure clear communication.

3. ___ As organizations grow, communication problems tend to decline.

4. ___ Communication takes place within the business itself and also between the business and outside audiences.

5. ___ Encoding is anything that reduces the accuracy or fidelity of a message.

Learning Goal 10.8: Compare the different types of communication.

True or False

1. ___ Formal communication channels within the organization generally follow the chain of command.

2. ___ In general, when verbal and nonverbal communication cues conflict, a communicator tends to believe the verbal elements.

3. ___ The grapevine is more rapid than formal communication channels and is surprisingly reliable.

4. ___ Oral communication can include meetings, voice mail, telephone conversions, and videoconferences.

5. ___ Gestures, facial expressions, posture, and body language generally have little impact on the meaning derived from oral communication.

6. ___ In today's team environment, most organizations depend almost exclusively on formal communication.

Self Review

True or False

1. ___ Team conflict is generally reduced when resources are scarce.

2. ___ When team goals are clear and communication within the team is good, greater cohesiveness can be expected.

3. ___ Vague assignments and roles are common causes of team conflict.

4. ___ A team leader can reduce conflict by clarifying member tasks and focusing members on broad common goals.

5. ___ Noise is anything that reduces the accuracy or fidelity of a message.

6. ___ Messages must be encoded into symbols that are capable of being transmitted.

7. ___ When the intended audience receives a communicated message, the message must still be decoded.

8. ___ The feedback a sender receives may cause the sender to alter or cancel the original message.

9. ___ Good communication depends little on active listening.

10. ___ The clothing you wear or the car you drive can be a form of nonverbal communication.

11. ___ Research has demonstrated that the greater part of understanding a message is linked to the verbal, rather than nonverbal, cues the audience receives.

12. ___ The grapevine is a good example of an informal communication channel.

13. ___ In a high-context culture, communication depends more on nonverbal cues and the relationship between the communicators.

14. ___ American business people may need to temper their dependence on explicit spoken or written messages when dealing with people from high-context cultures.

15. ___ People from all over the world share the same perception of what is an appropriate physical distance between people engaged in communication.

Name _____ Instructor _____

Section _____ Date _____

16. ___ The United States is a good example of nation that has a low-context communication culture.

17. ___ While communications problems can easily occur when translating into different languages, all English speaking people use the identical vocabulary.

Multiple Choice

1. The first stage of team development, in which members get acquainted and oriented, is known as:

   a. forming
   b. storming.
   c. norming.
   d. performing.
   e. adjourning.

2. As teams develop, members may differ as they try to clarify expectations and roles in the stage of group development known as:

   a. forming.
   b. storming.
   c. norming.
   d. performing.
   e. adjourning.

3. When team members resolve differences and reach a consensus about the roles of the team leader and other participants, the group has reached the stage of group development known as:

   a. forming.
   b. storming.
   c. norming.
   d. performing.
   e. adjourning.

4. In the adjourning stage of group development:

   a. the group often disbands.
   b. the team's experience and accomplishments are often summarized.
   c. participants' contributions are often recognized with some type of ritual.
   d. all of the above.

5. Extracting the meaning from a received message is known as:

   a. encoding.
   b. decoding.
   c. transmitting.
   d. noise.
   e. sending.

6. When team members communicate freely and reach decisions collectively, they are part of:

   a. a centralized communication network.
   b. a decentralized communication network.
   c. a low-context culture.
   d. a high-context culture.

7. In communication theory, a message:

   a. may be oral.
   b. may be written.
   c. may be transmitted electronically.
   d. must be encoded and decoded during the process.
   e. all of the above.

8. Studies have found that work teams made up of a diverse group of people:

   a. tend to find broader solutions.
   b. tend to be more innovative.
   c. are an important asset in our culturally diverse global environment.
   d. all of the above.

9. When an unpopular decision must be implemented or an emergency arises, the most suitable approach to conflict resolution is often the:

   a. competing style.
   b. avoiding style.
   c. compromising style.
   d. accommodating style.
   e. collaborating style.

10. The compromising style of conflict resolution is best applied when:

   a. two opposing goals are equally important.
   b. the parties to the conflict are equally powerful.
   c. the team feels pressure to achieve some sort of immediate solution and has no time to find the optimal solution.
   d. all of the above.

Name _____ Instructor _____

Section _____ Date _____

Application Exercises

1. Tony Tavernelli is a product development engineer at an electronics company. He has come up with a new idea that top management believes could be the company's next big winner, but he is meeting resistance from marketing, production and finance personnel within his company. Some of their concerns are legitimate, and Tony feels unqualified to make recommendations in areas outside his engineering expertise.

    Do you think Tony's firm might benefit from the team approach in this situation? If so, what sort of team would your recommend, and why?

2. Consider the following situations. What has each of the people communicated to you?

    a. Jill is speaking very rapidly and in a high pitch.

    b. Jim believes he presents his ideas clearly but he doesn't give others a chance to respond.

    c. Gina is listening to Tom, and has stepped back from him and crossed her arms.

    d. The customers listening to David's sales presentation are doodling or looking out the window.

    e. Your professor smiles, looks various students in the eye, and moves around the room while lecturing.

Short Essay Questions

1. What are the essential steps in any communication process? How important is listening to being an effective communicator?

2. What are teams, and why have they become more important in modern organizations?

CHAPTER 11

Production and Operations Management

Chapter Summary: Key Concepts

Strategic Importance of the Production Function

Production

The process that converts people, machinery, and other resources into marketable finished goods and services.

Mass production

Utilizing specialization, mechanization and standardization to produce large quantities at lower prices.

Flexible production

This cost effective way to produce smaller batches uses modern information technology and programmable equipment to quickly make a variety of goods.

Customer-driven production

Uses data about customer sales to forecast and schedule production.

Team concept

The team approach combines employees from various departments and functions within the organization, and often includes representatives of suppliers and customers. They work together to design and build products.

Technology and the Production Process

Production processes

Systems based on the means and time used to create output. They include analytic system, synthetic system, continuous process, and intermittent process.

Robots

A reprogrammable machine capable of performing a variety of jobs that require manipulations of materials and tools. Often used to replace boring or dangerous jobs.

Computer-aided design and computer-aided manufacturing	Computer-aided design (CAD) systems allow interactions between a designer and a computer to design a product, facility, or part that meets predetermined specifications. Computer-aided manufacturing (CAM), often used with CAD, enables a manufacturer to analyze the steps needed to implement a design, followed by electronic transmission of instructions to production equipment.
Flexible manufacturing system	A production facility that workers can quickly modify to manufacture different parts, typically consisting of computer-controlled machines and powerful software to run the machines.
Computer-integrated manufacturing	Companies integrate robots, CAD/CAM, FMS, computers, and other technologies to design products, control machines, handle materials, and control the production function.

The Location Decision

Location of facility	Considerations include proximity to raw materials and markets, availability of personnel, transportation, energy resources, taxes, and living conditions.
Environmental impact study	Local regulatory agencies may require a study to determine how a proposed facility will impact the quality of life in the surrounding area, taking into account such things as energy, water, sewage treatment, natural plant life and wildlife, and potential pollution.

The Job of Production Managers

Planning the production process	Production and operations managers must plan what to produce and how to produce it.
Determining the facility layout	The three basic types of layouts are process, product, and fixed position. A fourth, customer-oriented layout, is typical of service providers' production systems.

Implementing the production plan

Implementing a production plan involves making the decision of whether to make, buy, or lease components, selecting the best suppliers, and controlling inventory.

Inventory control

Inventory control methods include maintaining a perpetual inventory, vendor managed and CPFaR inventory control systems, just-in-time (JIT) inventory systems, and computerized materials requirement planning (MRP).

Controlling the production processes

Controlling production follows five steps: planning, routing, scheduling, dispatching and follow-up.

Importance of Quality

Quality control

Some means of quality control must be devised. Common methods include benchmarking, inspections, customer surveys, and constant improvement in production processes.

ISO standards

This international organization promotes the development of standardized products to facility trade and cooperation across national borders.

Name _____ Instructor _____

Section _____ Date _____

Business Vocabulary

assembly line
benchmarking
CPFaR
computer-aided design (CAD)
computer-aided manufacturing
  (CAM)
computer-integrated
  manufacturing (CIM)
critical path
dispatching
environmental impact study
flexible manufacturing system
  (FMS)
follow up
International Organization for
  Standardization (ISO)
inventory control
just-in-time (JIT)

make, buy, or lease decision
mass production
materials requirement
  planning (MRP)
perpetual inventory
program evaluation and review
  technique (PERT)
production
production and operations
  management
production control
production planning
quality control
robot
routing
scheduling
vendor managed inventory (VMI)

Application of Vocabulary

Select the term from the list above that best completes the statements below. Write that term in the space provided.

1. _____ is the general term applied to operations that use people, machinery, and other resources to convert materials into finished goods and services.

2. The industrial development of the United States involved the manufacture of large quantities of standardized goods using specialized labor and mechanization in an approach known as _____.

3. The _____ is a manufacturing technique, first used by Henry Ford, wherein the product passes through several work stations, each with a specialized task.

Name _____ Instructor _____

Section _____ Date _____

4. A _____ makes it possible to quickly modify production methods as different products are manufactured.

5. Designers can use computers to create and modify a part or product before producing an actual prototype using _____.

6. When computers are used to analyze a CAD and electronically transmit instructions to production processing equipment, a _____ is in use.

7. The use of computers to design products, control machines, handle materials, and control the production function in an integrated fashion is called _____.

8. _____ involves balancing the costs of holding raw materials, work in progress, and inventory against the costs involved in carrying the inventory.

9. _____ is the process of identifying best practices in a field or industry, and then using those standards to continually measure and improve performance.

10. _____ is a computer-based planning system for ensuring that the needed amount of parts and materials is available at the right time and place, and in the right amounts.

11. Producers must make a _____ about whether it is advisable to manufacture, purchase, or lease a needed component, product, or material.

12. _____ is the phase of production control that develops timetables specifying how long each operation in the production process takes and when it should be performed.

13. The management of people, machinery, and other resources used in converting inputs into finished goods and services is called _____.

14. During the phase of production control known as _____, managers develop a bill of materials and a determination of other resources needed to produce a certain quantity of good or service.

15. _____ is the phase of production control that specifies where and by whom each aspect of production will be performed.

16. The measurement of products or services produced against established quality standards is referred to as _____.

17. A study undertaken to determine what effect a proposed plant will have on the quality of life in a given area is known as an _____.

18. _____ is a scheduling technique developed by the military, used to minimize production delays by coordinating all aspects of a complex task.

19. The _____ phase of production control spots problems and informs management of needed adjustments.

20. A _____ inventory system supplies the needed parts to the production line on a last-minute basis.

21. A _____ system makes it possible to continuously update the list of items in inventory.

22. The sequence of operations in a PERT diagram requiring the longest time for completion is called the _____.

23. Once routing and scheduling have been completed, each department is instructed on what work is to be done and the time allowed for its completion in a phase of production control known as _____.

24. A _____ is a smart machine capable of performing numerous or dangerous tasks without getting hungry, tired, or sick.

25. _____ is a well-defined set of procedures for coordinating people, materials, and machinery to provide maximum production efficiency.

26. The organization established to ensure consistent standards for products and to facilitate trade and cooperation among its 130 member nations is called the _____.

Name _____ Instructor _____

Section _____ Date _____

27. When inventory control decisions are turned over to a supplier, the _____ _____ system is in use.

28. _____ is an approach to inventory management where vendors and purchasers collaborate in the planning, forecasting and replenishment of inventory.

Analysis of Learning Goals

Learning Goal 11.1: Outline the importance of production and operations management.

True or False

1. ___ Production and operations managers oversee the conversion of inputs (labor, materials, machines) into outputs (goods and services).

2. ___ Production and operations managers are needed by business, but are rarely used in the not-for-profit sector.

3. ___ Effective production and operations management can reduce production costs and increase profits.

4. ___ Production management applies to manufacturing but not to service businesses.

5. ___ Unfortunately, flexible production systems offer no means to integrate the information technology and programmable equipment used in mass production.

6. ___ Customer-driven production techniques allow a firm to alter its production plans continuously in response to customer demands.

Learning Goal 11.2: Explain the role of computers and related technologies in production.

True or False

1. ___ With the use of computer-integrated manufacturing (CIM), production can be integrated by a centralized computer system that designs products, controls machines, handles materials, and controls production processes.

2. ___ Computer controlled machining centers, powerful software, and other technologies make it possible to quickly modify systems to manufacture different products.

3. ___ Materials requirement planning (MRP) integrates data from a variety of departments to produce a master business plan for the whole organization.

4. ___ In computer-aided design (CAD), users can sketch, analyze and modify three dimensional designs on a computer screen.

5. ___ In computer-aided manufacturing (CAM), the user can analyze the steps that will be needed in manufacturing the product designed using the CAD program.

6. ___ Robots are reprogrammable machines that have replaced many production workers in the performance of repetitive or dangerous tasks.

7. ___ Integration of modern technology in production allows firms to produce items so fast that customers can keep a lower stock on hand and place more frequent orders.

Learning Goal 11.3: Identify the factors involved in a plant location decision.

Short Answer

What are the nine factors that should be considered when selecting a location?

1.

2.

3.

Name _____ Instructor _____

Section _____ Date _____

4.

5.

6.

7.

8.

9.

Learning Goal 11.4: Explain the major tasks of production and operations managers.

Short Answer

Describe the four major tasks of production managers.

1.

2.

3.

4.

Learning Goal 11.5: Compare alternative layouts for production facilities.

Fill in the Blank

1. The type of layout that groups materials and equipment by function, allowing the production of a variety of nonstandard products in relatively small batches is called
   _____.

2. The layout that is designed to accommodate only a few product designs, such as in the automobile industry where each product has its own layout is the _____
   _____.

3. When the workers, material, and machines are transported to and from the product, such as in bridge construction or missile assembly, the _____
   is in use.

4. When interaction between providers and customers of services is important, a
   _____ layout may be used.

Learning Goal 11.6: List the steps in the purchasing process.

True or False

1. ___ Producers must first determine if they will make their own products and components, or buy or lease them from outside vendors.

2. ___ The major objective of the purchasing process is to have the right materials in the right amounts available at the right time and place.

3. ___ Today, firms increasingly get bids from as many suppliers as possible, rather than developing long-term relationships with one or two suppliers.

Name _____ Instructor _____

Section _____ Date _____

4. ____ Firms avoid purchasing raw materials or component parts by long term contract since availability over a one or two year period is not a worry.

5. ____ Quality control standards are a major factor in selecting the right supplier.

Learning Goal 11.7: Outline the advantages and disadvantages of maintaining large inventories.

True or False

1. ____ Inventory control balances the need to have inventory on hand with the costs of carrying that inventory.

2. ____ Extra inventory is more costly than inadequate inventory.

3. ____ JIT systems try to maximize inventory on hand to insure against production delays.

4. ____ Inventory costs must take into account warehousing, taxes, insurance, and maintenance.

5. ____ The scanning devices used in many supermarkets are often linked to inventory systems that can automatically reorder needed merchandise.

Learning Goal 11.8: Identify the steps in the production control process.

Fill in the Blank

Identify the following steps in the production control process. Write the name of the step in the space provided.

1. _____ is the phase of production control that determines the amount of inventory needed to produce a certain amount of product.

2. The phase that spots problems in the production process and informs management of needed adjustments is called _____.

3. _____ instructs each department on what work is to be done and the time allowed for completion.

4. The phase of production control that determines the sequence of work throughout the facility is known as _____.

5. PERT networks are used in the phase of production control known as

_____ _____.

Learning Goal 11.9: Explain the benefits of quality control.

True or False

1. ___ Investing more money up front in quality design and development ultimately lowers the costs of maintaining high quality.

2. ___ The most efficient way to control quality is to spot check output and fix any mistakes.

3. ___ X-rays, electronic sensors, and robots can help automate quality control inspections.

4. ___ Benchmarking involves recognizing best practices and doing what it takes to achieve and even exceed these standards.

Self Review

True or False

1. ___ Production can be defined as the use of people, machinery, and other resources to convert materials into finished products and services.

2. ___ Plant location can contribute to the difference between profit and loss for a firm.

3. ___ Refining crude oil is an example of an analytic production process.

4. ___ Mass production was based in part on the specialization of labor and tasks.

Name _____ Instructor _____

Section _____ Date _____

5. ___ Mechanization refers to using machines to perform work previously done by people.

6. ___ In a process layout, the facility is designed so that the product stays in one place while workers, materials and machines come to it.

7. ___ Customers and suppliers are increasingly involved in forecasting and implementing production schedules.

8. ___ Automobiles are manufactured by means of an analytic process.

9. ___ Proximity to customers should be a determining factor in the location of service facilities.

10. ___ Transportation is an important factor to be considered when selecting a location.

11. ___ Production control is a three step process: planning, scheduling, and dispatching.

12. ___ Synthetic production involves putting various parts together to make a finished product.

13. ___ Continuous-process production is used in petroleum refineries.

14. ___ One of the advantages of flexible manufacturing systems is that they enable the users to produce small batches at mass production speed.

15. ___ In a PERT network, the critical path is the sequence of operations requiring the shortest time for completion.

Multiple Choice

1. Producing uniform, interchangeable goods and parts is called:

   a. dispatching.
   b. standardization.
   c. routing.

   d. quality control.
   e. none of the above.

2. Under a _____, machines and equipment are grouped by function.

   a. process layout.   d. PERT layout.
   b. static product layout.   e. quality control layout.
   c. product layout.

3. An important consideration in plant location is:

   a. transportation.
   b. taxes and regulations in the area.
   c. adequate labor supply.
   d. quality of life in the community.
   e. all of the above.

4. The step in production control that involves developing the timetables for each operation is:

   a. planning.   d. dispatching.
   b. routing.   e. mechanization.
   c. scheduling.

5. The PERT network method is most useful for:

   a. prototype building.   d. service centers.
   b. routine jobs.   e. none of the above.
   c. complex projects.

6. A synthetic system is the opposite of:

   a. a basic system.   c. an intermittent system.
   b. a fixed position system.   d. an analytic system.

7. If the price and quality of an item are similar, what other factors should determine the selection of the supplier?

   a. speed of delivery.
   b. previous experience.
   c. warranties on purchases.
   d. the supplier's commitment to quality control.
   e. all of the above.

Name _____ Instructor _____

Section _____ Date _____

8. JIT has to do with:

    a. inventory control.   d. product design.
    b. quality control.   e. plant layout.
    c. production control.

9. Managers of the production function are responsible for:

    a. planning overall production processes.
    b. determining the best layout for the production facilities.
    c. implementation of the production plan.
    d. maintaining quality control standards in production.
    e. all of the above.

10. Today, production planning:

    a. is confined to the production department.
    b. involves only the production and marketing departments.
    c. increasingly utilizes the team concept.
    d. never includes customer or supplier input.
    e. excludes evaluation of production processes.

11. Standards set to ensure standardization of components and goods sold in 140 countries are set by the:

    a. ISO.   c. CIM.
    b. MRP.   d. JIT.

12. A firm that relies on its supplier to manage inventory for it is using:

    a. a perpetual inventory system.
    b. a vendor-managed inventory system.
    c. a JIT inventory system.
    d. poor judgment.

13. Historically, mass production relied upon:

   a. specialization of labor.   c. mechanization.
   b. standardization.   d. all of the above.

Application Exercises

Pat and Todd Doty own a small but growing manufacturing firm. The firm produces custom-made products and is becoming more mechanized. Currently, the company's employees are trained on a variety of tasks. Most of them can literally perform every step in the manufacturing process. The employees enjoy the variety of work. However, the training time for new employees is very long and thus expensive.

The firm is considering going to the specialization of labor. They have asked you to outline the advantages and disadvantages of specialization and suggest a method that would not completely devastate the morale of the present employees and, at the same time, reduce the cost of training new employees.

1. What are the advantages of specialization?

2. What are the disadvantages of specialization?

3. What suggestions can you make?

Name _____ Instructor _____

Section _____ Date _____

Short Essay Questions

1. What are the tasks of production and operations management? How important are these techniques in the creation of services?

2.   Computers have vastly changed the way production and operations management works. Write a brief essay detailing the various computer techniques used by modern production managers.

CHAPTER 12

Customer-Driven Marketing

Chapter Summary: Key Concepts

What is Marketing?

Marketing

The process of determining customer wants and needs and then providing the goods and services that meet or exceed expectations.

Creating utility

Marketing creates the "want satisfying power" of goods and services by researching what will provide form utility, and directly producing time, place and ownership utility.

Evolution of the Marketing concept

Marketing concept

Companywide customer orientation in which all of the organization's efforts are aimed at satisfying customer needs over the long run.

Delivering added value through customer satisfaction

Firms today focus on adding value by meeting or exceeding customers' quality expectations. Providing good value at a fair price leads to customer satisfaction and enduring loyalty.

Customer satisfaction and feedback

Successful companies seek and respond to customer feedback to ensure the satisfaction of their customers.

Expanding Marketing's Traditional Boundaries

Not-for-profit marketing

Both public and private not-for-profit organizations employ marketing strategies to reach audiences, secure funding, improve their images, and accomplish their overall missions.

Nontraditional marketing

Person, Place, Event, Cause, and Organization marketing are examples of marketing efforts that go beyond traditional product-oriented appeals. They are used primarily by the not-for-profit sector, but also have gained increased use in the private sector.

Developing a Marketing Strategy

Market

People with needs and wants, purchasing power, and the willingness and authority to buy. Markets are usually classified as consumer (B2C) or business (B2B) markets.

Selecting a target market

The target market is the group of potential customers toward whom an organization directs its marketing efforts.

Developing a marketing mix

Taking aim at a particular target market involves developing product, price, promotion and distribution strategies.

Developing a marketing mix for international markets

Marketing a good or service in foreign markets means deciding whether to offer the same mix in every market--*standardization*, or to develop a unique mix to fit each market--*adaptation.*

Marketing Research for Improved Marketing Decisions

Marketing research

Links marketers to the environment by collecting internal and external data and developing information systems to aid in marketing decision making.

Obtaining marketing research data

Internal financial records provide useful information regarding inventory levels, sales, and profitability. External data can be collected from secondary (previously published) sources, or by doing one's one external marketing research (collecting primary data).

Applying marketing research data	Computer-based marketing research systems allow firms to increase the accuracy of information at hand as they develop their marketing strategies. UPC reported information, and data mining using sophisticated customer databases (data warehouses) are widely used techniques.

Market Segmentation

Market segmentation	Dividing the total undifferentiated market for a good or service into several relatively homogeneous groups.
How it works	B2B and B2C market segments must each be measurable, accessible for communications, and large enough to offer profit potential.
Segmenting consumer markets	Consumer markets are segmented on the basis of geographic, demographic, psychographic, and product related bases.
Segmenting business markets	Business marketers use geographic, customer-based (demographic), and end-use segmentation.

Buyer Behavior: Determining What Customers Want

Buyer behavior	The process by which consumers and business buyers make purchase decisions.
Determinants of consumer behavior	Consumer behavior is governed by interpersonal determinants, (cultural, family, and social influences), as well as by personal determinants (needs and motives, perceptions, attitudes, learning, and self-concept.)
Determinants of business buying behavior	Business buyers face a variety of organizational influences, and these decisions often involve the combined judgment of people from many areas of the organization.

Steps in the consumer behavior process	Consumers first recognize a problem or opportunity. They then search for and evaluate alternatives. They make a purchase decision, and then complete the transaction (the purchase act). Then they generally perform a postpurchase evaluation. Each step is influenced by the personal and interpersonal determinants mentioned above.

Creating, Maintaining, and Strengthening Marketing Relationships

Relationship Marketing	Modern firms increasingly attempt to develop long-term, cost-effective links with individual customers, suppliers, employees, and other partners for mutual benefit.
Benefits of relationship marketing	These efforts, enhanced by modern information technology, allow firms to identify their best customers, add value, and provide a competitive edge by providing superior customer service.
Tools for nurturing customer relationships	Frequency marketing, affinity marketing programs, comarketing, cobranding, and one-on-one marketing are commonly used tools.

Business Vocabulary

affinity program
business products (B2B)
buyer behavior
buyer's market
cobranding
comarketing
consumer behavior
consumer products (B2C)
customer satisfaction
data mining
data warehouses
exchange process
frequency marketing
lifetime value of a customer

market
market segmentation
marketing
marketing concept
marketing mix
marketing research
marketing strategy
relationship marketing
seller's market
target market
transaction marketing
utility
value-added

Name _____ Instructor _____

Section _____ Date _____

Application of Vocabulary

Select the term from the list on the preceding page that best completes the statements beginning below. Write that term in the space provided.

1. A(n) _____ is composed of people with authority, ability, and desire to purchase goods and services.

2. The _____ is a combination of product, pricing, distribution, and promotional strategies.

3. A(n) _____ is a market characterized by a shortage of a sought-after product.

4. The need satisfying power of a good or service is known as its _____.

5. The _____ takes place when two or more parties trade something of value.

6. _____ is the collection and use of information to help make marketing decisions.

7. Searching through customer information files to detect patterns that guide marketing decision making is known as _____.

8. _____ involves defining and selecting a target market and then devising a marketing mix aimed at that target.

9. When a firm directs its marketing efforts toward a select group of customers, that group is called the _____.

10. A(n) _____ exists when supply for a product exceeds the demand for that product.

11. _____ are defined as products purchased by consumers for personal, non-business use.

12. A firm that figures out what the customer wants and needs, and then takes a customer orientation in all of its activities is utilizing the _____.

13. _____ is the process of dividing the total market into several relatively homogeneous groups.

14. _____ are products purchased by industry for business or industrial use.

15. _____ is the total process of determining customer wants and needs and then providing the goods and services that meet or exceed customer expectations.

16. Data mining uses _____, which are sophisticated customer databases combining data from several different organizational functions.

17. _____ is the process by which consumers and business buyers make purchase decisions.

18. The buying behavior of ultimate consumers is called _____.

19. _____ is the ability of a good or service to meet or exceed customer needs and expectations.

20. A _____ program rewards purchasers with cash, rebates, merchandise, or other premiums to enhance and protect customer relationships.

21. _____ is the increased worth of a good or service when a company adds features, reduces its price, enhances customer service, strengthens its warranty, or makes other marketing mix improvements that increase customer satisfaction.

22. The _____ measures the revenues and other benefits over the duration of a customer relationship, less the costs of acquiring and servicing that customer.

23. In _____, buyer and seller exchanges are based entirely on lowering costs and/or maximizing profits on each deal.

24. Companies who develop long-term, mutually beneficial, cost-effective links with customers are engaged in _____.

25. A(n) _____ builds emotional links with customers by soliciting involvement by people who share common interests, activities, or affiliations.

Name _____ Instructor _____

Section _____ Date _____

26. When two businesses jointly market each other's products, _____ is in use.

27. When two or more businesses team up to closely link their names for a single product, _____ is in use.

Analysis of Learning Goals

Learning Goal 12.1: Summarize the ways in which marketing creates utility.

True or False

1. ___ Utility in marketing is defined as "want satisfying power."

2. ___ Retailers create ownership utility when they accept credit cards as a method of payment.

3. ___ A presence on the Internet can help a firm to create utility.

4. ___ Getting a product to market when the customer wants it creates time utility.

5. ___ Marketing is really nothing more than selling.

Learning Goal 12.2: Explain the marketing concept and relate how customer satisfaction contributes to added value.

True or False

1. ___ The marketing concept requires organizations to take a customer orientation in all the organization's activities to achieve long term success.

2. ___ The marketing concept has little application in not-for-profit organizations.

3. ___ A good or service provides added value when its price is higher than the offerings of competing producers.

4. ___ Customer satisfaction is defined as the degree of excellence or superiority of an organization's good and services.

5. ___ Value is the customers' perception of what they got for their money.

6. ___ Quality is judged by what producers decide it should be, not by what customers want or expect it to be.

7. ___ Marketing campaigns can focus on people, places, causes, events, and organizations.

8. ___ In marketing, partnerships between for-profit and not-for-profit organizations are illegal.

Learning Goal 12.3: Describe the components of a market and distinguish between B2B and B2C marketing.

True or False

1. ___ A market consists of people with needs and wants, money to spend, and the willingness and authority to spend.

2. ___ When you buy a personal computer for business use you have made a purchase in the consumer (B2C) market.

3. ___ Consumer and business markets are distinguished by the buyer's intended use of the product or service purchased.

4. ___ When you purchase a CD for your listening pleasure you have made a purchase in the business (B2B) market.

Learning Goal 12.4: Outline the basic steps in developing a marketing strategy.

Multiple Choice

1. The first step in developing a marketing strategy is:

   a. creating a product to sell.
   b. selecting a target market.
   c. developing a price strategy.
   d. developing a distribution strategy.
   e. planning a promotional campaign.

Name _____ Instructor _____

Section _____ Date _____

2.   Package design, branding and labeling, and customer service are all components of:

a.   product strategy.   d.   promotional strategy.
b.   price strategy.   e.   all of the above.
c.   distribution strategy.

3.   Advertising, personal sales, sales promotion, and public relations comprise:

a.   product strategy.   d.   promotional strategy.
b.   price strategy.   e.   all of the above.
c.   distribution strategy.

4.   Deciding which wholesalers and retailers to use in bringing a product to market is part of:

a.   product strategy.   d.   promotional strategy.
b.   price strategy.   e.   all of the above.
c.   distribution strategy.

5.   The marketing mix is comprised of:

a.   product strategy.   d.   promotional strategy.
b.   price strategy.   e.   all of the above.
c.   distribution strategy.

Learning Goal 12.5: Describe the marketing research function.

True or False

1. ___   Marketing research requires the collection and interpretation of data for use in marketing decisions.

2. ___   Marketing research focuses exclusively on external data.

3. ___   The U.S. government provides little if any useful information to private firms doing market research.

4. ___   Observational studies and surveys are means of collecting primary data.

5. ___ Data mining is a way for a company to avoid maintaining costly data warehouses.

6. ___ Information technology has greatly aided the development of responsive marketing strategies by improving the quantity, quality, and accuracy of marketing data.

Learning Goal 12.6: Identify each of the methods for segmenting consumer and business markets.

Multiple Choice

1. Market segmentation:

   a. combines differing groups into one mass market.
   b. divides the varied total market into groups with similar characteristics.
   c. has little application in defining target markets.
   d. is done for the consumer market but not for the business market.

2. Segmenting markets on the basis of age, race, gender, occupation, household type, or ethnic group is called:

   a. demographic segmentation.   c. psychographic segmentation.
   b. geographic segmentation.   d. product-related segmentation.

3. Psychographic segmentation divides markets on the basis of:

   a. socioeconomic characteristics.   c. where people live or buy.
   b. behavioral and life-style profiles. d. perceived product benefits.

4. Product-related segmentation divides markets on the basis of:

   a. customer usage rates.   c. perceived product benefits.
   b. brand loyalty levels.   d. all of the above.

5. Business market segmentation:

   a. uses the identical segmentation criteria used in consumer markets.
   b. can rely on geographic, demographic, or end-use segmentation.
   c. avoids having to use the NAICS system of business classification.
   d. all of the above.

Name _____ Instructor _____

Section _____ Date _____

Learning Goal 12.7: Distinguish between buyer behavior and consumer behavior.

True or False

1. ___   While consumer behavior refers to the behavior of ultimate consumers, buyer behavior concerns the behavior of both consumers and businesses as they make purchase decisions.

2. ___   Cultural, social, and family influences are considered personal determinants of consumer behavior.

3. ___   Like consumer purchases, industrial purchasers tend to rely on a single person to make the purchase decision.

4. ___   Consumer purchases are influenced by a person's attitudes, needs, motives, and past experiences.

5. ___   Business buyer behavior is influenced less by relationship marketing than is consumer buyer behavior.

Learning Goal 12.8: Discuss the benefits of relationship marketing.

True or False

1. ___   Retaining customers is important in a successful marketing strategy

2. ___   The goal of relationship marketing is to achieve customer satisfaction that creates repeat business.

3. ___   Studying current customers' buying habits and preferences can help marketers target their best customers.

4. ___   Information technologies such as computers, databases, and the Internet provide critical support in relationship marketing.

5. ___   Relationship marketing applies to customers, but not to employees or suppliers.

Self Review

True or False

1. ___ A firm that makes products of high quality and exceptional value need not be concerned with marketing research.

2. ___ The business products market can be segmented on a geographical basis.

3. ___ In a buyer's market, supply exceeds demand.

4. ___ Market segmentation based on the income of potential buyers is rarely used.

5. ___ Person marketing is visible in political campaigns.

6. ___ A membership drive for a non-profit organization is an example of organization marketing.

7. ___ Advertising campaigns that discourage drug or alcohol abuse are examples of cause marketing.

8. ___ Marketers of services need not be concerned with developing a distribution strategy.

9. ___ Promotional strategy involves advertising and sales promotion, but excludes personal selling.

10. ___ Relationship marketing relies less on customer feedback than does transaction marketing.

11. ___ In the long run, the consumer is "king."

12. ___ The marketing concept focuses on production, not the customer.

13. ___ Firms may have more than one target market for a given product.

14. ___ Relationship marketing seeks to benefit the sellers, but provides no new benefits to buyers.

15. ___ Geographical segmentation is useful in both business and consumer markets.

16. ___ Value is the customer's perception of the balance between the quality of goods and services and the prices of those goods and services.

Name _____ Instructor _____

Section _____ Date _____

17. ___ Quality is whatever the customer says it is.

18. ___ In marketing products abroad, standardization can bring reliable marketing performance at lower cost.

19. ___ In marketing products abroad, adaptation lets marketers vary their marketing mix to suit local conditions and preferences.

Multiple Choice

1. A seller's market is characterized by:

    a. more supply than demand.   d. high advertising expenditures.
    b. much competition.   e. shortages.
    c. low prices.

2. If an organization adopts the marketing concept as its general policy, this means that:

    a. marketing personnel will dominate the organization.
    b. the organization will hire an advertising manager.
    c. all areas of the organization will try to satisfy the potential buyer or user.
    d. the organization will stress quality at low prices.
    e. the marketing director will be come the organization's president.

3. The dividing of a market into submarkets is called:

    a. market partitioning.   d. market conceptualization.
    b. market mix.   e. market segmentation.
    c. market division.

4. A market consists of:

    a. people with the financial ability to buy.
    b. people with the authority to buy.
    c. people with the willingness to buy.
    d. all of the above.

5. A viable market segment must:

   a. be a measurable group.
   b. be accessible for communications.
   c. be large enough to offer profit potential.
   d. all of the above.

6. Whether a product is a consumer or business product depends on the:

   a. price.
   b. seller.
   c. demography.
   d. end user.
   e. economic environment.

7. Which of the following is *NOT* one of the major strategies in the marketing mix?

   a. distribution
   b. competition
   c. product
   d. price
   e. promotion

8. The first step in the consumer decision making process is to:

   a. seek out information about a product.
   b. talk to others about product features.
   c. look at all the brands that are available.
   d. recognize a need or desire to be met.
   e. evaluate competitive products.

9. Examples of cause marketing would include all of the following *EXCEPT:*

   a. gun control.
   b. neighborhood watch groups.
   c. drunken driving.
   d. abused children.
   e. a subscription to the local newspaper.

10. Organizational marketing involves:

   a. influencing people to accept an organization's goals.
   b. receiving the services offered.
   c. getting people to contribute to the organization.
   d. attracting new members.
   e. all of the above

Name _____ Instructor _____

Section _____ Date _____

11. A marketing effort aimed at sustaining ongoing, mutually beneficial relations with customers is called:

    a. relationship marketing.   c. market segmentation.
    b. transaction marketing.   d. data mining.

12. In modern business, marketing strategy must take into account external factors such as:

    a. the competitive and socio-cultural environments.
    b. the economic and political-legal environments.
    c. technological innovations.
    d. all of the above.

Application Exercise

The owner of a new toy manufacturer will be a guest speaker in your class. The subject of her talk will center on marketing strategies.

In preparation for the speaker, your professor divided the class into small groups. Each group has a chairperson and five students. The chairperson's duty is to make sure that his or her group is completely versed about one facet of marketing. The chairperson must also prepare a list of five questions to ask the speaker.

You have been selected as a chairperson, and have been given the subject of market segmentation.

1. What information will you give your group?

2.   What five questions would you ask the speaker?

Short Essay Questions

1.   What is the marketing concept? How did this approach to marketing arise? What difference does the marketing concept make to producers? to customers?

Name _____ Instructor _____

Section _____ Date _____

2.   What is the marketing mix? Carefully define each component strategy.

3.   What is marketing research, and what are five reasons for doing it?

Notes:

CHAPTER 13

Product and Distribution Strategies

Chapter Summary: Key Concepts

Product Strategy

Product strategy The part of marketing that deals with product/service development. It also manages package design, trademarks and other product identification, warranties, product life cycle, and new-product development.

Classifications of consumer (B2C) products The classification is based on consumer buying habits, and includes convenience, shopping, and specialty products.

Classifications of business (B2B) products Business products are classified by their basic characteristics and use. The five categories are raw materials, component parts and materials, accessory equipment, installations, and supplies.

Marketing strategy implications Once a product has been classified, marketers have a better idea of its promotion, pricing, and distribution needs.

Product lines and produce mix A firm's product line is a group of related products marked by similarities or intended for a similar market. The product mix is the complete assortment of lines and individual goods and services that a firm offers its customers.

The Product Life Cycle

Stages of the product life cycle The cycle begins with the introductory stage, advances through the growth and maturity stages, and ends in the decline stage.

Marketing implications of the product life cycle	Price, promotion and distribution strategies will differ as the product moves through its life cycle. The life cycle will be extended, (finding new uses is an example) as long as it remains profitable.
Stages in new-product development	The new-product development process involves six distinct activities: 1) idea generation; 2) screening; 3) business analysis; 4) product development; 5) test marketing; and 6) commercialization.

Product Identification

Selecting an effective brand name	Products are identified by brands, brand names, and trademarks. Good brands are easy to pronounce, recognize and remember. They should also convey benefits of the product, and be legally protectable.
Brand categories	Brands can carry the manufacturer's name (national brands) or the wholesaler or retailer's name (private brands). Marketers must also decide whether to use the same name for many goods (family branding) or to use a unique name for each offering (individual branding).
Brand loyalty and brand equity	The three levels of brand loyalty are brand recognition, brand preference, and brand insistence. A highly respected and widely recognized brand name gives a brand added value, known as brand equity.
Packages and labels	Distinctive packages and labels also contribute to product identification, and offer other marketing tools such as the UPC code on most labels.

Distribution Strategy

Distribution channels	The pathway that goods and ownership of them follow from the producer to the consumer or industrial user. There are four channels each for consumer and business goods, and two for services. The appropriate channel in any situation will be determined by market factors, product factors, producer factors, and competitive factors.

Direct distribution	Distribution channel that moves goods directly from producer to consumer. Common in the business-to-business market and in delivery of services.
Marketing intermediaries	Also known as middlemen, includes wholesalers and retailers.

Wholesaling

Wholesaling intermediaries	Persons or firms that sell to retailers and/or to other wholesalers or to industrial users. Manufacturers may operate sales offices or sales branches to serve their wholesaling needs. Independent wholesalers include merchant wholesalers and agents and brokers. Retailers can also band together to form their own wholesaling operations.
Retailer-owned cooperatives and buying offices	Retailers sometimes band together to reduce costs or to share functions like shipping or warehousing.

Retailing

Retailers	Distribution channel member that sells goods and services to individuals for their personal use rather than for resale.
Nonstore retailers	Retailers using Internet retailing, automatic merchandising, direct-response retailing, and direct selling are examples of nonstore retailers.
Store retailers	Ninety-five percent of all retail sales take place in retail stores. In the process called the _wheel of retailing_, new retailers enter the market by offering lower prices and fewer services. As they businesses mature, they gradually add services, ultimately becoming the target for new retailers.
How retailers compete	After identifying their target market, retailers must choose merchandising, customer service, pricing, atmosphere and location, and promotional strategies that will attract their targeted customers.

Distribution Channel Decisions and Physical Distribution

Selecting distribution channels   Marketers may select direct channels, or channels involving middlemen. In general, products that are complex, expensive, custom made, or perishable use shorter channels. Standardized products or items with low unit values usually pass through relatively long distribution channels.

Selecting distribution intensity   There are three categories of market coverage: intensive, exclusive, and selective distribution.

Logistics and physical distribution   Physical distribution is the actual movement of goods from producer to consumer or industrial user, and is the last link in the supply chain. The process of coordinating the flow of goods, services, and information among members of the supply chain is called logistics. Physical distribution includes the functions of transportation, warehousing, materials handling, inventory control, order processing, and customer service.

Transportation   The prevalent modes of transportation include rail, water, truck, pipeline and air. The mode of transportation used depends upon the type of product, the distance, cost, and timing.

Name _____ Instructor _____

Section _____ Date _____

Business Vocabulary

brand
brand equity
brand loyalty
brand name
category manager
direct distribution channel
distribution channels
distribution strategy
exclusive distribution
family brand
individual branding
intensive distribution
label
logistics

manufacturer's (national) brand
physical distribution
private (store) brand
product
product life cycle
product line
product mix
retailers
selective distribution
supply chain
trademark
warranty
wheel of retailing
wholesalers

Application of Vocabulary

Select the term from the list above that best completes the statements beginning below. Write that term in the space provided.

1. A _____ is a bundle of physical, service, and symbolic attributes designed to satisfy customer wants.

2. A _____ is a name, term, sign, symbol, design, or some combination thereof used to identify a product or service.

3. A good _____ is easy to recognize, pronounce, remember, should attract attention and suggest product image, and be legally protectable.

4. The _____ begins in the introduction stage, proceeds through growth and maturity, and ends in the decline stage.

5. A _____ is a brand name that is owned by a wholesaler or a retailer.

6. A _____ is a brand or other product identifying feature that has been given exclusive legal protection.

7. The assortment of products offered by a firm is known as its _____.

8. A _____ is a series of related products or services offered by a firm.

9. A brand offered and promoted by a manufacturer is known as a _____ _____.

10. Brand recognition, brand preference, and brand insistence are the levels of _____ _____.

11. When a firm gives an entirely different brand name to each product in a line of products, the firm is following the strategy of _____.

12. When a single brand name is used for several related products, the firm has decided to use a _____.

13. _____ is the added value that a brand names gives to a product.

14. The descriptive part of a product's package that shows the brand name or symbol, name and address of the manufacturer or distributor, product composition and size, the bar code, and recommended uses is the _____.

15. A _____ is a legal promise that a good or service will serve the purpose for which it is intended.

16. Someone who oversees a line of related products and assumes profit responsibility for his or her product group is called a(n) _____.

17. The overall plan to get the right product to the firm's customers, including decisions regarding transportation, warehousing, inventory control, order processing and the selection of the marketing channels is called _____.

18. The _____ are the paths that goods and services and the legal ownership of them, travel through from the producer to the customer.

19. Distribution includes the actual movement of goods and services from the producer to buyers, which is called _____.

20. _____ are channel members who sell primarily to retailers, other marketing intermediaries, or business users.

Name _____ Instructor _____

Section _____ Date _____

21. _____ are channel members who sell goods and services directly to consumers for their own personal use.

22. The complete sequence of suppliers that contribute to creating and delivering a good or service is called the _____.

23. _____ are the business activities involved in managing movement of goods through the supply chain.

24. A distribution channel that moves goods directly from producer to ultimate user without the aid of any other channel members is called a(n) _____ _____.

25. The _____ is a concept of retailing evolution based on new types of retailers gaining competitive footholds by emphasizing low prices in exchange for limited services.

26. When a firm places its products in nearly every available outlet, it is using _____.

27. The market-coverage strategy in which a manufacturer selects only a limited number of retailers to distribute its product is known as _____.

28. When distribution of a product is limited to a single retailer or wholesaler in a specific geographical region, _____ is in use.

Analysis of Learning Goals

Learning Goal 13.1: Explain the marketing conception of a product and list the components of product strategy.

True or False

1. ___ A product is defined as a bundle of symbolic, service, and physical attributes designed to satisfy consumer wants.

2. ___ Product strategy does not include warranties or customer service.

3. ___ New-product development is an important part of product strategy.

4. ___ Product identification and packaging are part of promotional, not product, strategy.

5. ___ It is important for a firm to anticipate and manage the product life cycle.

Learning Goal 13.2: Describe the classifications of consumer and business goods and services.

Multiple Choice

1. The division of consumer goods into convenience, shopping, and specialty categories is based upon:

   a. what consumer need the good meets.
   b. when the product is used.
   c. the buying habits of consumers.
   d. the types of production processes used.

2. Products that consumers purchase quickly and with minimum effort are called:

   a. shopping goods.   d. specialty goods.
   b. brand goods.   e. quick goods.
   c. convenience goods.

3. A new airplane purchased by an airline is classified as a(n):

   a. raw material.   d. supply.
   b. accessory equipment. e. installation.
   c. component part.

4. A car stereo or TV set falls into which of the following classifications of products:

   a. convenience products. d. materials.
   b. shopping products.   e. expense item.
   c. specialty products.

Name _____ Instructor _____

Section _____ Date _____

5.   What type of industrial product is usually used up within a short period of time?

   a.   supplies   d.   accessory equipment
   b.   capital items   e.   installations
   c.   convenience goods

6.   Services:

   a.   can be stockpiled in inventory.
   b.   can be easily standardized.
   c.   are intangible and inseparable from the service provider.
   d.   all of the above.

Learning Goal 13.3: Distinguish between a product mix and a product line.

True or False

1. ___   The assortment of goods and services a firm offers its customers is called the
         product line.

2. ___   A series of related products is called the product mix.

3. ___   In order to ensure company growth, marketers should continually assess their
         product mix and adjust their offerings.

4 ___   If a firm develops and markets a unique product for an industrial customer it has
         expanded its product mix.

5. ___   Once a firm has a profitable product mix, it rarely makes a change.

Learning Goal 13.4: Identify and briefly describe each of the four stages of the product life cycle.

Multiple Choice

1. The stage of the product life cycle in which promotional costs are high and losses are common is:

    a. introduction.   c. maturity.
    b. growth.   d. decline.

2. The product life cycle stage in which sales climb rapidly, the producer begins to earn a profit, and competitors begin to enter the field, is known as:

    a. introduction.   c. maturity.
    b. growth.   d. decline.

3. During what stage of the product life cycle will industry sales reach a saturation level because of intense competition and price cutting?

    a. introduction   c. maturity.
    b. growth   d. decline

4. Strategies that can be used to extend the product life cycle include:

    a. increasing frequency of use.   c. changing the product.
    b. finding new users.   d. all of the above.

5. Most firms try to manage the product life cycle so that:

    a. all their products are in the growth stage at the same time.
    b. none of their products go into the decline stage.
    c. service features and warranties are unimportant.
    d. by regularly adding new products their offerings span all the stages of the product life cycle.

Name _____ Instructor _____

Section _____ Date _____

Learning Goal 13.5: List the stages of new-product development process.

Short Answer

Below is a list of the stages in the new-product development process. Briefly describe what is involved in each stage.

1. Stage One: New-product idea generation

2. Stage Two: Screening

3. Stage Three: Business analysis

4. Stage Four: Product development

5. Stage Five: Testing

6. Stage Six: Commercialization

Learning Goal 13.6: Explain how firms identify their products.

True or False

1. ___   A good brand name should be easy to spell, pronounce, and remember.

2. ___   A private brand carries the manufacturer's name.

3. ___   The only important consideration in packaging is how well it protects the product.

4. ___   When a company uses a single brand name for several related products it is using a family brand strategy.

5. ___   The stage of brand loyalty in which customers refuse to accept a substitute is known as brand preference.

6. ___   If a brand name becomes an everyday term, that is, a generic term for that type of product, it is still legally protectable.

7. ___   A trademark is legally protected.

8. ___   Packaging represents one of the biggest elements of production costs for many consumer products.

Learning Goal 13.7: Identify and briefly describe each of the major components of an effective distribution strategy and the impact of Internet commerce on distribution channels.

True or False

1. ___   Producers must first decide whether to sell products directly to customers or to use marketing intermediaries to bring the product to market.

2. ___   Consumer convenience goods are usually intensively distributed.

3. ___   Exclusive distribution is used by manufacturers who favor a single retailer handling their products in a given geographic area.

4. ___   Achieving market saturation by placing products in every available outlet makes use of selective distribution.

Name _____ Instructor _____

Section _____ Date _____

5. ___ Managing distribution channels means building positive, lasting relationships among channel members.

6. ___ Internet retailing is a form of nonstore retailing.

7. ___ Distribution strategy involves selecting channels of distribution as well as managing physical distribution.

8. ___ Distribution channels are the final link in the supply chain.

9. ___ The Internet can streamline distribution channels in both B2C and B2B markets.

Learning Goal 13.8: Identify the various categories of distribution channels and discuss the factors that influence channel selection.

Short Answer

1. What is direct distribution?

2. Your text notes that there are different types of channels for consumer goods, business goods, and services. Why do these channels differ?

3. There are four important factors that impact the selection of the appropriate distribution channel. Name and define each below.

    a.

   b.

   c.

   d.

Self Review

True or False

1. ___ When seeking shopping goods, the consumer generally wants to look at several like products.

2. ___ A brand helps assure the customer of comparable quality when they buy the same product again.

3. ___ A national brand carries the manufacturer's name.

4. ___ A trademark gives a product legal protection from infringement by other companies.

5. ___ A locomotive is an example of an expense item.

6. ___ Magazines, milk, soft drinks, and candy bars are all considered shopping products.

7. ___ Most supermarkets tend to specialize in specialty products.

8. ___ It is not unusual for a firm to suffer a loss during the introductory stage of a product's life cycle.

9. ___ An article might be considered a shopping product to one person and a specialty product to another person.

Name _____ Instructor _____

Section _____ Date _____

10. ___ The stage of new-product development when the product is launched is called the development stage.

11. ___ Convenience goods are products that consumers purchase frequently and with a minimum of shopping effort.

12. ___ Specialty goods are products for which the consumer will not accept a substitute.

13. ___ Component parts and materials are finished products that become part of a final product.

14. ___ Even when a company makes no express warranty, certain rights are always guaranteed to consumers by law.

15. ___ Services are products too.

16. ___ Activities to extend the product life cycle usually take place during the decline stage.

17. ___ A brand name and a trademark are the same thing.

18. ___ Each manufacturer should select the one best channel for distributing its output and stick to it.

19. ___ The first and most important consideration in locating a retail store is the cost of rent.

20. ___ Sellers of services generally utilize at least two wholesalers in their distribution channels.

21. ___ A retailer is classified as a middleman.

22. ___ Air is the most expensive mode of transportation.

Multiple Choice

1. Profits peak at which product life cycle stage?

    a. introduction   c. maturity
    b. growth   d. decline

2. The highest degree of brand loyalty is called:

    a. brand preference.   c. brand insistence.
    b. brand recognition.   d. brand awareness.

3. Timber products, iron ore, and farm products such as wheat or corn are classified as:

    a. installations.   d. accessory equipment.
    b. raw materials.   e. supplies.
    c. component parts and materials.

4. Classifying business products is important because:

    a. each group of business products requires a different marketing strategy.
    b. convenience goods must be distinguished from specialty goods.
    c. quality, price, and promotional strategies are identical for all business products.
    d. all of the above.

5. The total assortment of goods and/or services a firm offers its customers is called its:

    a. product life cycle.   d. product line.
    b. product mix.   e. family brand.

6. New-product development is:

    a. expensive and risky.
    b. time consuming.
    c. important because old products do not remain viable forever.
    d. all of the above.

7. When a manufacturer restricts the number of retail outlets handling its products, allowing only one per geographic area, it is using:

    a. intensive distribution.   d. contractual distribution.
    b. selective distribution.   e. restrictive distribution.
    c. exclusive distribution.

Name _____ Instructor _____

Section _____ Date _____

8. The distribution strategy used to obtain maximum exposure to consumers is:

   a. intensive distribution.   d. contractual distribution.
   b. selective distribution.   e. restrictive distribution.
   c. exclusive distribution.

9. The most flexible mode of transport is:

   a. air.   d. water.
   b. rail.   e. pipeline.
   c. truck.

10. If a firm wants to ship a bulky product the least expensive way, which of the following would be selected as the mode of transportation?

   a. railroads.   d. water.
   b. trucks.   e. air.
   c. pipeline.

11. Which of the following is usually the most expensive means of transporting goods?

   a. railroad.   d. water.
   b. trucks.   e. air.
   c. pipeline.

12. The supply chain:

   a. is the channel of distribution.
   b. begins with raw materials and ends when producers distribute to final customers.
   c. is always a vertical marketing system.
   d. all of the above.

13. The use of wholesalers:

   a. adds another member to the channel of distribution, and so simply increases costs.

   b. can significantly cut the number of transactions needed to move goods from several manufacturers to several retailers.

   c. generally adds nothing significant to the efficiency and effectiveness of distribution.

   d. all of the above.

Application Exercises

1. Sara Kline is Marketing Director for Alta Products, Inc., a producer of consumer products. She is analyzing the sales data on the firm's most successful product. The product got off to a great start, and sales grew dramatically over the first two years. But as major competitors developed similar products, sales began to fall off. Now industry sales are down, and the sales figures for her product in the latest quarter are particularly discouraging. Sara wonders what action she should recommend to top management.

   a. What stage of the product life cycle has the product apparently reached? How can you tell?

   b. What options should Sara consider before making her recommendations to top management?

Name _____ Instructor _____

Section _____ Date _____

2. Todd has been writing music for years, and has produced a cassette tape of songs he has written for children. He is wondering how to bring his product to market, and is considering mailing advertisements to potential customers and then filling any orders himself. He feels he can do this work at night after his full-time job, and that this way he won't have to share his proceeds with anyone else. Evaluate Todd's marketing plan. Can you make any suggestions that might help him distribute his product more effectively?

Short Essay Questions

1. How are products divided into Consumer and Business products? What are the classifications of consumer goods, and on what is the classification based? What are the classifications of business goods, and on what basis are they distinguished?

2.   What are the components of distribution strategy? How important is this strategy to the overall success of a marketing plan?

3.   What are the tasks that must be managed in physical distribution?

CHAPTER 14

Promotion and Pricing Strategies

Chapter Summary: Key Concepts

Integrated Marketing Communications

Promotion

The function of informing, persuading, and influencing a purchase decision.

Integrated Marketing Communications (IMC)

Coordination of all promotional activities to produce a unified customer-focused message.

The Promotional Mix

Promotional mix

Elements include personal selling, advertising, sales promotion, and public relations.

Objectives of promotional strategy

Objectives include providing information, differentiating the product or service, increasing sales, stabilizing sales, and accentuating the value of the product or service.

Promotional planning

Marketers identify the right blend of promotional mix elements for the situation. Some marketers also use nontraditional techniques such as product placements and guerrilla marketing.

Advertising

Advertising

A nonpersonal sales presentation directed at a large number of people using print and/or electronic media.

Types of advertising

Product advertising promotes a particular good or service. Institutional advertising involves messages that promote concepts, ideas, philosophies, or goodwill for organizations. Advocacy advertising promotes a specific viewpoint on a public issue.

Advertising and the product life cycle

Informative advertising is used primarily to build initial demand for a product in the introductory stage of the life cycle. Persuasive advertising, often incorporating comparative advertising, is more commonly used during the growth and maturity stages. In the late maturity and decline stages, reminder-oriented advertising may appear.

Advertising media

Marketers must choose how to allocate their advertising budgets among the various media available, including television, newspapers, direct mail, radio, magazines, outdoor, interactive media, and other miscellaneous media.

Sales Promotion

Consumer-oriented promotions

Forms of promotion used to enhance and supplement the sales and advertising effort aimed at consumers. Includes premiums, coupons, rebates, samples, games and contests, and promotional products.

Trade-oriented promotions

Trade promotion is geared to marketing intermediaries, encouraging them to buy, restock and promote the product. Common methods include point-of-purchase advertising, trade shows, or other methods that provide financial incentives to middlemen.

Personal Selling

Personal selling

A promotional presentation made on a person-to-person basis with a potential buyer.

Sales Tasks   The three areas of sales tasks include order processing, creative selling, and missionary selling.

The sales process   There are seven steps: prospecting and qualifying, approach, presentation, demonstration, handling objections, closing, and follow up.

Recent trends in personal selling Telemarketing, relationship selling, consultative selling, team selling and sales force automation (SFA) are recent trends.

Public Relations

Public relations   Having broader objectives, public relations communicates with the organization's various publics, including customers, vendors, news media, employees, stockholders, government, and the general public. It can be used to publicize products and create and maintain a positive image of the firm.

Publicity   This promotional technique disseminates news or obtains favorable unpaid media coverage for the firm.

Promotional Strategies

Selecting a promotional mix   The appropriate promotional mix will depend on the target market, the value of the product, the time frame, and other factors.

Pushing and pulling strategies   A pushing strategy encourages middlemen to carry and promote the product, and may involve cooperative advertising offers. A pulling strategy attempts to promote a product by generating consumer demand. An effective promotional strategy will should address both pushing and pulling.

Ethics in Promotion

Puffery and deception

Deception involves deliberately making promises that are untrue. Puffery uses doubtful, subjective, or vague statements to exaggerate claims of a product's superiority.

Promotion to children and teens

Because children and teens have huge purchasing power, they are natural targets for marketers. Since young people are not as sophisticated at evaluating promotional messages, special ethical questions arise.

Promotion in public schools and on college campuses

In-school promotion, including product placements, promotional messages in school publications, and revenues from privately owned vending machines, has raised ethical questions.

Price in the Marketing Mix

Price

The price, or exchange value of a good or service, is an important aspect of the marketing mix.

Pricing objectives

Price strategy can be used to meet profitability, volume, and prestige objectives, or to meet the competition.

Pricing Strategies

Price determination in practice

Most businesses use some form of cost-based pricing to make pricing decisions. Breakeven analysis is a commonly used tool in helping a firm understand how price will affect sales and profit.

Alternative pricing strategies

Skimming pricing, penetration pricing, everyday low pricing, discount pricing, and competitive pricing are alternatives that may be used.

Name _____ Instructor _____

Section _____ Date _____

Consumer perceptions of prices Research shows that a consumer's perception of quality is closely related to price. Odd pricing, or using uneven amounts, makes prices sound lower than they really are.

Business Vocabulary

advertising

advocacy advertising

breakeven analysis

breakeven point

comparative advertising

competitive pricing

consultative selling

cooperative advertising

cost-based pricing

creative selling

every day low pricing (EDLP)

infomercial

institutional advertising

integrated marketing
   communications (IMC)

missionary selling

nonpersonal selling

odd pricing

order processing

penetration pricing strategy

personal selling

point-of-purchase (POP) advertising

positioning

price

product advertising

product placement

profitability objectives

promotion

promotional mix

promotional products

publicity

public relations

pulling strategy

pushing strategy

relationship selling

sales force automation (SFA)

sales promotion

skimming pricing strategy

sponsorship

team selling

telemarketing

trade promotions

volume objectives

Application of Vocabulary

Select the term from the list above that best completes the statements beginning on the following page. Write that term in the space provided.

1. Nonpersonal marketing activities such as trade shows, coupon offers, samples, premiums, and point-of-purchase displays that stimulate consumer purchasing and dealer effectiveness are known as _____.

2. _____ is the nonpersonal promotional technique where firms pay for media messages that inform and persuade members of a particular audience.

3. When the promotional strategy is designed to get middlemen to aggressively promote a product, a _____ is in use.

4. The _____ is the combination of personal sales and non-personal selling appeals such as advertising, sales promotion, and public relations.

5. _____ is the promotional strategy used to differentiate a good or service from those of competitors in the mind of a prospective buyer.

6. The promotional strategy that is aimed at customers in order to create a demand for a product, thus encouraging middlemen to stock that product, is called a
_____.

7. _____ involves all the activities necessary to inform, persuade, and influence a purchase decision.

8. When personal selling is conducted entirely by telephone, _____ is in use.

9. The sales task performed when orders are received and handled is _____
_____.

10. _____ is a sales promotion technique that places a display or demonstration at the location where the potential customer will make the purchase decision.

11. _____ is advertising that supports a specific viewpoint on a public issue and is designed to influence public opinion or the legislative process.

12. _____ is a persuasive advertising approach in which direct comparisons are made with competing goods and services.

13. _____ involves making a promotional presentation on a person-to-person basis with a potential buyer.

Name _____ Instructor _____

Section _____ Date _____

14. When salespersons market the goodwill of a company and/or provide technical or operational assistance, they are engaged in _____.

15. _____ is a persuasive promotional presentation to potential customers needed when the benefits of a good or service are not readily apparent, or when the purchase is based on a careful analysis of alternatives.

16. Efforts designed to promote goods or services to retailers, wholesalers, international buyers, and other resellers in the distribution channel are called _____.

17. _____ is the nonpersonal selling technique aimed at promoting a particular good or service.

18. Advertising aimed at promoting an idea, concept, philosophy, or the goodwill of an industry, company, organization, or government entity is called _____
_____.

19. _____ are useful items imprinted with the donor's name, logo, or message, that are given away as sales promotions.

20. When organizations communicate with their various publics, they are engaged in
_____.

21. _____ involves sharing of local advertising costs between the manufacturer and the marketing intermediary.

22. _____ involves providing cash or other resources to an event or activity in exchange for a direct association with it.

23. Coordination of all promotional activities to produce a unified customer-focused message constitutes _____.

24. _____ involves applying computers and other technologies to improve the efficiency and competitiveness of the sales function.

25. The unpaid placement of significant news in print or broadcast media to stimulate demand is known as _____.

26. _____ means establishing a sustained buyer-seller relationship through regular contracts over an extended period of time.

27. Engaging in _____ means meeting customers' needs by listening, understanding, and solving their problems, paying attention to details, and following through after the sale.

28. When salespeople combine with specialists from other functional areas to promote a product, _____ is in use.

29. A commercial for a single product that resembles a regular television program running 30 minutes or longer is called a(n) _____.

30. Advertising, sales promotion, direct marketing, and public relations are the various forms of _____ .

31. Marketers sometimes pay a fee to have their products showcased in movies and television shows, a promotional practice known as _____.

32. The exchange value of a good or service is known as its _____.

33. In pricing strategy, using _____ means that management sets the price and/or reduces the costs of a product or service with certain net gain objectives in mind.

34. If market share goals are the key focus in pricing decisions, the firm is following _____ to set prices.

35. _____ adds a markup to the base cost of a product to cover unassigned costs and provide a profit.

36. _____ is a method of determining the minimum sales volume needed at a certain price level to cover all costs.

37. Once a company has reached its _____, it will begin to earn a profit on each additional unit of sales.

38. A(n) _____ maximizes profit per unit and establishes product prestige by setting a high price relative to competing offerings.

39. A(n) _____ sets a relatively low price compared with competing offerings to promote initial market acceptance and maximize sales volume.

Name _____ Instructor _____

Section _____ Date _____

40. _____ de-emphasizes price as a competitive variable by pricing a good or service at the same general level as competitive offerings.

41. _____ is a strategy devoted to maintaining continuous low prices rather than relying on short-term price-cutting techniques.

42. When uneven prices are used to make the product seem less expensive, _____ _____ is in use.

Analysis of Learning Goals

Learning Goal 14.1: Discuss how integrated marketing communications relates to a firm's promotional strategy.

Short Answer

1. What is integrated marketing communications (IMC)?

2. What are the key components in an IMC plan?

Learning Goal 14.2: Explain the concept of a promotional mix and outline the objectives of promotion.

True or False

1. ___   The promotional mix includes advertising, personal selling, sales promotion and public relations.

2. ___   Advertising, sales promotion and public relations are all personal selling techniques.

3. ___   In marketing, promotional strategy and sales promotion mean the same thing.

Short Answer

4.   List and define the five objectives of promotional strategy.

    a.

    b.

    c.

    d.

    e.

Name _____ Instructor _____

Section _____ Date _____

Learning Goal 14.3: Summarize the different types of advertising and advertising media.

True or False

1. ___ Informative advertising is primarily used to attract stockholders.

2. ___ Comparative advertising can be considered a type of persuasive advertising.

3. ___ Institutional advertising promotes the ideas, philosophies and goodwill of an organization.

4. ___ Reminder-oriented advertising is used in the late-maturity and decline stages of the product life cycle.

5. ___ Persuasive advertising is generally most useful in the introductory stage of the product life cycle.

6. ___ Internet advertising receives the largest dollar amount of advertising revenue.

7. ___ Magazines can target audiences for advertising better than most other media.

8. ___ E-mail is a cheaper form of direct mail advertising since it eliminates printing and postage costs.

9. ___ Interactive media advertising is the fastest-growing media segment.

10. ___ Sponsorships of sports or cultural events may be good advertising, but they do little to enhance relationship marketing.

11. ___ About 20% of advertising expenditures go for advertising in Yellow Pages and other miscellaneous publications.

Learning Goal 14.4: Describe the role of sales promotion, personal selling, and public relations in promotional strategy.

True or False

1. ___ The term "promotional products" refers to giveaway items that are imprinted with the donor's company name and/or logo.

2. ___ Sales promotion is a promotional technique that includes personal selling and advertising.

3. ___ While customer oriented sales promotion aims to increase sales to consumers, trade promotion encourages marketing intermediaries to aggressively promote a product.

4. ___ Personal selling involves creative selling, order processing, and missionary selling tasks.

5. ___ Creative selling uses prospecting, qualifying, and the approach to develop better sales techniques aimed at the specific needs of potential customers.

6. ___ Public relations often works to generate positive publicity for a company through media releases, news conferences, article placements, and story ideas in the media.

7. ___ Firms have to pay for any publicity they generate in the media.

Learning Goal 14.5: Identify the factors that influence the selection of a promotional mix.

True or False

1. ___ Most firms selling low cost items will tend to use personal selling rather than advertising.

2. ___ Sellers of business products would normally use advertising rather than personal selling.

3. ___ Advertising is often needed to precondition a potential customers for a sales presentation.

Name _____ Instructor _____

Section _____ Date _____

4. ___ One consideration that influences the selection of the elements in the promotional mix is the firm's marketing budget.

5. ___ The end user of the product will to some extent determine the components of the mix.

6. ___ While advertising is an important pre-sale activity, it plays no role in assuring customers they've made the right choice or in promoting repeat business.

Learning Goal 14.6: Discuss the major ethical issues involved in promotion.

True or False

1. ___ Promotion raises no more ethical questions than do the other elements of the marketing mix.

2. ___ While advertising to children may raise some ethical concerns, advertising to adults does not.

3. ___ Puffery is the practice of exaggerating product claims in advertising.

4. ___ Anyone can easily distinguish advertising from entertainment when watching television or going online.

5. ___ Many consumers believe that advertising exerts too much influence on buyers.

6. ___ Since schools can generate much needed revenues by allowing sponsorships and other promotions on campus, these practices raise no ethical concerns.

Learning Goal 14.7: Outline the different types of pricing objectives and discuss how firms set prices in the marketplace.

Multiple Choice

1. If marketers attempt to increase the percent of industry sales their product will attract, they are using:

    a. breakeven analysis.
    b. profit maximization objectives.
    c. market share objectives.
    d. return on sales objectives.
    e. cost-benefit analysis.

2. Competitive pricing:

    a. seeks to undercut the competitor's price.
    b. seeks to enhance the product's prestige.
    c. matches the prices of a firm's offerings to that of the competition.
    d. focuses competitive efforts primarily on pricing variables.

3. Pricing an item high relative to competing products to achieve an image of quality makes use of:

    a. breakeven analysis.
    b. prestige objectives.
    c. profit objectives.
    d. volume objectives.

4. In cost-based pricing:

    a. a markup over costs is used to determine price.
    b. the markup includes some amount to help cover overhead.
    c. the markup includes some amount to generate a profit.
    d. all of the above.

5. In breakeven analysis, the breakeven point in units is found by:

    a. dividing total costs by the number of units sold.
    b. dividing fixed costs by the unit contribution to fixed costs.
    c. dividing sales revenue by variable cost per unit.
    d. dividing sales price by variable costs.

Name _____ Instructor _____

Section _____ Date _____

6. If a company has fixed costs of $50,000, a selling price of $10 per unit, and variable costs per unit of $5, how many units must be sold to breakeven?

   a. 5,000   c. 15,000
   b. 10,000   d. 20,000

7. Using the figures in #6 above, suppose the company makes and sells 5,000 units. It will realize a:

   a. loss of $10,000.   c. profit of $10,000.
   b. loss of $25,000.   d. profit of $25,000.

8. Again using the figures in #6 above, now suppose the company makes and sells 20,000 units. It will realize a:

   a. loss of $25,000.   c. profit of $25,000.
   b. loss of $50,000.   d. profit of $50,000.

9. In modified breakeven analysis:

   a. breakeven points at several possible prices are calculated.
   b. sales estimates at different prices are considered.
   c. customer demand, not just costs, are used in setting the price.
   d. all of the above.

Learning Goal 14.8: Summarize the four alternative pricing strategies.

True or False

1. ___ A penetration price policy is used by firms attempting to earn the largest possible profit upon introduction of the product.

2. ___ The skimming price strategy involves starting out at a high price.

3. ___ A skimming strategy allows the firm to recover its costs rapidly by maximizing the revenue earned early in the product life cycle.

4. ___ In competitive pricing, price becomes the most important competitive factor.

5. ___ EDLP relies on short-term price reductions.

Learning Goal 14.9: Discuss consumer perceptions of price.

Short Answer

1. How are price and perceived quality related?

2. What is odd pricing, and why is it employed?

Self Review

True or False

1. ___ Informative advertising is most effective during the decline stage of the product life cycle.

2. ___ Product advertising is the major focus of public relations efforts.

3. ___ Television receives the largest total dollar amount of advertising revenue in the U.S.

4. ___ In most cases, promoting a product to vast numbers of people requires the use of nonpersonal selling.

5. ___ An example of a point-of-purchase sales promotion is the magazine rack at the checkout counters in a supermarket.

Name _____ Instructor _____

Section _____ Date _____

6. ___ Rather than aiming at increased sales, some advertisements are aimed at increasing the sponsor's image.

7. ___ The pulling strategy uses advertising and sales promotion techniques.

8. ___ The only major objective of promotion is to increase sales.

9. ___ Because modern promotion uses so many different methods and media, integrated marketing communications (IMC) is employed so customers don't get mixed messages.

10. ___ Companies that sell highly technical products will typically do a lot of missionary selling.

11. ___ In sales, prospecting means finding potential customers.

12. ___ Samples are particularly useful in promoting new products.

13. ___ A good creative salesperson avoids allowing customers to raise objections during the sales process.

14. ___ Sales promotion includes both activities directed at consumers and trade promotions aimed at marketing intermediaries.

15. ___ Interactive advertising creates two-way communication between marketers and consumers, and seems to enhance sales more than other types of advertising.

16. ___ Public relations is usually aimed at customers, but not at vendors, news media, employees, stockholders, government or the general public.

17. ___ In cost-based pricing, marketers total all costs associated with offering a product and add an amount to cover overhead, unexpected expenses, and profit.

18. ___ The amount added to total cost to arrive at selling price is called *markup*.

19. ___ When promotional strategies aim to develop consumer desire for a general product category, such as milk, they are trying to stimulate primary demand.

Multiple Choice

1.   Which type of advertising promotes the ideas, philosophies, and goodwill of a firm?

    a.   product advertising.
    b.   institutional advertising.
    c.   selective demand advertising.
    d.   restrictive advertising.
    e.   specialty advertising.

2.   The promotional strategy designed to generate customer demand is called:

    a.   a pushing strategy.
    b.   a pulling strategy.
    c.   a specialty strategy.
    d.   an institutional strategy.

3.   The most critical point in the sales process is:

    a.   the approach.
    b.   the presentation.
    c.   the demonstration.
    d.   qualifying prospects.
    e.   the close.

4.   A car salesperson invites the customer to take a test drive. This would be an example of which stage of the sales process?

    a.   the approach.
    b.   the presentation.
    c.   the demonstration.
    d.   qualifying prospects.
    e.   the close.

5.   The sales step that reassures the customer about the purchase decision and checks satisfaction is the:

    a.   follow-up.
    b.   prospecting.
    c.   approach.
    d.   demonstration.
    e.   close.

6.   The objectives of promotion include:

    a.   providing information.
    b.   differentiating the product.
    c.   stabilizing or increasing sales.
    d.   accentuating the value of the product.
    e.   all of the above.

Name _____ Instructor _____

Section _____ Date _____

7. A company that launches a promotion in the normal slack period for its product is attempting to:

   a. provide information.
   b. differentiate the product.
   c. stabilize sales.
   d. accentuate the value of the product.
   e. improve the firm's image.

8. If a bank offers its customers a calendar with the bank's name imprinted on it, this gift is called a:

   a. promotional product.
   b. trade item.
   c. premium.
   d. sample.

9. Sales force automation (SFA):

   a. utilizes e-mail, laptop computers, and specialized software to enhance customer service.
   b. can often access order information or company databases.
   c. can improve consistency, reduce response times, and provide better customer service.
   d. all of the above.

10. Contests and premiums are sales promotional efforts designed to:

   a. build positive public relations.
   b. build patronage loyalty.
   c. serve as institutional advertisements.
   d. all of the above.

11. Infomercials:

   a. are 30 minute programs that sell goods or services.
   b. are a form of broadcast direct marketing.
   c. often allow immediate response by featuring toll-free numbers.
   d. All of the above.

12. Expenses that do not vary with volume are called:

    a. marginal costs.   d. per unit costs.
    b. variable costs.   e. cyclical costs.
    c. fixed costs.

13. When a new product is priced low as compared with a substitute item as a means of gaining market acceptance and discouraging competition, the firm is following the pricing strategy of _____.

    a. prestige pricing.   d. skimming the cream pricing.
    b. marked up pricing.   e. penetration pricing
    c. competitive pricing.

14. A pricing strategy used by discounters to make products appear less expensive is _____.

    a. odd pricing.   d. skimming the cream pricing.
    b. penetration pricing.   e. competitive pricing.
    c. marginal pricing.

15. Total revenue for a product is found by:

    a. deducting expenses from sales revenue.
    b. multiplying the price by the quantity sold.
    c. adding fixed and variable costs together.
    d. subtracting the breakeven point from total units sold.

16. When comparative advertising is used to promote brand preference, the marketers are attempting to stimulate:

    a. primary demand.   c. selective demand.
    b. price consciousness.   d. publicity.

Name _____ Instructor _____

Section _____ Date _____

Application Exercises

The promotional mix includes advertising, personal sales, sales promotional activities, and public relations. Most organizations utilize a combination of these strategies, though a smaller business might focus on one or two. Consider each of the following businesses, and recommend which promotional techniques you feel should be the focus of promotion. Explain your selection.

1. A chewing gum manufacturer that distributes its products nationally.

2. A small local beauty supply store.

3. A grocery shopping service for people who have neither the time nor the desire to do their own shopping.

4. A soft-drink maker who distributes its products globally.

5. An aircraft manufacturer.

6. An oil refinery owned by a large oil company.

Short Essay Questions

1. What is the promotional mix? Define and distinguish the main elements.

2. Comment on the following statement: "Since we live in a country that recognizes the right to freedom of speech, advertisers should be able to sell anything to anybody and say anything they think will help sell the product."

3. What are the objectives that can be achieved through pricing policy?

CHAPTER 15

Using Technology to Manage Information

Chapter Summary: Key Concepts

Management Information Systems

Management Information System (MIS)	An organized method for providing past, present and projected information on internal operations as well as external intelligence to support managerial decision making.
Databases	A database is an electronic filing cabinet, containing the centralized integrated collection of data resources.
Information systems for decision making	These programs link users to data, allowing them to develop information for decision making. Types of programs include Decision Support Systems (DSSs), Executive Support Systems (EISs), and expert systems.
Trends in information systems	Computers can be linked using local area networks (LANs), and/or wide area networks (WANs). Enterprise resource planning (ERP) unifies and integrates all of a firm's computer systems. Application service providers (ASPs) specialize in providing both the computers and the application support for managing information systems of clients.

Computer Hardware and Software

Computer hardware	Hardware consists of the tangible machines in a computer system, including processors, storage, input, and output devices. Major types are mainframes, supercomputers, minicomputers, and personal computers (PC's), including desktop computers, notebook computers, tablet PCs and handheld devices.

Computer software

Software provides the instructions that tell the hardware what to do. The basic workings of the computers are managed by operating systems. Applications software can perform myriad business functions, including word processing, desk top publishing, spreadsheets, e-mail, and presentation graphics.

How Computers Help Business

Word processing

Computer applications software that uses computers to input, store, retrieve, edit, and print various types of documents.

Desktop publishing

This technology allows users to design and produce brochures, newsletters, and other sophisticated documents as professionally as if they had been sent to a printer.

Spreadsheets

These software packages create the computerized equivalent of an accountant's worksheet, allowing the user to manipulate variables and see the impact of alternative decisions on operating results.

Electronic mail

Also known as e-mail, this application (sometimes supplemented with instant messaging) allows people to communicate via their computers, overcoming time and distance barriers.

Presentation graphics

Presentation graphics software provides graphs and charts that help businesspeople see patterns in data.

Multimedia and interactive media

Multimedia computing refers to technologies that integrate two or more types of media, such as text, voice, sound, video, graphics, and animation into computer-based applications. Interactive media goes a step further, allowing users to interact with computer displays.

Groupware

This software combines information sharing through a common database with communications via e-mail.

Intranets, virtual private networks, and broadband technology	Intranets allow employees to share information on a company network. Virtual private networks provide secure Internet connections for accessing network information. Broadband technology includes digital, fiber-optic, and wireless network technology that compresses data and transmits them at far greater speed than traditional telephone lines.

Protecting Information Systems

Computer crime	Ranging from employees to outsiders, computers offer many opportunities to invent data, produce inaccurate or misleading information, conduct illegal transactions, or otherwise disrupt business. Protections against this type of crime include encryption, passwords, and firewalls.
Computer viruses	A computer virus is a program that secretly attaches itself to other computer programs or files and changes them or destroys data. Anti-virus programs can be installed to constantly monitor for and eliminate viruses, but these programs must be regularly updated to provide protection against new viruses.
Disaster recovery and backup	Disaster recovery planning, focuses on how to prevent system failures and how to continue operations if computer systems should fail. The most basic precaution is routinely backing up software and data, often storing it at a remote location.

Name _____ Instructor _____

Section _____ Date _____

Business Vocabulary

application service providers (ASPs)
application software
broadband technology
chief information officer (CIO)
computer virus
database
decision support system (DSS)
desktop publishing
disaster recovery plan
encryption
enterprise resource plan (ERP)
executive information system (EIS)
expert system
firewall
groupware
hardware
interactive media

intranet
local area network (LAN)
management information system (MIS)
mainframe computer
minicomputer
multimedia computing
operating system software
personal computer (PC)
presentation software
software
spreadsheets
supercomputers
virtual private network (VPN)
wide area networks (WAN)
Wi-Fi
word processing

Application of Vocabulary

Select the term from the list above that best completes the statements beginning below.
Write that term in the space provided.

1. The organized method of providing information for decision making is known as the

    _____.

2. The _____ is the top management executive
    responsible for directing a firm's management information system and related
    computer operations.

3. Programs that perform specific tasks desired by a user, such as word processing or
    preparing presentations, are collectively known as _____.

Name _____ Instructor _____

Section _____ Date _____

4. Today the most common type of computer is the _____, which includes desktop, notebook, tablet, and even pocket-size handheld computers.

5. _____ stands for "wireless fidelity," and refers to wireless networks that connect various devices and allows them to communicate with one another through radio waves.

6. _____ applications allow computer users to write, store, retrieve, edit, and print documents.

7. The _____ is the software that controls the basic workings of a computer system.

8. A(n) _____ is a network that connects computers in the same building or within a limited area.

9. Applications designed to print documents with high quality type, graphics and layouts are known as _____ software.

10. _____ software is particularly useful when a user wants to manipulate decision variables to determine their impact.

11. A(n) _____ is a computer system that quickly provides relevant facts for use in decision making.

12. A(n) _____ is a company network that links employees through Internet tools like e-mail, hypertext links, and searches using Web browsers.

13. A user-friendly decision-oriented computer system designed for use by senior management is known as a(n) _____.

14. A computer system that imitates human hypothetical reasoning through the use of "if...then" rules is known as a(n) _____.

15. _____ includes all the tangible equipment in a computer system.

16. _____ includes the programmed instructions that tell a computer what to do.

17. Electronic technology that allows users to interact with computer displays is known as _____.

18. Electronic technologies that facilitate the integration of two or more types of media are called _____.

19. _____ is computer software that combines networked databases with technologies such as e-mail to enable employees to share data and collaborate on projects.

20. A(n) _____ is the computer integrated collection of an organization's data resources.

21. Software that provides tools and graphics files for creating a variety of charts, graphs, and pictures as visual aids is called _____.

22. A(n) _____ involves deciding how to prevent information system failures or continue operating if failures occur.

23. Software that prevents entry to an intranet from an unauthorized location or by an unauthorized person is called the _____.

24. A(n) _____ is a program that secretly attaches itself to other programs or files and changes them or destroys data.

25. The largest type of computer system with the most extensive storage capacity and fastest processing speeds is called a(n) _____.

26. _____ are powerful mainframes that can handle extremely rapid, complex calculations involving thousands of variables that is particularly useful in scientific research.

27. A(n) _____ is an intermediate size computer with slower processing speeds and less storage capacity than a mainframe.

28. Networks that tie together geographically dispersed computers using telephone lines, microwave or satellite transmission are called _____.

29. _____ are outside suppliers that provide both computers and application support for managing information systems.

Name _____ Instructor _____

Section _____ Date _____

30. Digital, fiberoptic, and wireless network technologies that compress data and transmit them more rapidly than traditional telephone lines are known as _____.

31. A(n) _____ designs an organization's computer system so that the systems from all functional areas are unified and integrated.

32. Companies seeking to achieve secure connections between many points on the Internet but who want a cheaper, ready-made service would use a(n) _____ instead of a WAN.

33. _____ software encodes or scrambles messages for secure transmission.

Analysis of Learning Goals

Learning Goal 15.1: Distinguish between data and information.

True or False

1. ___ Raw facts and figures are called data.

2. ___ Information is knowledge gained from processing data.

3. ___ Modern information technologies allow large firms to access data and information for a global market, but unfortunately, cannot do the same for small businesses.

Learning Goal 15.2: Explain the role of management information systems in business.

True or False

1. ___ An information system can turn data inputs into information outputs to be used for decision making.

2. ___ Databases can include both internally generated data and outside subscription services.

3. ____ Because small firms are better able to track their day-to-day operations, an information system is less critical to them than to large firms.

4. ____ Chief information officers (CIOs) who report directly to the chief executive officer (CEO) are becoming commonplace in large and medium size organizations.

5. ____ A well designed information system can integrate decision making in all major departments of an organization.

6. ____ A planned management information system (MIS) can keep track of past and present information, but cannot help make the projections needed for good decisions.

Learning Goal 15.3: Identify and briefly describe each of the different types of information system programs.

Multiple Choice

1. A DSS (decision support system) typically involves:

   a. software to retrieve information from the database.
   b. software to allow computer simulations of changing business conditions.
   c. presentation software that allows users to include graphs and charts as they output their findings.
   d. all of the above.

2. A computer program that can imitate human hypothetical reasoning by using a complicated series of "if...then" rules is known as a(n):

   a. expert system.   c. DSS.
   b. EIS.   d. ERP.

3. Executive Information Systems (EISs):

   a. are complex, detailed information systems that take executives a long time to master.
   b. allow top managers to access information from the company's database quickly and easily.
   c. can print text reports but not graphs or figures.
   d. can only access financial data.

Name _____ Instructor _____

Section _____ Date _____

4. Linking computers in the same building or in a limited area creates a(n):

    a. WAN.   c. ASP.
    b. LAN.   d. ERP.

5. A company that links geographically separated computers via telephone lines, microwave, or satellite technology creates a(n):

    a. WAN.   c. ASP.
    b. LAN.   d. ERP.

6. A system of integrated programs to collect, process, and provide information about all business operations is a(n):

    a. WAN.   c. ASP.
    b. LAN.   d. ERP.

7. A firm that engages an outside supplier to provide both computers and applications support for managing information systems is using a(n):

    a. WAN.   c. ASP.
    b. LAN.   d. ERP.

Learning Goal 15.4: Describe the hardware and software used in managing information.

True or False

1. ___   Fax machines, personal computers, and printers are all good examples of software.

2. ___   Input devises include keyboards and voice recognition systems.

3. ___   Printers are good examples of output hardware.

4. ___   Desktop computers, notebook computers, and hand held devices are collectively known as minicomputers.

5. ___   The software that controls the basic workings of the computer is its operating
            system.

6. ___   Word processing, spreadsheets, and desktop publishing software are known as
            applications software.

Learning Goal 15.5: Identify how specific types of software can help businesspeople.

Multiple Choice

1. The computer application that includes the typing, storing, retrieving, editing, and
    printing of documents is:

    a. the decision support system.   c. the spreadsheet.
    b. word processing.   d. electronic mail.

2. If a manager wants to see how a change in one variable will change the outcome of a
    calculation, he or she will probably need to use:

    a. word processing.   c. desktop publishing.
    b. electronic mail.   d. a spreadsheet.

3. Technologies that integrate two or more types of media into a computer based
    application are known as:

    a. multimedia computing.   c. voice mail systems.
    b. expert systems.   d. e-mail.

4. Groupware:

    a. allows users to collaborate with one another.
    b. is an interactive computer application.
    c. combines database and e-mail capabilities.
    d. all of the above.

Name _____ Instructor _____

Section _____ Date _____

Learning Goal 15.6: Explain the importance of special network technologies.

Multiple Choice

1. Linking employees using tools of the Internet, such as e-mail and Web browser searches creates a(n):

    a. extranet.   c. intranet.
    b. LAN.   d. firewall.

2. Tools used to prevent unauthorized access to a company's information over the Internet are known as:

    a. firewalls.   c. mainframes.
    b. computer viruses.   d. applications software.

3. Digital, fiberoptic and wireless networks that can rapidly transmit large amounts of data make use of:

    a. broadband technology.   c. VPNs.
    b. LANs.   d. ERPs.

4. A firm that wants to exchange information securely over the Internet should explore developing a(n):

    a. broadband technology.   c. VPN.
    b. LAN.   d. ERP.

Learning Goal 15.7: List the ways that companies can protect themselves from computer crimes.

True or False

1. ____ All computer crime involves the deliberate use of computer viruses.

2. ____ Computer crime is on the rise.

3. ___ Organizations can limit unauthorized access to confidential data by using passwords, firewalls, and encryption.

4. ___ Companies need not carefully scrutinize the security protections provided by their Internet service providers.

5. ___ Theft of computer hardware is not common since the equipment is so large.

Learning Goal 15.8: Explain steps that companies go through in anticipating, planning for, and recovering from information system disasters.

True or False

1. ___ An effective disaster recovery system should enforce policies for frequently backing up data.

2. ___ Organizations need to be prepared with back-up plans so they can continue operations if their computer systems fail.

3. ___ When computers are connected to a network a problem at any location can affect the entire network.

4. ___ The best plan is to have all hardware and software assets in the same location.

5. ___ Most businesses whose computer systems were affected by 9/11 were up and running within days thanks to their disaster recovery systems.

Self Review

True or False

1. ___ Software usually refers to programs.

2. ___ Hardware can operate without software.

3. ___ The most common computers in use today are mainframe computers.

4. ___ The visual display device used with computers, similar to a television screen, is called a monitor.

Name _____ Instructor _____

Section _____ Date _____

5. ___ A database is essentially an electronic filing cabinet.

6. ___ Electronic mail ("e-mail") is a system for both sending and receiving messages through computers.

7. ___ A major use of databases is to enable managers to find information they already have.

8. ___ A computer virus is an equipment failure caused by bad wiring.

9. ___ While word processing applications have become commonplace, no voice processing systems have yet been developed.

10. ___ When computers in many different cities are linked into one network, a LAN is in use.

11. ___ Information is manipulated to produce data.

12. ___ A microprocessor is a small silicon chip that can contain the entire central processing unit of a computer.

13. ___ A computer network is a system in which interconnected computers can both function individually and communicate with each other.

14. ___ The computerized equivalent of an accountant's worksheet is called e-mail.

15. ___ Since only technical people use computers, you can expect to find a good job even if you have no computer skills.

Multiple Choice

1. Software that can create graphs, charts, and pictures as visual aids for reports and sales demonstrations is called:

   a. word processing software.   c. spreadsheet software.
   b. groupware.   d. presentation software.

2. All of the following are applications software, *EXCEPT*:

   a. word processing software.
   b. spreadsheet software.
   c. operating system software.
   d. presentation software.

3. We can expect that computers and telecommunications will:

   a. reduce the time necessary to transmit data.
   b. speed up the pace of work.
   c. overcome geographic barriers.
   d. all of the above.

4. When using word processing, the user can:

   a. edit the text material.
   b. store the text material.
   c. retrieve the text material.
   d. print the text material.
   e. all of the above.

5. Software that permits manipulation of decision variables is called:

   a. spreadsheet.
   b. e-mail.
   c. voice mail.
   d. word processing.

6. Computers are capable of:

   a. measuring.
   b. storing information.
   c. interpreting information.
   d. working in logical sequence.
   e. all of the above.

7. Supercomputers:

   a. are the newest generation of powerful mainframe computers.
   b. can handle extremely rapid, complex calculations involving thousands of variables.
   c. are most commonly used for scientific research.
   d. all of the above.

8. The software application that combines high-quality type, graphics, and layout tools used to create brochures and newsletters is known as:

   a. word processors.
   b. presentation software.
   c. spreadsheets.
   d. desktop publishing

Name _____ Instructor _____

Section _____ Date _____

9. Enterprise resource planning:

    a. integrates information from all areas of the firm into one information system.
    b. is integral to an overall *knowledge management* strategy.
    c. avoids duplication and inconsistencies in collecting and processing data among a firm's various departments.
    d. all of the above.

10. Due to the complexity and expense of information management, many firms decide to outsource this activity to outside suppliers known as:

    a. Application service providers (ASPs)
    b. Virtual private networks (VPNs).
    c. Executive information systems (EISs).
    d. Enterprise resource planners (ESPs).

Application Exercises

Your chapter has discussed several computer applications. Consider the situations below and recommend an appropriate computer application for each..

1. You need to turn in a term paper.

2. You want to produce a new brochure about your company's products.

3. You wonder how a change in costs will potentially affect price and sales.

4. You want to store large amounts of customer and sales data so that it can be retrieved later.

5. You want to be able to send and receive written messages using your computer.

6. You want to incorporate pie charts and pictures as visual aids for a report you will be giving at tomorrow's meeting.

Short Essay Questions

1. What contributions can information management make to the success of any organization?

2. What are the security issues that modern information technologies must address?

CHAPTER 16

Understanding Accounting and Financial Statements

Chapter Summary: Key Concepts

Accounting: Its Uses and Users

Accounting	The process of measuring, interpreting, and communicating financial information.
Users of accounting information	Managers and employees use accounting information to make better decisions and improve operations. People outside the organization also rely on its accounting information. Investors, lenders, suppliers, regulators, unions, economic planners and consumer groups all use an organization's accounting information to make decisions about that organization.
Uses of accounting information	Accounting plays a key role in each of the three basic activities all organizations must perform: financing, investing, and operating.

Accounting Professionals

Public accountants	Public accountants are independent organizations or individuals who provide accounting services to other firms or individuals for a fee.
Management accountants	Management accountants provide accounting services within their own firm.
Government and not-for-profit accountants	Government and not-for-profit accountants perform many of the same functions as management accountants, focusing on the effectiveness of their organization or agency rather than on profit or loss.

The Accounting Process

The process

The process is a cycle of activities used by accountants to record, classify, and summarize financial data. It involves all the steps needed to convert data on individual transactions into financial statements.

Impact of computers and the Internet on the accounting

Computers have simplified and speeded the accounting process. Specialized software has been developed to handle the accounting for small businesses, large firms, and those engaged in international transactions. The Internet can be used to compile and share accounting information.

The foundation of the accounting system

Standards have been developed to ensure reliable, consistent, and unbiased accounting information. These standards, known as "generally accepted accounting principles" (GAAP), are set by the Financial Accounting Standards Board (FASB.) Recently, additional federal oversight by the Public Company Accounting Oversight Board was enacted.

Financial Statements

Balance sheet

Accounting statement that shows the financial position of a company as of a particular date and makes explicit the basic accounting equation (Assets = Liabilities + Owners' Equity).

Income statement

Accounting statement that shows the income, expenses, and profits or losses of a company during a period of time.

Statement of cash flows

Accounting statement that provides investors and creditors with information about a company's cash receipts and payments during an accounting period.

Financial Ratio Analysis

Ratio analysis	Reduces dissimilar dollar or quantity amounts from the financial statements of a firm to a ratio, making it possible to compare the firm's activities and performance to previous periods and with other companies.
Liquidity ratios	Measure a firm's ability to meet it's short term obligations. Two commonly used liquidity ratios are the current ratio and the acid-test ratio.
Profitability ratios	Used to compare the firm's earnings to its revenues, sales, investments or other measures.
Leverage ratios	Measure the extent to which a firm relies on debt financing.
Activity ratios	Measure the effectiveness of management's use of the firm's resources. How fast inventory is moving or how much sales is generated from each dollar invested in assets can be measured using activity ratios.

Budgeting

Budget	Financial plan for a future time period that reflects expected revenues, expenses, receipts, and outlays. It serves as a planning and control tool.
Types of budgets	The master operating budget of a firm is a composite of budgets from all areas of the organization. Typical component budgets include production budgets, cash budgets, capital expenditures budgets, advertising budgets, and sales budgets.

International Accounting

Exchange rates	Fluctuating currency exchange rates must be accounted for as international transactions are recorded and analyzed.

Name _____ Instructor _____

Section _____ Date _____

International accounting standards	The International Accounting Standards Committee (IASC) provides worldwide consistency in financial reporting practices.

Business Vocabulary

accounting
accounting process
accrual accounting
activity ratio
asset
basic accounting equation
balance sheet
bottom line
budget
cash budget
certified public accountant (CPA)
free cash flow
government accountant

income statement
leverage ratio
liability
liquidity ratio
management accountant
owners' equity
profitability ratio
public accountant
Public Company Accounting Oversight
     Board
ratio analysis
statement of cash flows

Application of Vocabulary

Select the term from the list above that best completes the statements beginning on the following page. Write that term in the space provided.

1. _____ is the activity of measuring, interpreting, and communicating financial information for internal and external decision making.

2. A(n) _____ is a professional who has met specified educational and experiential requirements, and passed a comprehensive examination on accounting theory and practice.

3. An independent professional who provides accounting services for both business and individuals is a(n) _____.

Name _____ Instructor _____

Section _____ Date _____

4. A(n) _____ is defined as anything of value owned or leased by a business.

5. A claim against the assets of the business; excess of assets over liabilities is _____.

6. _____ is the term that describes any creditor's claims against the business.

7. A _____ is the term that identifies accountants employed by government agencies.

8. The _____ shows the financial position of an organization as of a given date and makes explicit the basic accounting equation.

9. A professional accountant employed by a firm to develop financial information used by the firm's own management is called a(n) _____.

10. The _____ is the financial statement that reflects the income, expenses, and profits of a business over a period of time.

11. The _____ is the method of converting information about individual transactions into financial statements.

12. The _____ is the final profit or loss earned by a business.

13. A _____ is a planning and control tool that reflects projected revenues, operating expenses, cash receipts and outlays for a future time period.

14. An important statement that tracts the firms inflows and outflows of money, indicating when loans may be needed or when there will be excess funds to invest, is the _____.

15. The accounting concept upon which the balance sheet is based, in which Assets = Liabilities + Owner's Equity is called the _____.

16. _____ involves the use of relative quantitative measures to evaluate various aspects of a firm's financial performance.

17. A(n) _____ is used to measure a firm's ability to meets it short-term obligations.

18. A(n) _____ is used to measure the "bottom line" financial performance of a firm.

19. A(n) _____ measures the extent to which a firm relies on debt financing in its operations.

20. A(n) _____ measures the effectiveness of the firm's use of its resources.

21. The _____ reports the firm's cash receipts and cash payments, presenting information on the sources and uses of cash.

22. _____ is the method of accounting that recognizes revenues and costs when they occur, not when actual cash changes hands.

23. The cash flow from operations, less capital expenditures, measures a firm's _____.

24. In response to cases of accounting fraud, the _____ was created by the Sarbanes-Oxley Act of 2002 to set audit standards, and to investigate and sanction accounting firms that certify the books of publicly traded firms.

Analysis of Learning Goals

Learning Goal 16.1: Explain the functions of accounting and its importance to the firm's management, investors, creditors, and government agencies.

True or False

1. ___ Accountants measure, interpret, and communicate financial information.

2. ___ If a firm is seeking a loan, it will need to show the potential lender accounting information.

3. ___ Accounting is important in profit oriented businesses but it cannot be used to evaluate the performance of not-for-profit organizations.

Name _____ Instructor _____

Section _____ Date _____

4. ___ Accountants produce information used by both the firm's managers and by outside parties.

5. ___ Today, few firms share accounting information with the firm's non-accounting employees.

Learning Goal 16.2: Identify the three basic business activities involving accounting.

Short Answer

Describe how accounting data is used in each of the following business activities.

1. Financing activities.

2. Investing activities.

3. Operating activities.

Learning Goal 16.3: Describe the roles played by public, management, government, and not-for-profit accountants.

True or False

1. ___ Accountants who own their own accounting firms and who provide accounting services to other organizations are known as management accountants.

2. ___ Since public accountants involved in an audit do not work for the firm under inspection, their findings are expected to be unbiased.

3. ___ Government and not-for-profit accountants are concerned with an organization accomplishing its objectives rather than measuring the organization's profit or loss.

4. ___ Management accountants prepare and report financial information for use by people who work in their own firm.

5. ___ Management accountants may work as costs accountants, tax accountants, or internal auditors within their own firm.

Learning Goal 16.4: Outline the steps in the accounting process.

Multiple Choice

1. A chronological record of day-to-day transactions is called the:

    a. ledger.
    b. budget.
    c. journal.
    d. balance sheet.

2. Separate accounts to which transactions are posted are:

    a. ledger accounts
    b. budget accounts.
    c. journal accounts.
    d. balance sheet accounts.

3. The final step in the accounting process is:

    a. preparing the financial statements.
    b. recording day-to-day transactions
    c. determining which types of ledgers to set up.
    d. bringing the owner's equity up to date.

Name _____ Instructor _____

Section _____ Date _____

4.   In modern computerized accounting systems, point-of-sale terminals:

     a.   are increasingly replacing cash registers.
     b.   record transactions and keep inventory in one step.
     c.   are linked to systems that can automatically prepare and analyze financial statements based on the original transaction entry.
     d.   all of the above.

Learning Goal 16.5: Describe the impact of recent ethical scandals and the Sarbanes-Oxley Act on the accounting profession.

Fill In

1.   This piece of legislation was passed to regulate _____
after serious cases of accounting fraud and questions about the independence of auditors came to light.

2.   The Sarbanes-Oxley Act created the _____
to set audit standards and monitor the practices of accounting firms who certify the financial statements of publicly traded firms

3.   This Board has _____ members.

4.   Members of the Board are appointed by the _____.

Learning Goal 16.6: Explain the functions and major components of the three principal financial statements: the balance sheet, the income statement, and the statement of cash flows.

True or False

1. ____   In the basic accounting equation, assets equal liabilities plus owners' equity.

2. ____   The balance sheet is a summary statement of the revenue received and the expenses incurred.

3. ___ The statement of cash flows summarizes the cash effects of a firm's operating, investing, and financing activities during a specific accounting period.

4. ___ The balance sheet shows the financial position of the firm as of a particular date.

5. ___ Owners' equity is another name for profits.

6. ___ Long-term liabilities are debts that are due in one year or more after the preparation of the balance sheet.

7. ___ Not-for-profit organizations do not need to prepare income statements.

8. ___ An income statement deducts all expenses and taxes from total sales revenue to yield after tax net earnings (or losses).

9. ___ The famous "bottom line" refers to the last figure on the income statement.

Learning Goal 16.7: Discuss how financial ratios are used to analyze a firm's financial strengths and weaknesses.

Completion

For each of the following ratios, answer the following questions:

    a. What does it measure?
    b. What is the equation for determining the ratio?
    c. Where do the numbers come from?
    d. How should you evaluate the ratio?

1. Current ratio:

    a.

    b.

    c.

    d.

Name _____ Instructor _____

Section _____ Date _____

2. Acid-test (quick) ratio:

    a.

    b.

    c.

    d.

3. Earnings per share:

    a.

    b.

    c.

    d.

4. Net Profit Margin:

    a.

    b.

    c.

    d.

5. Return on equity:

    a.

    b.

    c.

    d.

6. Total liabilities to total assets:

    a.

    b.

    c.

    d.

7. Inventory turnover ratio:

    a.

    b.

    c.

    d.

Learning goal 16.8: Describe the role of budgets in a business.

True or False

1. ___   Only underfinanced organizations have a need for a budget.

2. ___   The budget serves as the standard with which actual performance is compared.

3. ___   The budget is a firm's short-term financial plan.

4. ___   In large organizations, many people in various departments aid in preparing the overall budget.

5. ___   Typically, budgets are prepared on a daily basis.

6. ___   A budget should match income and expenses in a way that meets a firm's goals while correctly timing cash inflows and outflows.

7. ___   Accounting departments generally provide much of the data needed in the budgeting process.

Name _____ Instructor _____

Section _____ Date _____

Learning Goal 16.9: Explain how exchange rates influence international accounting practices and the importance of uniform financial statements for global business.

True or False

1. ___   The IASC sets international accounting standards which are used exclusively in Europe and North America.

2. ___   It is possible for a firm to earn a profit on an international transaction but still lose money due to shifts in currency exchange rates.

3. ___   Today's sophisticated accounting programs can track transactions in many different countries at once, but they are still not able to automatically account for the affect of currency fluctuations.

4. ___   Data about international financial transactions must be translated into the currency of the country in which the parent country resides.

Self Review

True or False

1. ___   Modern computerized accounting programs have made the accounting process much more efficient and effective.

2. ___   Accountants produce financial statements that can impact a firm's ability to start or expand a business.

3. ___   While accountants produce information useful for financial and investment decisions, they are rarely called upon to analyze the operations activities of a firm.

4. ___   In order to provide reliable, consistent, and unbiased information, accountants follow guidelines known as "generally accepted accounting principles (GAAP)."

5. ___   The four categories of financial ratios relate balance sheet and income statement items to one another to help pinpoint the organization's strengths and weaknesses.

6. ___   Leverage ratios measure the extent to which a firm is using debt financing.

7. ___   The current ratio and acid test ratio measure the organization's profitability.

8. ___   The inventory turnover ratio is a good example of a liquidity ratio.

9. ___   On the balance sheet, liabilities should equal equity minus assets.

10. ___   Accounts receivable is an example of a current asset.

11. ___   The income statement presents a summary of the firm's operations over a period of time.

12. ___   A business can show a large profit and still run out of cash.

13. ___   Public accountants can be external auditors.

14. ___   The statement of cash flows deals with the sources and uses of cash.

15. ___   The inventory turnover rate for a grocery store should be higher than for a furniture store.

16. ___   Accountants who work for the government and not-for-profit organizations do not have to be concerned about the organization's expenses and revenue.

17. ___   Depreciation is added to net income to calculate an accurate cash flow.

Multiple Choice

1. The basic accounting equation includes all of the following, *EXCEPT*:

    a. owner's equity.
    b. gross sales.
    c. assets.

    d. liabilities.
    e. all of the above are on a balance sheet.

Name _____ Instructor _____

Section _____ Date _____

2. On an income statement:

   a. cost of goods sold is added to sales.
   b. cost of goods sold is deducted from sales.
   c. gross income is found by deducting taxes from net earnings.
   d. profit is found by deducting operating expenses from sales.

3. Money due from customers is counted as:

   a. accounts payable.   d. current liabilities.
   b. accounts receivable.   e. none of the above.
   c. long-term liabilities.

4. In accounting, long-term means:

   a. due in a year or longer.   c. due in less than a year.
   b. due in a month or longer.   d. due in less than six months.

5. The debts of a business are known as:

   a. liabilities.   d. revenue.
   b. assets.   e. accounts receivable.
   c. equity.

6. The difference between gross income and operating income are the:

   a. assets.   c. operating expenses.
   b. liabilities.   d. equity.

7. Modern computerized accounting systems:

   a. adopt a "do-it-once" approach to data entry.
   b. can post, summarize, and analyze transaction data automatically.
   c. can track transactions in many different currencies at once and automatically
       calculate the differences that result from currency fluctuations.
   d. all of the above.

8. A firm with a high current ratio would have:

   a. high liquidity.   d. a low total debt ratio.
   b. low equity.   e. a low earnings per share.
   c. a high inventory turnover.

9. The net profit margin ratio:

   a. divides net income by net sales.
   b. is a measure of the firm's efficiency.
   c. should be evaluated in relation to profit forecasts, past performance, or more
      specific industry standards.
   d. all of the above.

10. A firm generally has two sources of funds: liabilities and equity. The things these
    funds are used to buy are called:

   a. assets.   c. net income.
   b. accounts payable.   d. liquidity ratios.

Application Exercises

1. The following is a list of the major sections of an income statement. Arrange the
   sections in the proper sequence, noting which sections are subtracted in order to
   arrive at the final figure.

   Cost of goods sold
   Operating expenses
   Gross income
   Income taxes
   Operating income
   Net income
   Sales

Name _____ Instructor _____

Section _____ Date _____

2. If a firm has current assets of $46,000 and current liabilities of $10,000, what is its current ratio? Is this acceptable or not?

3. If a firm has $150,000 in assets, $100,000 in stockholders' equity, and $50,000 in liabilities, what is the ratio of total liabilities to total assets for this firm? Is it acceptable or not?

4. A firm has total current assets of $60,000, an inventory valued at 50,000, and current liabilities of $20,000. What is its current ratio? What is its quick ratio? Evaluate this firm's liquidity.

Short Essay Questions

1. What is the accounting process? Detail each step and explain the importance of the financial statements that are eventually produced.

2.   What are budgets, and what role do they play in business?

CHAPTER 17

Financial Management and Institutions

Chapter Summary: Key Concepts

The Role of the Financial Manager

Financial management
Financial management is the business activity of developing and implementing the firm's financial plan and finding the best sources and uses of funds. Key financial managers include the Chief Financial Officer (CFO), a vice president for financial management, the treasurer, and the controller.

The financial plan
This document specifies the funds a firm will need for a period of time, the timing of inflows and outflows, and the most appropriate sources and uses of funds.

Characteristics and Functions of Money

Money
Money is anything generally accepted as a means of payment for goods and services.

Characteristics of money
Modern money must be divisible, portable, durable, difficult to counterfeit, and it should have a stable value.

Functions of money
Money serves as a medium of exchange, a common denominator for measurement of value (unit of account), a method of keeping accumulated wealth (store of value), and is highly liquid, that is, it can be obtained and disposed of quickly and easily.

The money supply
Amount of money in circulation. Common measures are M1 and M2. M1 includes coins, currency, traveler's checks, and demand deposits (checking accounts). M2 is a broader measure. It includes M1, savings accounts, certificates of deposit, and money market mutual funds. These additional components of M2 are not as liquid as those counted in M1, and

generally must go through some transaction before
they can fulfill all the functions of money.

Why Organizations Need Funds

Uses of funds

Firms use funds for day-to-day operations, to
purchase inventory, land, plant and facilities, to pay
dividends to stockholders, and to make investments,
such as marketable securities that earn a return while
acting as a temporary substitute for cash.

Sources of funds

There are two main sources of funds for a firm:
equity capital and debt capital. Equity capital is
generated from owner investment, the sale of stock,
accumulated retained earnings, and venture capitalist
investment. Debt capital can come from short term
sources, such as trade credit, secured and unsecured
bank loans, commercial paper, or from long term
sources, such as mortgages or the sale of bonds.

The Financial system and Financial Institutions

U.S. financial system

Made up of deposit institutions, including federal and
state chartered commercial banks, savings banks, and
credit unions; and nondeposit institutions, including
insurance companies, pension funds, and commercial
and consumer finance companies.

Commercial banks

By far the largest and most important financial
institution in most nations, commercial banks raise
money from depositors and lend those funds to
borrowers. The make both consumer and business
loans. Many transactions now occur through
electronic funds transfer systems, and many
households do some or all of their banking online.

Bank regulation

Banks are regulated by the Federal Reserve, the
Federal Deposit Insurance Corporation (FDIC), and
the Comptroller of the Currency.

Savings banks and credit unions In addition to standard commercial banks, savings banks (formerly called Savings and Loans or Thrifts) focus on mortgage loans rather than lending to business. Credit unions are cooperatives, and again focus on services for consumers, not businesses.

Nondepository financial institutions Insurance companies, pension funds, and finance companies accept funds from businesses and households, but they generally do not offer demand deposit accounts. Instead they offer financial services such as insurance, retirement benefits, and short-term loans to borrowers.

The Federal Reserve System (Fed)

Organization of the Fed The Federal Reserve System is a network of twelve regional banks controlled by a board of governors who each serve 14 year terms. The Federal Open Markets Committee (FOMC) of the Fed is responsible for setting most policies concerning monetary policy and interest rates.   As the Fed has its own sources of revenue, it does not depend on congressional appropriations for an operating budget.

Check clearing and the Fed The Fed centralizes the process by which funds are transferred from the check writer to the recipient, and sees to it that all checks clear within two business days.

Monetary policy The Fed's most important function is controlling the money supply and credit. Using tools such as reserve requirements, the discount rate, federal funds rate targets, and open market operations, the Fed promotes economic growth and a stable dollar through monetary policy.

U.S. Financial Institutions: A Global Perspective

Global finance Financial services have become a global industry, and international banks and financial service firms play an important role in global business.

Financial services International banks and other providers of financial services help transfer purchasing power from buyers to sellers and from lenders to borrowers in different countries. They provide credit to importers, and reduce the risk associated with changes in exchange rates.

Business Vocabulary

bonds
certificate of deposit (CD)
check clearing
Chief Financial Officer (CFO)
commercial bank
commercial paper
controller
debt capital
demand deposits
depository institutions
discount rate
equity capital
electronic funds transfer system (EFTS)
Federal Deposit Insurance
  Corporation (FDIC)
federal funds rate
Federal Reserve System (Fed)
finance
financial managers

financial plan
financial system
leverage
M1
M2
monetary policy
money
open market operations
private placements
reserve requirement
risk-return trade-off
trade credit
treasurer
Treasury Bills (T-Bills)
underwriting
venture capitalists
Vice President for financial
  Management

Name _____ Instructor _____

Section _____ Date _____

Application of Vocabulary

Select the term from the list on the previous page that best completes the statements below. Write that term in the space provided.

1. _____ is the business function of planning, obtaining, and managing the company's use of funds in order to effectively accomplish its objectives.

2. People responsible for developing and implementing a firm's financial plan and determining the most appropriate sources and uses of funds are called

    _____ .

3. A high risk investment should be expected to generate a high return, while a low risk investment will generally produce only a modest return. This relationship is known as the _____ .

4. _____ is anything generally accepted as a means of paying for goods and services.

5. The _____ includes all financial institutions that participate in the process by which money flows from savers to users.

6. The funds obtained through borrowing are called _____ .

7. Funds invested by a firm's owners, stockholders, retained earnings, or venture capitalists are called _____ .

8. The _____ is a document that specifies the funds needed by a firm for a period of time, the timing of inflows and outflows of funds, and outlines the most appropriate sources and uses of funds.

9. _____ are certificates of indebtedness sold to raise long-term funds.

10. In a typical organization, the _____ is responsible for preparing financial forecasts and analyzing major investment decisions.

11. _____ is the method of increasing the rate of return on investment by adding borrowed funds to invested funds.

12. The financial manager who manages cash, taxes, the sale of new securities to investors, and shareholder relations, typically holds the title of _____.

13. The _____ is the chief accounting officer.

14. A(n) _____ is a computerized method for making purchases and paying bills by electronically depositing or withdrawing funds.

15. The U.S. central bank, consisting of 12 regional banks that regulates banking in the United States is called the _____.

16. The Fed's most important function, _____, involves controlling the supply of money and credit in the overall economy.

17. The Fed helps facilitate _____, that is, the process by which funds are transferred from the check writer to the recipient.

18. The _____ is the interest rate charged by the Federal Reserve System on loans to member banks.

19. _____ are used by the Federal Reserve System to control the money supply through the purchase and sale of government bonds.

20. The _____ is the percentage of a bank's deposits that must be kept in the bank or on deposit at the local Federal Reserve district bank.

21. _____ are the short-term notes issued by major corporations with high credit ratings that are backed solely by the reputation of the issuing firm.

22. If a business makes purchases on credit or open account, it is making use of _____.

23. _____ are short-term U.S. Treasury borrowings issued each week and sold to the highest bidder. They are virtually risk-free and easy to resell.

24. Commercial banks, savings banks, and credit unions are collectively known as _____.

25. _____ raise money from wealthy individuals and institutional investors, and invest these funds in promising new firms.

Name _____ Instructor _____

Section _____ Date _____

26. New issues of bonds or stocks that are offered only to a small select group of large investors, but not to the public at large, are known as _____.

27. The _____ is the corporation that insures bank depositors' accounts up to a maximum of $100,000 per account and sets requirements for sound banking practices.

28. Checking accounts are also known as _____.

29. A time deposit at a financial institution is known as a(n) _____.

30. Financial institutions that accept savings from depositors and make loans to both businesses and individuals are known as _____.

31. _____ is a narrow measure of the money supply, and includes coins, currency, and demand deposits.

32. When the amount in savings accounts, CD's, and money market mutual funds is added to M1 we get a broader measure of the money supply known as _____.

33. The vice-president for financial management, the treasurer, and the contoller all report to the _____, who then reports directly to the CEO.

34. The process called _____ is used by insurance companies to determine whom to insure and what to charge.

35. The rate at which banks lend money to one another overnight is called the _____.

Analysis of Learning Goals

Learning Goal 17.1: Identify the functions performed by a firm's financial managers.

True or False

1. ___   Financial managers seek to balance financial risks with expected returns.

2. ___   The highest ranking financial manager in a large organization is the CFO.

3. ___   Financial managers are responsible for obtaining any needed funds, but play no role in planning expenditures.

4. ___   The chief accounting manager typically holds the title of Treasurer.

5. ___   Financial managers are responsible for both raising and spending the firm's money.

Learning Goal 17.2: Describe the characteristics a form of money should have, and list the functions of money.

Short Answer

1. List and define the characteristics of modern money:

    a.

    b.

    c.

    d.

    e.

2. List and discuss the functions of money.

    a.

    b.

Name _____ Instructor _____

Section _____ Date _____

    c.

    d.

Learning Goal 17.3: Explain each of the various measures of the money supply.

True or False

1. ___ A checking account is considered to be money, and is counted as part of M1.

2. ___ M2 is a broader measure of the money supply than M1.

3. ___ The assets included in M2 are all as liquid as the assets counted in M1.

4. ___ Money market mutual funds and savings deposits are counted in M1.

Learning Goal 17.4: Explain how a firm uses funds.

True or False

1. ___ Firms use funds to finance day-to-day operations, to purchase inventory and long-term assets, and to make payments on loans.

2. ___ Financial managers generally invest excess cash in marketable securities until the funds are needed.

3. ___ The dividends paid to stockholders are not usually counted as expenditures of funds.

4. ___ If cash inflows fall below cash needs, a financial manager should buy commercial paper.

5. ___ Treasury bills generally pay a higher rate of interest than can be earned from commercial paper.

6. ___ A certificate of deposit (CD) is a short term note issued by a bank, thrift, or credit union.

Learning Goal 17.5: Compare the two major sources of funds for a business.

Multiple Choice

1. Sources of equity capital include:

    a. owner contributions or stock sold.
    b. contributions by venture capitalists.
    c. retained earnings.
    d. all of the above.

2. Debt capital refers to:

    a. owners' investments in the firm.   d. residual funds.
    b. retained earnings.   e. venture capital.
    c. borrowed funds.

3. Which of the following matures (i.e. must be repaid at a stated time)?

    a. stock   c. bonds
    b. retained earnings   d. all of the above

4. Equity capital is referred to as:

    a. ownership funds.   c. borrowed funds.
    b. debt capital.   d. residual funds.

5. Who has the first claim to the assets and income of a firm?

    a. lenders.   c. venture capitalists.
    b. stockholders.   d. owners.

Learning Goal 17.6: Identify likely sources of short-term and long-term funds.

Fill in the Blank

1. _____ are stocks and bonds sold to a select group of large investors, such as pension funds, but not to the general pubic.

2. Major corporations can save 1-2% on borrowing costs by selling _____
    _____ to other corporations.

Name _____ Instructor _____

Section _____ Date _____

3. Open-account purchases from suppliers are called _____.

4. In a(n) _____, borrowers need not pledge collateral.

5. _____ sources of funds must be repaid within one year.

6. Long-term sources of funds must be repaid _____.

7. Bonds, loans that mature in a year or more, and equity funds all constitute _____.

8. Firms that raise money from wealthy individual investors and institutional investors to invest in new firms are called _____.

Learning Goal 17.7: Describe the financial system and the major financial institutions.

Multiple Choice

1. A profit-making business that holds deposits for individuals and business firms and makes loans to individuals and business firms is a:

    a. commercial bank.   c. commercial finance company.
    b. credit union.   d. consumer finance company.

2. A form of cooperative that acts as a depository and grants loans to its members is a(n):

    a. commercial bank.   c. insurance company.
    b. commercial finance company. d. credit union.

3. An institution that offers both saving and checking accounts and that has historically been the major source of home loans is now called a:

    a. consumer finance company.   c. savings bank.
    b. commercial bank.   d. credit union.

4. What type of financial institution offers short-term loans to businesses but not to individuals?

    a. credit unions
    b. consumer finance companies
    c. savings and loan associations

    d. commercial banks
    e. commercial finance companies

5. These types of institutions provide financial protection for their policyholders, make commercial and real estate mortgage loans, and purchase government bonds:

    a. mutual savings banks.
    b. insurance companies.
    c. commercial banks.

    d. credit unions.
    e. consumer finance companies.

6. All of the following are deposit institutions, *EXCEPT*:

    a. pension funds.
    b. credit unions.

    c. commercial banks.
    d. savings banks.

Learning Goal 17.8: Explain the functions of the Federal Reserve System and the tools it uses to control the money supply.

True or False

1. ___ The most essential function of the Federal Reserve System is to control the supply of money and credit in order to promote economic growth and a stable dollar.

2. ___ An increase in the reserve requirement or the discount rate will increase the money supply.

3. ___ The Fed is theU.S. Central Bank.

4. ___ If the Fed buys government bonds on the open market, the money supply will increase.

5. ___ The Federal Reserve System has no control over interest rates.

6. ___ The Fed is designed to be politically dependent on the current administration and congressional appropriations process.

Name _____ Instructor _____

Section _____ Date _____

Learning Goal 17.9: Describe the global financial system.

True or False

1. ___ Virtually all nations have a central bank.

2. ___ American banks make up the majority of the global financial giants.

3. ___ Transactions in international markets have no impact on the domestic money supply.

4. ___ Foreign currencies and securities held by the Fed are counted as part of the U.S. banking system's reserves.

Self Review

True or False

1. ___ Financial control is the process that periodically checks actual revenues, costs, and expenses against a firm's forecasts and plans.

2. ___ Commercial paper is another name for long-term debt.

3. ___ Having too much cash on hand can be costly.

4. ___ Not having enough cash on hand can be costly.

5. ___ The amount and timing of borrowing are important aspects of the financial plan.

6. ___ Leverage is a technique of increasing the return on investment.

7. ___ If the Federal Reserve Bank buys government bonds on the open market, the money supply will decline.

8. ___ Commercial banks and Savings Banks both focus on business banking.

9. ___ A demand deposit is another name for a checking account.

10. ___ Commercial finance companies usually make long-term loans to businesses.

11. ___ All national banks must belong to the Federal Reserve System.

12. ___ If the Federal Reserve Bank increases the reserve requirements, member banks will have less funds available to make loans.

13. ___ With a debit card, consumers' purchases are deducted directly from their accounts.

14. ___ In a secured loan, borrowers need not pledge collateral.

15. ___ Loans repaid over one year or longer, bonds, and equity funds are all considered long term sources of funds.

16. ___ Commercial paper is more risky than T-Bills; thus it pays a higher rate of interest.

17. ___ Banks examiners are trained representatives who inspect the financial records and management practices of financial institutions.

18. ___ Equity capital is obtained through the sale of bonds.

19. ___ Insurance companies are depository institutions.

20. ___ Money serves as a medium of exchange, eliminating the need for a barter system.

Multiple Choice

1. Money should have which of the following characteristics?

   a. durability
   b. divisibility
   c. stability
   d. portability
   e. all of the above

2. The functions of money include:

   a. a store of value.
   b. a medium of exchange.
   c. a unit of account.
   d. all of the above.

Name _____ Instructor _____

Section _____ Date _____

3. The owner of a cow who wishes to exchange it for a loaf of bread is faced with the problem of:

    a. portability.
    b. divisibility.
    c. currency exchange rates.

    d. counterfeiting.
    e. stability of value.

4. Which of the following has no maturity date?

    a. debt.
    b. equity.

    d. both debt and equity mature.
    e. neither have a maturity date.

5. The largest and most common financial institutions in the U.S. are:

    a. commercial banks.
    b. commercial finance companies.

    c. savings banks.
    d. consumer finance companies.

6. Accounts similar to checking accounts that are offered by credit unions are called:

    a. time deposits.
    b. Now accounts.

    c. share draft accounts.
    d. deposit accounts.

7. The clearinghouse for checks is the:

    a. Internal Banking System.
    b. Bank of America.
    c. Federal Reserve System.

    d. Federal Check Regulatory Commission.
    e. Internal Revenue Service.

8. Which of the following is *NOT* true of commercial paper?

    a. It is issued by major corporations to raise money.
    b. It is a secured short-term loan.
    c. It is a short-term promissory note.
    d. It is backed by the reputation of the issuing company.
    e. All of the above are true.

9. Corporate bonds are a form of:

   a. long-term debt financing.
   b. short-term debt financing.
   c. long-term equity financing.
   d. short-term equity financing.
   e. commercial paper.

10. If you are saving money for a trip after graduation, which function of money are you utilizing?

    a. medium of exchange
    b. unit of account
    c. store of value
    d. liquidity
    e. all of the above

11. Money eliminates the need for a barter system and makes trade easier by serving as a(n):

    a. unit of account.
    b. medium of exchange.
    c. store of value.
    d. substitute for time.
    e. all of the above.

12. Banks:
    a. raise money by accepting deposits.
    b. pool deposits and use them to make loans to consumers and businesses.
    c. make money by charging a higher rate on loans than they pay on deposits.
    d. make money on fees they charge to customers for services performed.
    e. all of the above.

Application Exercises

1. Alice Brown is a recent widow who received $100,000 from her husband's life insurance policy. She plans to use the money as a down payment for a new home in about a year, and wants to put the money in a safe place until then. Her inclination is to put it in the bank, but she has also heard that sometime banks fail. What can you tell her about the safety of her proposed deposit? What should she look for when selecting a bank? An investment vehicle?

Name _____ Instructor _____

Section _____ Date _____

2. In each of the cases below, calculate the rate of return on stockholders' investment.

    a.   Stock $80,000
           Bonds   0
           Earnings   40,000
           Rate of return to stockholders =

    b.   Stock $60,000
           Bonds   20,000
           Earnings   40,000
           Annual rate of interest on the bonds: 8%
           Rate of return to stockholders =

    c.   Stock $80,000
           Bonds   40,000
           Earnings   50,000
           Annual rate of interest on the bonds: 10%
           Rate of return to stockholders =

Short Essay Questions

1. Define financial management and discuss its components and importance to modern organizations.

2. Define debt capital and equity capital. What are the chief sources and characteristics of each?

3. What is the Federal Reserve System and what role does it play in modern finance? Name and discuss the major tools the Federal Reserve System has at its disposal.

CHAPTER 18

Financing and Investing through Securities Markets

Chapter Summary: Key Concepts

Introduction to Securities and Markets

Securities	Common and preferred stocks, money market instruments, and the various types of bonds are all referred to as securities.
The Primary market	Markets in which new issues of securities are sold to the public for the first time.
The Secondary market	These markets include the New York Stock Exchange (NYSE), the American Stock Exchange (AMEX), the NASDAQ, and regional and foreign stock exchanges. In these secondary markets, securities are traded between investors.

Securities

Money market instruments	Short-term debt securities issued by corporations, financial institutions such as banks, and governments.
Bonds	By selling bonds, the seller obtains long-term debt capital. Bonds are sold by the U.S. Treasury (government), municipalities, and corporations. Bonds can be secured or unsecured (debentures).
Quality ratings for bonds	Standard & Poor's and Moody's rate corporate and municipal bonds with regard to risk. Higher risk bonds must pay higher interest to attract investors.
Retiring bonds	Bonds must eventually be repaid. Provisions for repayment of bonds include whether the bonds are convertible, serial, callable, or sinking fund.

Stock

Corporations generate equity capital when they sell stock and stockholders actually own a piece of the corporation. Corporations may issue, common stock, preferred stock, or convertible securities.

Securities Purchasers

Investors

Individual investors are people who buy securities for themselves. Institutional investors now account for about half of daily trading volume, and include mutual funds, pension funds, insurance companies, and not-for-profit organizations and foundations.

Investment motivations

The five primary motivations for investing in securities include potential growth in capital, stability of principal, liquidity, current income, and growth in income. Different securities will be selected depending on the investment objective.

Taxes and investing

Many institutional investors, such as pension funds, pay no taxes on investment returns. Individual investors may owe taxes on investment income and gains.

Securities Exchanges

The New York Stock Exchange

The NYSE or "Big Board" is the largest secondary market in the world. It is where most of the largest, best-known U.S. companies' stocks are traded. Trading involves face-to-face bidding between seated traders at posts on the exchange floor. Each listed stock is assigned to one of 42 specialists, who maintain orderly and liquid markets in the stocks on their posts.

The NASDAQ stock market

This National Association of Securities Dealers Automated Quotation system is a computerized communications network where buy and sell orders are executed electronically.

Other U.S. stock markets

The AMEX and several regional exchanges trade in the stocks of smaller firms, or offer additional trading venues for NYSE stocks.

Foreign stock markets

All developed countries, and many developing countries, have stock exchanges.

Direct trading and ECN's

Sometimes called the "fourth market", here buyers and sellers meet in a virtual stock market where they trade directly with one another.

Buying and Selling Securities

Placing an order

An investor can place a market order or a limit order in buying or selling a stock.

Costs of trading

Various types of brokerage firms offer different services and fee arrangements. In general, lower fees are charged by firms offering fewer services.

Direct investing

Some companies offer shares directly to investors and/or dividend reinvestment plans (DRIPs).

Reading the financial news

Investors should be able to read and understand stock and bond quotations, and to understand the meaning of important stock indexes (The Dow, the S&P 500, the NASDAQ).

Mutual funds

These organizations pool investment money from many purchasers to acquire a diversified portfolio of securities. More than 8000 funds exist, including stock funds, bond funds, money market funds, and hybrid funds.

Legal and Ethical Issues in Securities Trading

Government regulation and the securities markets

The Securities and Exchange Commission (SEC) is the primary federal regulatory agency. The SEC is charged with protecting fairness to all investors. It registers all new public issues of corporate stock. It regulates and monitors trading practices in the secondary markets, and it can restrain trading in times of excessive trading volatility.

Industry self-regulation

The National Association of Securities Dealers (NASD) has established rules of conduct for its members, prescribed penalties for breaking the rules, and devised methods for arbitrating investor/broker disputes. All securities markets use market surveillance techniques to spot possible violations of rules or laws. And market participants must keep detailed records, or "audit trails" of every transaction.

Business Vocabulary

bond rating
book value
brokerage firm
call provision
common stock
convertible security
debenture
Electronic Communications Network
  (ECN)
full and fair disclosure
government bonds
initial public offering (IPO)
insider trading
institutional investors
investment bankers
limit order

market order
money market instruments
municipal bonds
mutual funds
preferred stock
price-earnings ratio (P/E)
primary market
prospectus
regulation FD
secondary market
secured bond
securities
stock exchange (market)
underwriting
yield

Name _____ Instructor _____

Section _____ Date _____

Application of Vocabulary

Select the term from the list on the previous page that best competes the statements below. Write that term in the space provided.

1. A(n) _____ is a financial intermediary that buys and sells securities for individual and institutional investors.

2. _____ are firms who bring new issues of securities to market..

3. _____ is an illegal trade of securities by a person who profits from nonpublic information.

4. The _____, commonly referred to as "the market," is the means by which securities are traded between investors.

5. The _____ is a measure that assesses the riskiness of a corporate or municipal debt issue.

6. The _____ is found by dividing a stock's current market price by the issuer's annual earnings per share.

7. Part of what is known as the fourth market, a(n) _____ lets securities buyers and sellers meet in a virtual stock market where they trade directly with one another.

8. An investor can place a _____ that indicates that the stock purchase or sale be made at a specified price.

9. When an investor requests that a security be purchased or sold at the current market price, that investor has placed a(n) _____.

10. A(n) _____ is a document that describes a new issue and its underwriting agreement in detail, as well as providing a description of the company, that details financial data, products, research and development projects, and pending litigation.

11. Common stocks, preferred stocks, and bonds are collectively known as

_____.

12. _____ are credit instruments issued by cities or states.

13. The regulatory philosophy that investors should be told all relevant information so they can make informed decisions is known as _____.

14. To calculate the current _____, or percentage return earned from securities, you divide the annual dividend of a stock by its market price, or the annual interest payment of a bond by the bond's market price.

15. The _____ of a share of stock is determined by subtracting the liabilities and the value of any preferred stock from the firm's assets, and dividing the difference by the number of shares of common stock outstanding.

16. _____ provides owners voting rights for the board of directors of the corporation, but only a residual claim to company assets.

17. _____ provides owners preferential dividend payment and the first claim to assets after debts are paid, but seldom includes voting rights.

18. A(n) _____ allows the issuer to redeem a bond prior to its maturity at a prespecified price.

19. _____ include organizations such as pension funds, insurance companies, banks, and mutual funds that invest in securities.

20. _____ are short-term debt securities issued by corporations, financial institutions, and governments.

21. When securities are initially offered to the public, they are sold through the _____.

22. _____ are organizations that pool investor's money in order to purchase a diversified portfolio of securities.

23. A(n) _____ occurs when securities are offered for sale to the general public for the first time.

24. Investment bankers who purchase an entire new issue from the issuing firm or government and then resells the issue to investors is engaged in _____.

25. A(n) _____ is a bond backed by the reputation of the issuing corporation.

Name _____ Instructor _____

Section _____ Date _____

26. A(n) _____ is a bond backed by specific pledges of company assets.

27. The location at which stocks and bonds are bought and sold is called the _____ _____.

28. The U.S. government borrows by means of certificates of indebtedness known as _____.

29. A(n) _____ gives the owner the option to trade it in for a specified number of shares of common stock.

30. To help ensure full and fair disclosure, _____ requires that firms share information with all investors at the same time.

Analysis of Learning Goals

Learning Goal 18.1: Distinguish between the primary market for securities and the secondary market.

Multiple Choice

1. The initial issue of stock or bonds takes place in the:

    a. primary market.
    b. secondary market.

    d. American Stock exchange.
    e. all of the above.

2. When investors trade securities among themselves they do so by means of the:

    a. primary market.
    b. secondary market.

    c. Dow Jones Industrial Index.
    d. Standard and Poor's rating services.

3. Each time securities are traded on the secondary market, the issuing corporation receives:

    a. 100% of the selling price.
    b. 50% of the selling price.

    c. 25% of the selling price.
    d. none of the selling price.

4.   Rather than going directly to the public with a new issue of stock, most corporations use:

    a.   investment bankers.   c.   the New York Stock Exchange.
    b.   the secondary market.   d.   the American Stock Exchange.

Learning Goal 18.2: Compare money market instruments, bonds, and common stock, and explain why particular investors might prefer each type of security.

Multiple Choice

1.   The true owners of a corporation:

    a.   are the common shareholders.   c.   have a residual claim to assets.
    b.   have voting rights.   d.   all of the above.

2.   Preferred stockholders:

    a.   have a prior claim to assets.
    b.   usually have a vote.
    c.   are contributors of debt, not equity capital
    d.   all of the above.

3.   In the event of a firm's dissolution the first claim on its assets belongs to:

    a.   bondholders.
    b.   preferred stockholders.
    c.   common stockholders.
    d.   all investors have an equal claim to assets.

4.   A person who prefers being a creditor to being an owner would invest in:

    a.   common stock.   c.   bonds.
    b.   preferred stock.   d.   an IPO.

5.   Short-term debt securities sold by corporations and governments are:

    a.   bonds.   c.   preferred securities.
    b.   money market instruments.   d.   common stocks.

Name _____ Instructor _____

Section _____ Date _____

Learning Goal 18.3: Identify the five basic objectives of investors and the types of securities most likely to help them reach each objective.

Completion

Define each of the following investment objectives. What securities might an investor select to meet each objective?

1. Growth in capital.

2. Stability of principal.

3. Liquidity.

4. Current income.

5. Growth in income.

Learning Goal 18.4: Explain the process of buying or selling a security listed on an organized securities exchange.

True or False

1. ___   A market order is an investor request to buy or sell a stock at a specified price.

2. ___   The NYSE lists over 8000 stocks.

3. ___   A growing number of investors bypass the traditional exchanges and make their trades through computer trading networks.

4. ___   Discount brokers charge lower commissions but also offer fewer services than traditional brokers.

5. ___   Online trading is offered by special online brokerage firms, but is not available through more traditional full-service or discount brokerage firms.

Learning Goal 18.5: Describe the information included in stock, bond, and mutual fund quotations.

Multiple Choice

1. In a stock quotation, the PE:

   a.   is the price to earnings ratio.
   b.   is found by dividing today's closing price by the annual earnings per share.
   c.   is equal to the stock's annual yield.
   d.   all of the above.
   e.   a and b only.

2. Bond quotations show all the following information, *EXCEPT*:

   a.   the yield.   d.   the interest rate.
   b.   the closing price.   e.   the price-earnings ratio.
   c.   the maturity date.

3. On the stock quotations found in the newspaper, the high and low shown before the name of the issuer refers to:

   a.   the previous day's high and low.   d.   the all time high and low.
   b.   the last month's high and low.   e.   today's high and low.
   c.   the last year's high and low.

Name _____ Instructor _____

Section _____ Date _____

4. The last column in a stock quotation in the newspaper shows the net change between:

   a. the high and low for the day being reported.
   b. the high and low for the year being reported.
   c. the stock's closing price for the day being reported and its closing price on the previous trading day.
   d. the stock's all time high and low.

5. In a mutual fund quotation, the NAV column:

   a. gives the net assert value of one share of the fund.
   b. includes the sales charges or "load" for buying a share of the fund.
   c. shows the change in the fund's net asset value from the previous trading session.
   d. shows the earnings of the fund over the last year.
   e. gives the fund's yield.

Learning Goal 18.6: Explain the role of mutual funds in securities markets.

True or False

1. ___ The main advantage of mutual funds is that the investor cannot lose.

2. ___ Mutual funds are professionally managed investment companies that own securities of many different companies or government issuers.

3. ___ An investor gains greater diversification from buying a share of a mutual fund than from buying an individual stock or bond.

4. ___ Mutual funds have become an increasingly popular investment vehicle for individual investors.

5. ___ Over half of all American households own mutual fund shares.

Learning Goal 18.7: Evaluate the major features of regulations designed to protect investors.

Fill in the blank

1. The federal agency that regulates the securities markets is the _____.

2. Before a new security can be issued, the issuer must prepare and submit a

 _____.

3. The SEC tries to ensure _____, that is, investors should have access to all relevant information so they can make informed investment decisions.

4. If a company's officers, directors, lawyers, accountants, investment bankers, or even outside friends or reporters use material, nonpublic information about a company to make investment profits, they are engaged in _____.

5. The SEC recently issued _____ to ensure that no particular class of investor gets information about a company before it is available to everyone.

6. The securities industry uses market surveillance and adopts professional rules of conduct to ensure fair and orderly markets and promote investor confidence. These activities are collectively known as _____.

Self Review

True or False

1. ___ Moody's and Standard and Poor provide services that rate the quality of bonds.

2. ___ IPOs take place in the secondary market.

3. ___ Discount brokers deal only with junk bonds and low-cost stocks.

4. ___ When reading stock market quotes, the net change is the difference between the high price and the low price on the day being reported.

5. ___ All mutual funds invest in stocks.

6. ___ The yield on a particular security will vary with the market price of that security.

Name _____ Instructor _____

Section _____ Date _____

7. ___ Bondholders are creditors to the issuing organization.

8. ___ Today, about 10% of stock trades takes place online.

9. ___ The price-earnings ratio relates dividends to market value.

10. ___ A stockbroker can recommend an appropriate security for you before identifying your investment objectives.

11. ___ The Dow Jones Averages include all stocks traded that day.

12. ___ Some bonds and preferred stock are convertible.

13. ___ Bond prices move inversely to interest rates.

14. ___ Insider trading involves profiting from information that was not available to the general public.

15. ___ An IPO means *going public.*

Multiple Choice

1. The price of a stock is $20 per share, earnings are $4 a share, and dividends are $4 a share. Which of the following is correct?

   a. P/E 5, Yield 25%.
   b. P/E 4, Yield 25%.
   c. P/E 5, Yield 20%.
   d. P/E 4, Yield 20%.

2. If an investor wanted to pay no more than a specified amount for a stock the investor would:

   a. use a limit order.
   b. use a market order.
   c. change brokers.
   d. buy on margin.
   e. find a bookie.

3. An investor looking for maximum liquidity would most likely invest in:

   a. money market instruments.   c. common stocks.
   b. preferred stocks.   d. corporate bonds.

4. An investor looking for growth in capital would be most likely to invest in:

   a. common stock.   c. corporate bonds.
   b. preferred stock.   d. government bonds.

5. An investor seeking the highest current income available from securities would most likely purchase:

   a. common stock.   c. money market instruments.
   b. preferred stock.   d. bonds.

6. Junk bonds:

   a. offer higher yields in return for taking greater risks.
   b. generally earn lower interest rates than AAA rated bonds.
   c. are already in default.
   d. all of the above.

7. DRIPs:

   a. are direct investment programs offered by corporations.
   b. reinvest dividends immediately into additional stock of the company.
   c. allow investors to accumulate more shares without incurring brokerage fees.
   d. all of the above.

8. Sales charges levied on mutual funds are commonly called:

   a. loads.   c. DRIPs.
   b. commissions.   d. P/E ratios.

9. Program trading:

   a. means that computer systems are programmed to buy or sell securities if certain conditions arise.
   b. cannot be halted by the SEC during periods of extreme market volatility.
   c. is now illegal.
   d. all of the above.

Name _____ Instructor _____

Section _____ Date _____

10. Suppose you own a $1000 bond that matures in 10 years and pays an interest rate of 8%. You hear on the evening news that interest rates have risen to 10%. You should expect:

    a.   the current market value of your bond to increase.
    b.   the current market value of your bond to decline.
    c.   to earn more interest from your bond.
    d.   to earn less interest from your bond.

11. In daily newspaper stock quotes, the yield on a stock is calculated by:

    a.   dividing annual dividend per share by the stock's market price.
    b.   dividing annual earnings per share by the stock's market price.
    c.   multiplying the P/E ratio by the stock's market price.
    d.   subtracting broker's commission from the stock's market price.

Application Exercises

The various kinds of securities have characteristics that make them suitable for some investment objectives and unsuitable for others. Consider each of the following securities and suggest an investment objective it would meet.

1. common stock in a fast growing company.

2. a U.S. Treasury bond.

3. a municipal bond.

4. a junk bond.

5. a money market mutual fund.

6. a mutual fund that invests in both domestic and foreign securities.

Short Essay Questions

1. What are securities? What are the risks and rewards of investing in securities? What steps can an individual investor take to minimize risk?

2. What are primary markets? How do they differ from secondary markets?

APPENDIX A

Risk Management and Insurance

Summary: Key Concepts

Overview of Risk and Risk Management

Risk

Risk is the uncertainty about loss or injury, and falls into two major categories. Pure risk is when there is only a chance for a loss, while in speculative risk there is a chance for a gain or a loss.

Risk management

The four methods of managing risk are to avoid risk, reduce risk, self-insure against risk, or shift the risk to insurance companies.

Basic Insurance Concepts

Insurable interest

To purchase insurance, the policyholder must demonstrate that they will suffer a loss if some specified event occurs.

Insurable risk

Insurance companies impose five basic requirements for a pure risk to be insurable: the loss should be reasonably predictable, financially measurable, and accidental; also the risk should be spread over a wide geographic area, and the loss must meet the company's underwriting standards.

Law of large numbers

Insurance premiums are based on the statistical probability of a loss. Insurance underwriting involves the use of the law of large numbers to construct actuarial tables.   Insurance companies use these tables to predict the likelihood of loss (and hence claims they will have to pay), and they set premiums accordingly.

Sources of Insurance Coverage

Public insurance companies Public insurance companies are government agencies established at the state or federal level to provide specialized insurance protection for individuals and organizations. Unemployment insurance, worker's compensation insurance, and Medicare are examples.

Private insurance companies Private insurance companies are agencies that operate as either profit-seeking stock companies or as nonprofit mutual insurance companies. Policyholders shift risk to private insurance companies in exchange for the premiums they pay.

Types of Insurance

Property and liability insurance Individuals and businesses face many risks to their property and for damages done to others. Homeowners' insurance, auto insurance, commercial and business insurance, and liability insurance are ways individuals and businesses can shift those risks.

Health and disability insurance Health insurance covers risks to people from illness or injury. Many types of health insurance are available, including fee-for-service plans and managed-care plans such as health maintenance organizations (HMOs) and preferred provider organizations (PPOs).

Disability income insurance This insurance is designed to replace lost income when a wage earner cannot work due to an accident or illness.

Life insurance This type of insurance protects people against the financial losses that occur with premature death.

Name _____ Instructor _____

Section _____ Date _____

Business Vocabulary

actuarial table	managed care plans
business interruption insurance	Medicare
cash value policies	preferred provider plan (PPO)
disability income insurance	premium
fee for service plan	property and liability insurance
health insurance	public insurance agency
health maintenance organization (HMO)	pure risk
insurable interest	risk
insurable risk	self-insurance fund
insurance	speculative risk
key executive insurance	term policies
law of large numbers	underwriting
liability insurance	unemployment insurance
life insurance	workers' compensation insurance

Application of Vocabulary

Select the term from the list above that best completes the following statements. Write that term in the space provided.

1. _____ is defined as any uncertainty about loss or injury.

2. When an activity can bring the chance of either profit or loss, we say the activity involves _____.

3. Most insurance is sold to protect buyers in situations where there is a chance for loss but no chance for gain, known as _____.

4. When you buy _____, you trade a smaller known loss (the policy premium) for protection against a larger unknown loss (up to the limits of your policy).

5. Premiums are based on the _____, or probability calculation of the likelihood that the perils you are insuring against will occur.

6. Insurance companies construct _____ to predict the number of claims they can expect in any year for each category of risk they insure.

7. Before you can buy insurance, you must demonstrate that you have a(n) _____ _____, that is, that you stand to suffer loss.

8. _____ protects against financial losses resulting from fires, accidents, theft, or other destructive events. Included in this category are Home Owners', Auto, Commercial/Business, and Liability policies.

9. Companies that set up their own account to cover losses that might occur due to risk have established a(n) _____.

10. A policy that pays a benefit to surviving beneficiaries when someone dies is known as _____.

11. _____ policies are designed to replace lost income when a wage earner cannot work due to an accident or illness.

12. _____ provides coverage for the care needed if the insured gets sick or has an accident.

13. A(n) _____ is a managed care health plan that provides a comprehensive set of health care services to policyholders.

14. Before an insurance company will sell a policy to cover a risk, that risk must meet the requirements that make it a(n) _____.

15. _____ is life insurance designed to reimburse an organization for the loss of the services and cost of replacing a senior manager.

16. A policyholder pays a _____ to the insurance in order to receive coverage against losses.

17. A(n) _____ is a state or federal government unit established to provide specialized insurance protection for individuals and organizations.

18. Each state has a(n) _____ program that assists out of work persons by providing financial benefits, job counseling, and placement services.

Name _____ Instructor _____

Section _____ Date _____

19. Employers must provide _____ to guarantee payment of wages and salaries, medical care costs, retraining, job placement, and vocational rehabilitation to employees who are injured on the job.

20. _____ protects an individual or business against financial losses to others for which the individual or business was responsible.

21. The two types of _____ are HMOs and PPOs.

22. In a(n) _____ the insured people pick their own doctors and pay for their services; then they are reimbursed by the insurance company.

23. A managed care program where members choose their primary care physician, needed specialists, and hospitals from a list of approved health care providers is called a(n) _____.

24. _____ are life insurance products that pay a death benefit if the policyholder dies within a specified period of time, but they have no value at the end of that period.

25. Products that combine life insurance protection with a savings feature are known as

_____.

26. _____ is the federal program that provides health insurance for people 65 or older.

27. Insurance that protects firms from financial losses resulting from the interruption of business operations is called _____.

28. _____ is the process used by insurance companies to evaluate an applicant's risk profile with reference to the company's standards for accepting risks.

Self Review

True or False

1. ___ A firm that sets asides reserves to cover possible losses is self-insuring.

2. ___ Buying a lottery ticket is an example of pure risk.

3. ___ Since public insurance companies are owned by the government, the coverage is free to the insured.

4. ___ Very few states have unemployment insurance.

5. ___ Companies can purchase insurance that covers losses resulting from injuries caused by their products.

6. ___ Mutual insurance companies are profit organizations whose owners need not be policyholders.

7. ___ Insurance premiums are based on the law of large numbers.

8. ___ The only way to handle risk is to shift it to an insurance company.

9. ___ Many types of risk can be reduced or even eliminated by removing hazards or taking preventative measures.

10. ___ You must stand to suffer a loss to be eligible to buy insurance on property or another person's life.

11. ___ In general, cash value life insurance policies are cheaper than term policies.

12. ___ The higher auto insurance rates paid by younger people is simple discrimination.

13. ___ Employers are required to contribute to worker's compensation insurance plans, which cover employees for any illness or injury they suffer on or off the job.

14. ___ Managed care health insurance plans include HMOs and PPOs.

15. ___ Employers can generally purchase health insurance at more affordable rates than can individuals because they are offered insurance at group rates.

16. ___ It is important to be sure that the insurance company from which you purchase insurance is financially strong.

Name _____ Instructor _____

Section _____ Date _____

17. ___ Managed care health plans generally limit the choice of health care providers.

18. ___ Fee-for-service health plans typically have lower out of pocket expenses than managed care plans.

19. ___ Commercial and business insurance protects employers from employee dishonesty or loses resulting from the nonperformance of contracts.

Multiple Choice

1. Pure risk:

   a. involves the possibility of loss or gain.
   b. involves only the possibility of loss.
   c. involves only the possibility of gain.
   d. cannot be covered by buying insurance.

2. Speculative risk:

   a. involves the possibility of loss or gain.
   b. involves only the possibility of loss.
   c. involves only the possibility of gain.
   d. can be covered by buying insurance.

3. What type of insurance covers a business against injuries to its customers?

   a. liability insurance   c. health insurance
   b. property insurance   d. life insurance

4. A person or company that stands to suffer a financial loss due to fire, accident, lawsuit, or death, is said to have a(n):

   a. bad day.   c. insurable interest.
   b. assumed liability.   d. speculative risk.

5. A small firm that wishes to deal with the risk of loss by fire would probably:

   a. ignore it.   c. purchase fire insurance.
   b. self-insure.   d. move to another building.

6. Which of the following is *NOT* a recommended method of dealing with risk?

   a. avoid it.
   b. insure against it.
   c. ignore it.

   d. reduce it.
   e. recognize it.

7. The type of risk you take when investing in the stock market is:

   a. pure risk.
   b. speculative risk.

   c. probable risk.
   d. no risk.

8. Actuarial tables are based on:

   a. historic costs.
   b. mortality tables.

   c. the law of large numbers.
   d. the birth rate.

9. For a risk to be insurable:

   a. the likelihood of loss should be predictable and the losses financially measurable.
   b. the loss must be fortuitous or accidental.
   c. the risk should be spread over a wide geographic area.
   d. it must meet the insurer's underwriting standards.
   e. all of the above.

10. Most people and businesses:

    a. self insure.
    b. shift the risk of loss to an insurance company.
    c. can avoid paying insurance premiums.
    d. can eliminate risks entirely and hence don't need insurance.

11. Health Maintenance Organizations (HMOs) are:

    a. Preferred Provider Organizations.
    b. fee for service health insurers.
    c. primary providers of life insurance.
    d. managed care health insurance programs.

APPENDIX B

A Guide to Your Personal Finances

Summary: Key Concepts

The Meaning and Importance of Personal Finance

Personal finance

Study of the economic factors and personal decisions that affect a person's financial well-being.

The importance of personal finance today

Today many factors make prudent financial planning more important than ever. Changes in job security and the nature of work, the sluggish growth in personal income, and a far wider array of financial choices make personal financial planning a lifelong activity.

Setting financial priorities

The first step in financial planning is identifying financial priorities. Figure out where you stand financially, put yourself on a budget, insure against financial ruin, get debt under control, start saving for retirement, and set up a regular savings program.

A personal financial management model

A suggested model for financial planning begins with identifying short and long term monetary and and nonmonetary goals. Then, considering the changing external factors, one should develop plans in each of the financial planning areas.

Setting personal goals

Your financial goals will reflect your values, and they should be well defined, realistic, and attainable.

Personal Financial Planning Areas

Career choice

People pick careers based on financial considerations like income and job security. Other factors, such as job satisfaction and contributing to society also affect one's choice of careers.

Basic money management

Basic money management consists of regularly evaluating one's net worth, constructing and following a monthly budget, and managing bank accounts and other financial assets.

Credit management

Credit is borrowing money. While there are many good reasons to use credit for certain purchases and necessary services, borrowers must be sure they can repay their loans in a timely manner. Using credit to live beyond one's means is a wrong use of credit that can lead to financial problems.

Tax planning

We all pay a variety of taxes, including federal and state income taxes, Social Security and Medicare taxes, property taxes, and sales taxes. Good planning will help you understand what tax records to keep, what obligations you will face, and how you can take advantage of opportunities to reduce taxes owed.

Major purchases

Transportation and housing are major components of everyone's monthly budget, and the selection and financing of these items must be considered carefully.

Insurance

To protect against financial ruin, people use life, health, disability, and property and liability insurance. Whether coverage is employer-provided or individually purchased, careful comparison of costs and benefits is essential.

Investment planning

Money you have can be preserved and increased through investing. The proper mix of investments depends on investment goals, investment time horizon, and maintaining the proper balance between risk and return for your situation.

Financial planning for tomorrow

Everyone, even young people, should develop retirement and estate plans.

Creating your financial plan

Your plan should help guide you in meeting your goals. It should help you to monitor expenditures, use money effectively, and increase wealth.

Name _____ Instructor _____

Section _____ Date _____

Business Vocabulary

credit
defined benefit plans
defined contribution plan
financial plan
installment loan

lifestyle
net worth
personal finance
revolving credit
standard of living

Application of Vocabulary

Select the term from the list above that best completes the following statements. Write that term in the space provided.

1. _____ is the study of the economic factors and personal decisions that affect a person's financial well-being.

2. Good money management helps people attain a higher _____ _____, which is ability to get and keep the necessities, comforts, and luxuries of life.

3. The way you live your daily life, called _____, is affected by and has consequences for personal financial decisions.

4. Your _____ is the difference between what you own (assets) and what you owe (liabilities).

5. _____ is buying something or receiving money through borrowing at a specified interest rate for a specified time.

6. Credit cards and other credit that allow the consumer to pay some or all of the outstanding balance each month, with interest applied to any remaining balance, is called _____.

7. When using a(n) _____, a consumer repays the loan in regular specified payments over a specified period of time.

8. Retirement plans that guarantee workers a certain retirement benefit are called _____.

9. In a(n) _____ employees (often with matching contributions from employers) set aside certain amounts the employee can invest for the future, and the eventual benefit depends on how well the investments have done over time.

10. Each of us should develop a _____ to use as a guide in helping us reach our desired goals.

Self Review

True or False

1. ___ The reward of sound money management is an improvement in an individual's standard of living.

2. ___ The bewildering number of choices available today makes personal financial planning and management more important than ever before.

3. ___ Young people don't need to start thinking about retirement planning.

4. ___ The first step in any financial plan is figuring out what you would like to buy.

5. ___ Personal financial decisions can affect our achievement of both monetary and nonmonetary goals.

6. ___ Unless you pay the full balance each month, using a credit card is really borrowing money.

7. ___ There are proper uses for credit, such as buying a house.

8. ___ Since you should always have a savings plan, it is important to learn to "live beneath your means."

9. ___ The investments appropriate for meeting long term goals are usually identical to the ones used for meeting short term goals.

10. ___ Investments offering higher return carry higher risk.

Name _____ Instructor _____

Section _____ Date _____

Multiple Choice

1. The first step in any successful financial plan is to:

    a. figure out where you stand now.
    b. develop a budget.
    c. get the right mix of insurance.
    d. get debt under control.

2. Basic money management includes:

    a. preparing financial statements.
    b. budgeting.
    c. managing checking and other bank accounts.
    d. all of the above.

3. If you have to repay a loan in specified monthly payments that will end after a given period of time, you are using:

    a. revolving credit.   c. a defined contribution plan.
    b. installment credit.   d. your net worth.

4. In a most defined contribution plans:

    a. you are guaranteed a defined retirement benefit.
    b. employers usually don't contribute to the plan.
    c. your benefit at retirement depends on how well your investments have done.
    d. you generally have no responsibility to understand how the funds have been invested.

5. The ability to get and keep the necessities and luxuries of life is called your:

    a. lifestyle.   c. net worth.
    b. standard of living.   d. all of the above.

6. We measure _____ by subtracting someone's liabilities (debts) from the value of their assets.

    a. lifestyle   c. net worth
    b. standard of living   d. budgets

7. Your personal financial goals should:

   a. reflect your values.
   b. be realistic and attainable.
   c. be very specific and well defined.
   d. all of the above.

8. If you are using credit to meet your basic living expenses:

   a. you are increasing your net worth.
   b. you are making proper use of credit.
   c. you are living within your means.
   d. you are living beyond your means and will eventually have to face the financial consequences.

9. The proper mix of investments depends on:

   a. your time horizon.   c. your tolerance for risk.
   b. your investment goals.   d. all of the above.

10. Financial statements individuals need to develop include:

   a. a budget.   c. a balance sheet that shows net worth.
   b. an income statement.   d. all of the above.

APPENDIX C

Developing a Business Plan

Summary: Key Concepts

The Basics of Business Planning

Business Plan

The written document that articulates a company's objectives, the methods by which these objectives will be achieved, the financing process, and the amount of revenue the company can expect to bring in.

Importance of a business plan

A carefully constructed business plan serves several key functions. It organizes the business, validates its central idea, shows up the strong points and flaws of the plan, and summarizes the business and its strategy to obtain funding from investors.

Who needs a business plan

All businesses, large or small, benefit from articulating a clear business plan. The plan serves as a guide in business decision making and a tool for achieving objectives.

Writing the Business Plan

Collecting information

A good business plan demonstrates understanding of the business, the industry, and the market, and must be based on and backed up with specific information.

Self-evaluation

A plan should reflect careful evaluation of the strengths and weaknesses of the business, and demonstrate that there are plans in place to address these issues.

The document

Between 10 and 50 pages long, depending on the complexity of the firm, it should be well organized and easy to use. Pages should be numbered, there should be a table of contents, the format must be attractive and professional, and it is helpful to include charts and/or graphs to illustrate.

Components of a Business Plan

Executive Summary	One or two page attractive summary of what the plan will detail. Quickly answers the who, what, why, when, where, and how questions about the business.
Introduction	Describes the company and its history, the management team, and the product in detail.
Marketing strategy	This part of the plan details the market's need for the product and ways the business will go about capturing the intended market. It should examine demographics, trends, and intended market penetration and sales revenue.
Financing the business	Explains the cost of the product, the operating expenses, the sales revenue and profit that can be expected. This section should include a cash flow analysis, an income statement, and a balance sheet that shows the owner's own investment. These financial projections and documents must be detailed, accurate, and defensible.
Resumes of principals	Each member of the management team should include a detailed history of employment, accomplishments, business affiliations, professional memberships, and other information that show the ability and passion needed for success.

Resources

Research	The text suggests several excellent books and Web sites that offer advice, tips, and sample plans.

Name _____ Instructor _____

Section _____ Date _____

Planning software	Programs exist for creating plans, but care must be taken that the software is appropriate for your business and industry.
Associations and organizations	Many government and professional organizations can provide assistance and information, so it is worthwhile to explore what they have to offer.
Resources for women and minorities	Some resources specialize in assisting women and minorities in business planning.

Business Vocabulary

business plan
demographics
executive summary
financing section
introduction

market penetration
marketing strategy
potential sales revenue
trends

Application of Vocabulary

Select the term from the list above that best completes the following statements. Write that term in the space provided.

1. A carefully constructed document that spells out the what a company is, where it wants to go, and how it intends to get there is called the _____.

2. A one or two page section that offers an attractive synopsis of the business plan is called a(n) _____.

3. The detailed description of the company, the management team, and the product should go in the _____ of the business plan.

4. A business plan must include a section on _____ that explains the market's need for the product, and exactly how the business will go about capturing its intended market.

5. The statistical study of the characteristics of market segments is called
   _____.

6. A business plan must take account of _____, those consumer tendencies or patterns that can be exploited to gain market share in an industry.

7. _____ measures the percentage of the total market who can be expected to or have already purchased the company's product.

8. The _____ measures what your total dollar sales would be if everyone who is a potential customer purchased your product.

9. The _____ of the business plan presents all the numbers on costs, operations, cash flow, sources of investment, etc., in detail.

Self Review

True or False

1. ___ Large businesses need business plans more than new smaller businesses do.

2. ___ The only major purpose of a business plan is to attract investors.

3. ___ The Introduction should be the first section of the business plan.

4. ___ You should write the Executive Summary of a business plan last.

5. ___ Numbers you use in a business plan should be detailed and accurate, and you should be prepared to provide backup documentation for them.

6. ___ Research on markets and competitors provides helpful information when writing a business plan.

7. ___ Marketing plans and financial forecasts should be prepared once the business plan is in place.

8. ___ Demographics would help you decide if there are enough potential customers in your target market to make the business work.

9. ___ A cash flow plan demonstrates that the business owner understands and is prepared to respond to both slow and high-volume periods of the business.

Name _____ Instructor _____

Section _____ Date _____

Multiple Choice

1. A written document that identifies the business, its goals, and its strategies is called the:

    a. business plan.   c. marketing strategy.
    b. financial plan.   d. cash flow statement.

2. Constructing a business plan is important because:

    a. it organizes the business and offers validation for the central idea of the business.
    b. it provides guidance in day-to-day business decisions.
    c. it helps potential investors get a clear picture of the business and its prospects.
    d. all of the above.

3. A business plan should be:

    a. captivating but not very detailed.
    b. detailed, accurate, defensible, and professionally presented.
    c. designed for internal use exclusively.
    d. designed to show to outsiders, rather than for internal use.

4. When developing the marketing strategy, paying attention to trends means:

    a. understanding the size and characteristics of market segments.
    b. understanding how cash flow fluctuations will affect the business.
    c. understanding consumer tendencies or patterns that businesses can exploit to gain market share.
    d. all of the above.

5. The financing section of a business plan should include:

    a. a cash flow analysis.
    b. an income statement and balance sheet.
    c. detailed financial plans for all the operations and marketing plans in other areas of the business plan.
    d. all of the above.

6. A financial plan should include detailed resumes of:

   a. the CEO only.
   b. the financial people.
   c, the marketing people.
   d. all key members of the management team.

7. Help writing business plans can be obtained from:

   a. books on the subject.
   b. Web sites that offer advice, tips, and sample plans.
   c. government and professional organizations like the SBA.
   d. all of the above.

8. The actual business plan document should be:

   a. neat, professional, and include page numbers and a table of contents.
   b. between 10 and 50 pages long.
   c. written for use by both managers and outsiders.
   d. all of the above.

SOLUTIONS

CHAPTER 1

Vocabulary

1. a. private property
    b. profit
    c. freedom of choice
    d. fair competition
2. a. natural resources
    b. human resources
    c. capital
    d. entrepreneurship
3. Gross Domestic Product (GDP)
4. productivity
5. invisible hand of competition
6. competition
7. Competitive differentiation
8. consumer orientation
9. private enterprise system
10. Branding
11. business
12. outsourcing
13. Technology
14. Internet
15. Vision
16. value
17. Strategic alliances
18. Quality
19. customer satisfaction
20. entrepreneurs
21. diversity
22. Not-for-profit organizations
23. Relationship management
24. transaction management
25. Creativity
26. Critical thinking

Analysis of Learning Goals

LG 1.1:   1. T, 2. F, 3. F, 4. F.
LG 1.2:   1. T, 2. T, 3. T, 4. T.
LG 1.3:   1. F, 2. T, 3. F, 4. T.
LG 1.4:   1. d, 2. a, 3. a, 4. d.
LG 1.5:
1. Value is the balance between the positive traits of a good or service and its price as perceived by the consumer.
2. Quality is the degree of excellence or superiority of a firm's goods and services. It includes such things as durability and performance reliability, and most importantly, the ability of a good or service to meet and exceed customer expectations.

LG 1.6:   1. F, 2. T, 3. T, 4. F, 5. T.
LG 1.7:   1. F, 2. F, 3. T, 4. F, 5. T.

2. Critical thinking skills: the ability to analyze and assess information in order to pinpoint problems or opportunities. It involves the ability to look beneath the surface and determine the authenticity, accuracy, and worth of information, knowledge and arguments.
3. Creativity: the capacity to develop novel solutions and to see new and better ways of doing things.
4. Ability to steer change: the skill of recognizing employee strengths and motivating people to adapt to the changes brought about by technology, marketplace demands, and global competitiveness.

LG 1.9:   1. b, 2. c, 3. d.

Self Review

True or False: 1. T, 2. F, 3. T, 4. F, 5. T, 6. T, 7. F, 8. T, 9. F, 10. T, 11. T, 12. F, 13. T, 14. T, 15. F.

Multiple Choice: 1. c, 2. d, 3. a, 4. d, 5. c, 6. b, 7. d, 8. b. 9. c, 10. e, 11. a, 12. c, 13. a.

Application Exercises

1. The colonial society
   a. Mainly agricultural.
   b. The United States was importing manufactured products from England.
2. The Industrial Revolution.
   a. Rapid construction and expansion of the railroad system.
   b. Large scale production with rail transportation as means for wide distribution.
3. The age of industrial entrepreneurs.
   a. Advances in technology and increased demand for manufactured goods.
   b. Individuals began to act as risk takers, starting their own businesses.
4. The production era.
   a. Emphasis on producing more goods faster.
   b. Focus on internal processes such as assembly-line production.
5. The marketing era.
   a. The competitive business environment brought the need for identifying and satisfying target markets.
   b. Growth in advertising, market and consumer research.
6. The relationship era.
   a. Focus shifts to establishing long term relationships with customers, suppliers, and to building partnerships and strategic alliances to further competitive differentiation.
   b. Reliance on information technology to develop long-term relationships and sustain customer satisfaction.

Short Essay Questions

1. The world's nations and their economies are developing increasing interdependence, so the emphasis has changed from domestic markets to the global market. Many businesses, large and small, produce and/or market their output outside the U.S. The U.S. is also a popular place for foreign firms to invest and market their goods. One reason this trend is so important is that foreign economies have rising standards of living which create increasing customer demand for the latest goods and services.

2. The four basic rights awarded to citizens living in a private enterprise system are private property, profit, freedom of choice and fair competition. The right to private property is the right to own and use what one has earned, and is a primary motivation for hard work in private enterprise economies. The right to profit means that an entrepreneur can expect to keep after tax profits earned by taking a business risk. This is both the incentive and reward to taking the risk in the first place. The right to freedom of choice means people in a free enterprise system can select careers, change jobs, and even open their own businesses. It means that they will generally have a choice between competing producers when they want to make a purchase. Likewise, they will have many choices of investment opportunities, including owning all or part of a business. Finally, people living in a private enterprise system can expect that competition should be fair. The U.S. government, for example, has passed laws that outlaw price discrimination, fraud in financial markets, and deceptive practices in advertising and packaging. The intent of such laws is to eliminate "cutthroat" competition that might harm consumers, the competitive environment, the natural environment, etc.

3. In the 1990s business moved from transaction management to relationship management. Relationship management makes use of information technology, partnerships, and strategic alliances to build and sustain long-term relationships with customers, suppliers, and other outside groups. Relationship management also depends increasingly on a talented, diverse workforce to serve and understand the multicultural global market. Contributions and creativity of workers is crucial, so new employee-employer partnerships have arisen to develop and retain better relationships with customers and other outside groups. Finally, management must engage in ethical business practices and consider social responsibilities to the wider society to assure the firm's long-term success.

Notes:

CHAPTER 2

Vocabulary

1. family leave
2. Pollution
3. Recycling
4. code of conduct
5. Social audit
6. Consumerism
7. Equal Employment Opportunity Commission (EEOC)
8. conflict of interest
9. corporate philanthropy
10. social responsibility
11. Business ethics
12. Whistle-blowing
13. Sexual harassment
14. Sarbanes-Oxley Act
15. Integrity
16. Sexism
17. Genetic engineering
18. boycott
19. product liability
20. green marketing.

Analysis of Learning Goals

LG 2.1: 1. T, 2. T, 3. F, 4. T, 5. T.
LG 2.2: 1. d, 2. d, 3. a, 4, c.
LG 2.3: 1. preconventional 2. conventional 3. postconventional
LG 2.4: 1. a, 2. b, 3. d, 4. b.
LG 2.5: 1. T, 2. F, 3. T, 4. T.
LG 2.6: 1. F, 2. F, 3. T, 4. T.
LG 2.7: 1. F, 2. T, 3. T, 4. T, 5. T, 6. F, 7. F, 8. T, 9. F.
LG 2.8: 1. F, 2. T, 3. T, 4. T.

Self Review

True or False: 1. F, 2. T, 3. F, 4. F, 5. F, 6. T, 7. T, 8. T, 9. T, 10. T, 11. T, 12. F, 13. F. 14. F, 15. T.

Multiple Choice: 1. e, 2. c, 3. a, 4. d, 5. c, 6. b, 7. d, 8. e, 9. c, 10 c.

Application Exercises

1. It is probably unethical for these sales people to share such information since they each have a responsibility to protect the interests of their own employer.

2. Under the Americans with Disabilities Act (1991) this employer is obligated to make the appropriate accommodations so that the qualified candidate can work despite her disability.

3. This is an example of the continuing inequity in pay between the genders. This company needs to review it's salary schedules to eliminate pay differentials for jobs where people have like skills and responsibilities.

4. Patty may have to start smoking outside, even though this is her business. As the employer, if she exposes employees to second-hand smoke she may later be held liable for any smoke-related illness an employee develops.

Short Essay Questions

1. Business managers have a whole range of responsibilities. They include:

    a. Ethical treatment of employees. Such issues as equal opportunity, fair pay, a safe work environment, attention to the multicultural nature of the work force, prevention of sexual harassment, and developing employee skills are included.
    b. Protection of the environment. Business managers today need to be concerned with pollution control and abatement, conservation of scarce resources, ecological issues such as the rights of other species, and waste disposal issues such as proper disposal of toxic wastes and recycling .
    c. Ethical treatment of consumers. Business managers have an obligation to make certain that products are safe, that they have been truthful in advertising, labeling, etc., so that consumers can make informed choices; that they do not act in restraint of trade, so that consumers will have a choice in the marketplace, and to be open to consumer complaints and suggestions (i.e., respect the consumer's right to be heard.)
    d   Responsibilities to the general public. In addition to environmental protection, today's business manager should be aware of public health issues, and other needs of society that business may be in a unique position to meet.

2. Firms can help build ethical awareness by articulating a code of conduct. People within the organization must then learn how to apply critical thinking skills to reasoning out ethical issues. The organization's structure and processes must make it possible for workers to translate their ethical conclusions into concrete actions. Finally, ethical business practices depend on top management articulating and communicating the ethical standards expected of those within the organization. Managers must be personally committed to these ethical standards, and prepared to take action to enforce them. Above all, managers must themselves behave ethically. Employees are quick to notice when ethical standards get no more than "lip service" from managers.

CHAPTER 3

Vocabulary

1. economics	20. supply
2. macroeconomics	21. balanced budget
3. Microeconomics	22. national debt
4. Frictional unemployment	23. recession
5. Cost-push	24. communism
6. Consumer Price Index (CPI)	25. socialism
7. budget deficit	26. mixed market economy
8. inflation	27. oligopoly
9. Seasonal unemployment	28. monopoly
10. Monetary policy	29. monopolistic competition
11. supply curve	30. pure competition
12. demand curve	31. private enterprise system
13. cyclical unemployment	32. privatization
14. equilibrium price	33. Deregulation
15. fiscal policy	34. deflation
16. unemployment rate	35. producer price index (PPI)
17. demand-pull	36. gross domestic product (GDP)
18. Structural unemployment	37. productivity
19. demand	

Analysis of Learning Goals

LG 3.1:   1. T, 2. T, 3. F, 4. F.

LG 3.2:   1.   The factors that collectively determine demand are (see Table 3.1):

   a.   customer preference: if customers have increased or decreased preference for the product or service offered.

   b.   number of buyers: if the number of buyers for a product or service increases or decreases.

   c.   buyers' incomes: if buyer's incomes increase or decrease.

   d.   prices of substitute goods: where substitute goods have an increase or decrease in price, the demand for the good will be affected.

   e.   prices of complimentary goods: where complimentary goods increase or decrease in price, the demand for the original good or service will be affected.

   f.   future expectations: when they become more optimistic, demand increases, while as they become more pessimistic, demand will decline.

2. The factors that collectively determine supply are (see Table 3.2):

    a. costs of inputs: changes in the costs of factors of production, such as natural resources, capital, human resources and entrepreneurship, affect the amount of supply offered.

    b. costs of technologies: changes in the costs of new technologies can affect the supply of products or services using that technology.

    c. taxes: an increase or decrease in taxes levied will impact suppliers' willingness to supply the product or service.

    d. number of suppliers: where more suppliers enter the market the supply curve shifts right. The opposite occurs if the number of suppliers decreases.

LG 3.3: 1. F, 2. T, 3. T, 4. F, 5. T.

LG 3.4:
1. pure competition
2. monopolistic competition
3. monopoly
4. oligopoly

LG 3.5: 1. a, 2. b, 3. d, 4. c.

LG 3.6: 1. F, 2, T, 3. F, 4. T, 5. T. 6. T.

LG 3.7:
1. Monetary policy refers to government policies and actions concerning regulation of the money supply.
2. Fiscal policy refers to governmental actions concerning tax revenues and expenditures of public funds.
3. Examples of how monetary and fiscal policy are used to combat inflation and unemployment include:

    a. An expansionary monetary policy puts more money into circulation making business borrowing easier and often lowers interest rates. As businesses increase activity, more jobs may be created, thus decreasing the unemployment rate.

    b. A restrictive monetary policy reduces the money in circulation and could help reduce inflation.

    c. A fiscal policy that increases taxes will pull money out of circulation and could help reduce inflation.

    d. A fiscal policy that increases government purchases may create jobs, thus reducing unemployment.

LG 3.8: The five interrelated areas are:
1. The threat of international terrorism.
2. A global information economy that enable businesses to enhance the effectiveness of their use, management, and control of information. These technologies will necessitate a more highly trained work force.
3. The world's population is aging, and both business and governments must be prepared to meet the needs of these older people.

4. A global economy puts even greater competitive pressure on providing top quality products and outstanding customer service.

5. The more diverse and technologically advanced global market of the future will mean that workers will need greater levels of skill and education if their economies are to compete successfully.

Self Review

True or False: 1. T, 2. F, 3. T, 4. T, 5. T, 6. T, 7. F, 8. T, 9. T, 10. F, 11. T 12. T, 13. T, 14. F, 15. F. 16. T, 17. F, 18. T, 19. F, 20. T.

Multiple Choice: 1. d, 2. c, 3. a, 4. b, 5. c, 6. c, 7. d, 8. a, 9. e, 10. d, 11. c.

Application Exercises

1. Ron is experiencing structural unemployment.

2. Ron might try enrolling in an educational program to acquire new skills, or taking a lower paying job that offers him the opportunity to develop new skills.

Short Essay Questions

1. Market economies experience periods of growth, with expanded job opportunities, improved wages, and a rising standard of living. But no economy goes straight up, and differences in the business cycle affect business decisions and consumer buying patterns. In periods of economic prosperity, unemployment remains low, strong consumer confidence leads to strong sales of consumer products and services, while businesses expand to take advantage of marketplace opportunities. Economic downturns called recessions are cyclical economic contractions that last six months or longer. During such downturns consumers frequently postpone major purchases and shift buying patterns to basics. Businesses also slow expansion and may even layoff workers and/or reduce inventories. An extended downturn causes a depression. During the last depression in America in the 1930s unemployment hit 25%. But eventually economies reach the recovery stage, and consumer spending picks up steam, and business activity accelerates in response.
While the business cycle is an enduring feature of market economies, most economists believe that society is capable of preventing future depressions through effective economic policies. That is, good economic management hopefully reduces the intensity of any downturn, and leads instead to prolonged periods of growth.

2. Communism is an economic system in which the government owns and operates all the means of production. Government determines production objectives, prices, and resource allocation.

    Socialism is an economic system in which the government owns and operates key industries that are essential to the public welfare. Private enterprise is permitted to run other businesses.

    In Capitalism, all the means of production are privately owned, and all decisions on what to produce, how to produce it, and how it should be priced are determined by the market.

    Today most economies operate as mixed market economies. A mixed market economy is a combination of government and private ownership, planning, and resource allocation. The particular blend used by mixed market economies differs from country to country.

CHAPTER 4

Vocabulary

1. Exporting
2. importing
3. Balance of trade
4. Balance of payments
5. devaluation
6. exchange rate
7. absolute advantage
8. comparative advantage
9. floating exchange rates
10. Revenue tariffs
11. quota
12. embargo
13. currency control
14. franchise
15. dumping
16. North American Free Trade Agreement (NAFTA)
17. International Monetary Fund (IMF)
18. foreign licensing agreement
19. countertrade
20. Subcontracting
21. multinational company
22. protective tariffs
23. General Agreement on Trade and Tariffs (GATT)
24. World Bank
25. global business strategy
26. multidomestic business strategy
27. infrastructure
28. joint venture
29. maquiladora
30. European Union (EU)
31. World Trade Organization (WTO)

Analysis of Learning Goals

LG 4.1:   1. F, 2. T, 3. F, 4. T.

LG 4.2:   1. b, 2. a, 3. e.

LG 4.3:   1. F, 2. T, 3. F, 4. T, 5. F, 6. F.

LG 4.4:   1.   Social and cultural barriers.
Customs, language, education, social values, religious attitudes and consumer habits vary between countries. Difficulties in translation, or variances on when people eat or how they like their products packaged might be examples.

2. Economic Differences. Differences in standards of living, currency strength or weakness, birth rates, and weak infrastructures (transportation systems, water, utilities, etc.). An example might be market opportunities offered in developing nations with higher birth rates.

3. Political and legal obstacles. Countries engaged in the global marketplace must adhere to home country laws, host country laws, and various international regulations. For example, when American firms try to do

business in a country where "grease payments" (bribes) are common, they are prohibited from paying the expected bribes by American law.

4. Tariffs and trade restrictions. Tariffs are taxes on imports, levied to generate revenues for governments or to protect domestic industries. Trade restrictions include import quotas, currency exchange controls, and embargoes. An example might be an American shoe maker who finds it difficult to sell shoes in a developing country when protective tariffs designed to protect that country's shoe industry increase the price of the American product in that market.

LG 4.5:   1. T, 2. T, 3. T, 4. T, 5. F.
LG 4.6:   1. T, 2. T, 3. T, 4. T, 5. F.
LG 4.7:   1. T, 2. T, 3. F, 4. F.

Self Review

True or False: 1. T, 2. F, 3. T, 4. T, 5. T, 6. F, 7. F, 8. T, 9. T, 10. F, 11. T,
12. T, 13. T, 14. F, 15. F, 16. F, 17. F, 18. F, 19. F, 20. T.

Multiple Choice: 1. c, 2. d, 3. a, 4. c, 5. c, 6. a, 7. b, 8. b, 9. d, 10. d, 11. b.
12. c, 13. c.

Application Exercise

The director of the international division would include the definition of both a joint venture and foreign licensing. A joint venture involves sharing operational costs, risks, management, and profits with a foreign partner. Foreign licensing involves supplying such things as plant equipment, production assistance, or permission to use a brand or patent in exchange for a percentage of the profits. Using foreign licensing can reduce tariff barriers and other trade restrictions.

Short Essay Questions

1.   A trade deficit occurs when a country has an unfavorable balance of trade, that is, it imports more than it exports. If the U.S. currency is devalued against that of major trading partners with whom we have a deficit, their goods are more expensive for Americans to buy, and our goods are cheaper for their citizens to buy. This makes it likely that we will buy less of their goods and they will buy more of ours. Countertrade is another means by which the U.S. might open more foreign markets to our goods. U.S. innovation and skill in technology and services are important sources of additional exports. Finally, doing more to reduce trade restrictions and to make foreign markets as open to imports as the U.S. is to goods from other countries will help correct this situation.

2.   A comparative advantage occurs when a nation can produce a good more efficiently than it can other goods, and exports what it does best. If each nation were to follow this, all goods in the global market would be produced by the most efficient producers, reducing costs and improving the standard of living worldwide. While this works well in theory, many nations want to remain self-sufficient in certain commodities (e.g. food), and so continue to produce goods even when cheaper ones are available in the global market.

Notes:

Vocabulary

1. law
2. common law
3. statutory law
4. appellate court
5. contract
6. judiciary
7. Sales law
8. Taxes
9. breach of contract
10. damages
11. bankruptcy
12. copyright
13. patent
14. international law
15. tort
16. Business law
17. trial court
18. product liability
19. trademarks
20. negotiable instruments
21. agency

Self Review

True or False: 1. F, 2. F, 3. T, 4. T, 5. T, 6. F, 7. T, 8. T, 9. T, 10. T, 11. T, 12. T, 13. F, 14. F, 15. F, 16. T, 17. F, 18. F.

Multiple Choice: 1. a, 2. b, 3. b, 4. d, 5. b, 6. a, 7. c, 8. a, 9. e, 10. b, 11. c, 12. a, 13. d, 14. b, 15. d, 16. a, 17. b, 18. a, 19. c, 20. e.

Notes:

CHAPTER 5

Vocabulary

1. acquisition
2. franchise
3. franchisee
4. Franchisors
5. limited liability company (LLC)
6. domestic corporation
7. corporate charter
8. conglomerate merger
9. home-based business
10. Small Business Administration (SBA)
11. common stockholders
12. horizontal merger
13. Small business
14. corporation
15. sole proprietorship
16. cooperative
17. preferred stockholders
18. alien corporation
19. Public ownership
20. partnership
21. closely held corporation
22. board of directors
23. outside directors
24. S corporations
25. vertical merger
26. inside director
27. merger
28. set aside programs
29. business incubator
30. Small Business Investment Company (SBIC)
31. business plan
32. foreign corporation
33. joint venture

Analysis of Learning Goals

LG 5.1: 1. d, 2. d, 3. e, 4. c.

LG 5.2: 1. T, 2. T, 3. F, 4. T, 5. T, 6. F, 7. T.

LG 5.3:
1. disadvantage
2. advantage
3. advantage
4. disadvantage
5. disadvantage
6. advantage
7. advantage

LG 5.4:
1. Providing financial assistance: The SBA, guarantees some small business loans, makes some direct loans to businesses unable to find private financing, licenses SBIC's who make small business loans, and sponsors a website to bring entrepreneurs and investors together.
2. Help with government procurements, including online opportunities to find governement business as well as guidance on how to do business with the government, and set-aside programs.
3. Providing management training and consulting services: the SBA has many programs offering free or low cost consulting services to small business.

LG 5.5:	1. T, 2. F, 3. T, 4. T, 5. F, 6. T, 7. F.
LG 5.6:	1. b, 2. c, 3. c, 4. T, 5. T, 6. F, 7. T, 8. F.
LG 5.7:	1. T, 2. F, 3. T, 4. T.
LG 5.8:	1. d, 2. c, 3. a, 4. c, 5. b.
LG 5.9:	1. c, 2. b, 3. b, 4. b.

Self Review

True or False: 1. F, 2. T, 3. F, 4. T, 5. F, 6. T, 7. T, 8. T, 9. T, 10. F, 11. T, 12. T, 13. T, 14. T, 15. T, 16. F, 17. T, 18. T, 19. T, 20. F, 21. T.

Multiple Choice: 1. b, 2. a, 3. c, 4. c, 5. b, 6. c, 7. e, 8. c, 9. d, 10. b, 11. c, 12. a, 13. b, 14. c, 15. d.

Application Exercises

Application Exercise I:

1. People in this situation combine for mutual benefits of long-term growth. The assumption is that profits will increase and thus a higher tax burden is created. The S corporation form of ownership will lessen the tax burden while giving the owners all the advantages and protections of the corporate structure.
2. A general partnership is not recommended because of the unlimited liability of the owners.
3. A potential problem is the division of stock. If each contributes equally, then each would own one third. The problem is in defining "equally." The skills and dollar contributions of each would have to be evaluated and a total dollar value assigned. A second potential difficulty might be selecting who will be designated president, vice-president, etc.
4. The advantages for each include the combination of skills and resources with a potential for greater growth than each would enjoy separately. However, both Mr. Fox and Mr. Keller will be giving up the independence and flexibility of the sole proprietorship. Mrs. Reyes will gain the independence of working for her own company, but initially she may have to give up the benefits and steady salary of working for a larger firm.

Application Exercise II:

1. Because this is a general partnership, Al, like Carla, is responsible for all the debts of the firm.

2.   As a general partner, Carla is also responsible for the debts. However, the real
      problem is finding Carla and hoping she still has the money. If she cannot be
      found, or if she no longer has the money, Al will be fully responsible for all the
      debts of the firm.

3.   If Al sincerely wants to go into business with his winnings, the first thing he
      should probably do is enroll in this course! He would learn about the legal
      forms of business ownership, and perhaps avoid making an unprofitable
      investment.

Short Essay Questions

1.   Small business brings greater competition to the U. S. economy. It also creates new
      jobs, is a source of innovation, and fills isolated market niches. Small businesses
      often operate at lower costs than larger businesses because of lower overhead and
      staffing costs. Lower overhead is often the benefit of opening a business from the
      home. Lower staffing costs can occur when entrepreneurs and their families work
      without insisting on being paid for every hour contributed. Small business is a major
      contributor to the success of the U.S. free enterprise system. Still, small business
      faces many difficulties which must be overcome. First, it is often difficult to raise
      adequate capital for a small business enterprise. Also, many small businesses suffer
      from lack of management skill. And government paperwork and red tape are a
      particular burden to small businesses with their small staffs.

2.   Franchising is a method of expanding a business by allowing small business owners
      to purchase the right to market a product or service. The franchise is created by a
      contract between the franchisor (a company with a product or service it will allow
      others to market) and the franchisee (a small business person who purchases the right
      to market the franchisor's product or service). This contract establishes the methods
      to be used by the franchisee, and often also includes the help that can be expected
      from the franchisor. Franchises offer the benefits of a proven business model, a
      product or service with a track record, name recognition, and help from franchisors
      including training and help in finding financing and doing promotion. Franchises,
      however, require the franchisee to pay royalties and other fees, and to give up total
      independence in order to comply with the methods required by the franchisor.
      Franchisees may also find that their business unit suffers when other franchisees
      perform poorly. Overall, while franchising is a more costly way to enter a new
      business, it often brings greater likelihood of business success.

3.   Sole Proprietorship: a business owned and operated by one person. Advantages
      include flexibility, retention of all after tax profits, and ease of formation and

dissolution. Disadvantages include unlimited financial liability, lack of skill and financing, and lack of continuity.

Partnership: a business owned by two or more people who each have unlimited financial liability. Joint ventures are partnerships that are formed for a specific business purpose and then disbanded. The advantages of partnerships include ease of formation, greater financial ability, and complimentary management skills. Disadvantages include unlimited financial liability, potential conflict with partners, difficulty of dissolution, and lack of continuity.

Corporation: a form of business ownership, created by statute, in which the firm acts and is liable separately from its owners. The advantages include limited financial liability, expanded financial ability, and in large corporations, the benefits of professional management and economies of scale. The disadvantages include cost and difficulty in formation and dissolution, legal restrictions, and double taxation. The last disadvantage can be avoided by small corporations, who meet the requirements to be treated as S corporations, and are thereby taxed as partnerships.

4. Mergers: the combination of two or more firms into one. Horizontal mergers involve combinations of firms who are already in the same industry. Vertical mergers combine firms who formally did business with one another (i.e., were part of the same channel of distribution). Conglomerate mergers occur when two unrelated firms combine, usually in an effort to achieve diversification. Acquisitions: when all (or a majority) of a firm's stock (or assets) is purchased by another firm. Both mergers and acquisitions can occur across national boundaries to aid companies as they go global.

CHAPTER 6

Vocabulary

1. entrepreneurs
2. intrapreneur
3. Venture capitalists
4. Seed capital
5. angel investors
6. debt financing
7. equity financing
8. Intrapreneurship
9. vision
10. need to achieve
11. change agent
12. internal locus of control
13. classic entrepreneur
14. Gazelles

Analysis of Learning Goals

LG 6.1:   1. F, 2. F, 3. T, 4. F, 5. T.

LG 6.2:   1. classic entrepreneur: a person who identifies a business opportunity and allocates available resources to tap that market. This is what we usually mean when we speak of entrepreneurs.

2. intrapreneur: an entrepreneurially oriented person who develops innovations within the context of a large organization. More and more firms seek such people, and develop programs to encourage them to stay with the company rather than leaving to start their own businesses.

3. change agents: a manager who tries to revitalize an established firm to keep it competitive. Also known as turnaround entrepreneurs, since they often take over troubled firms and turn them around.

LG 6.3:   1. F, 2. T, 3. T, 4. T, 5. F, 6. T.

LG 6.4:   1. T, 2. F, 3. T, 4. F, 5. T.

LG 6.5:   1. d, 2. a, 3. d.

LG 6.6:   1. Vision: the overall idea for a business that gives direction and guidance to entrepreneurs as the open and grow a business venture. Vision may include many things, but especially what problem the venture will solve for its customers, or what role the venture will play in the marketplace.

2. High energy level: starting and building a company requires a lot of hard work and very long hours.

3. Need to achieve: Entrepreneurs have strong competitive drive, enjoy the challenge of reaching difficult goals, and are dedicated to personal success.

4. Self-confidence and optimism: entrepreneurs believe in their ability to succeed, and they instill their optimism in others.

5. Tolerance for failure: entrepreneurs view setbacks and failures as learning experiences. They are not easily discouraged or disappointed.

6. Creativity: entrepreneurs must have the ability to conceive new ideas and devise innovative ways to overcome business problems.

7. Tolerance for ambiguity: Entrepreneurs must expect and become expert in dealing with uncertainties and unexpected events.

8. Internal locus of control: Entrepreneurs tend to believe that they control their own fates, and like to take personal responsibility for the success or failure or their actions.

LG 6.7: 1. F, 2. T, 3. T, 4. T, 5. T, 6. F.

LG 6.8:
1. Firms must identify and disseminate company-wide goals relating to new ventures, and encourage managers to support spin-offs that advance those goals.

2. Firms must protect and reward employees who identify new business ideas, developing management attitudes that aid rather than hinder the intrapreneurial spirit.

3. Firms need to develop methods to quickly move proposals for new ventures through the approval process. Otherwise, people with innovative ideas and enthusiasm will leave the company and start their own ventures.

Self Review

True or False: 1. T, 2. T, 3. T, 4. F, 5. T, 6. T, 7. F, 8. F, 9. T, 10. F, 11. F, 12. F, 13. T, 14. F, 15. T.

Multiple Choice: 1. b, 2. c, 3. e, 4. b, 5. b, 6. d, 7. b, 8. e, 9. d, 10. a.

Application Exercise

1. Bill should be sure that the tasks of operating a restaurant are things he will like doing and be good at doing. He needs to understand the time demands of this kind of business, which will be quite different from those in the insurance industry (working weekends and evenings for example). He should also honestly evaluate himself with respect to the eight characteristics of successful entrepreneurs identified in Figure 6.9. He must have the right temperament, not just the desire, to be a successful entrepreneur.

2. Bill might read magazines and books on entrepreneurship and the restaurant industry to gain insight. He should search the Internet for information about his selected industry, and other resources for restaurant owners. And he should become aware of and contact trade associations for new entrepreneurs as well as those in his new industry. Visiting sites like those shown in Table 6.1 would be a big help.

3. If he hasn't already done so, Bill needs to get experience in the restaurant industry. There is no teacher like experience to help one decide if a particular field is really suitable.

Short Essay Questions

1. This statement is true, not only of the U.S. but worldwide. More people from diverse backgrounds are beginning their own businesses than ever before. Likewise, there is increased interest from investors in new ventures. The information technology revolution has made it possible for start-ups to have a presence on the Internet, to handle complex and detailed record keeping more easily, and to communicate with suppliers and customers around the world. The growth of the world economy, with more older people, more people attaining a higher standard of living, and more people with less time all have combined to create many new opportunities for entrepreneurs. And there is no shortage of people who want to take advantage of these opportunities: 30% of Americans report thinking about starting their own businesses.

2. The most common reasons people give are:

    a. to be their own boss or have greater control over their own lives.
    b. to make lots of money.
    c. to create something new.
    d. to prove to themselves that they can do it.
    e. to find greater rewards from self-employment that they did in their former jobs.

3. Entrepreneurship provides opportunity and innovation in the U.S. economy. New ventures are the most important creators of new job opportunities in the U.S., and also are important source of opportunity for minorities and women. Entrepreneurship also creates new products, finds new solutions to problems in the home or workplace, builds entirely new industries, and revitalizes old businesses and industries. Overall, entrepreneurship has enriched our economy, and is a major reason to be optimistic about the future of the U.S. economy.

CHAPTER 7

Vocabulary

1. Internet
2. World Wide Web (WWW)
3. Web site
4. domain name
5. Internet Service Provider (ISP)
6. DSL
7. server
8. client
9. Instant messaging
10. Online communities
11. newsgroup
12. portal
13. E-commerce
14. Business-to-business commerce (B2B)
15. electronic exchanges
16. extranet
17. private exchange
18. Business-to-consumer commerce (B2C)
19. electronic storefronts
20. electronic shopping cart
21. Encryption
22. electronic cash
23. Electronic wallets
24. smart cards
25. Electronic signatures
26. Children's Online Privacy Protection Act (COPPA)
27. firewall
28. Electronic data interchange (EDI)
29. web host
30. Click-through rates
31. conversion rate

Analysis of Learning Goals

LG 7.1: 1. c, 2. b, 3. d, 4. a.

LG 7.2: 1. F, 2. T, 3. F, 4. T, 5. T.

LG 7.3:

1. Communication: people can communicate over the Internet through e-mail, instant messaging, chat rooms, Internet telephony and videoconferencing. Example: staying in touch with family overseas.

2. Information Services: people can access information from anywhere in the world using search engines and portals, online publications and newsgroups. Example: doing research for a school term paper.

3. Net Entertainment: online gaming, radio and television programming, electronic publishing, music and movies are increasing available over the Net. Example: downloading and listening to a sample of a new CD over the Net.

4. E-commerce: doing business over the Net. Includes both business-to-consumer transactions and business-to-business information sharing and transactions. Example: buying a book or CD from an electronic storefront.

LG 7.4:   1. F, 2. T, 3. T, 4. F, 5. T, 6. d, 7, c, 8. b.
LG 7.5:   1. T, 2. F, 3. F, 4. T, 5. F.
LG 7.6:   1. T, 2. T, 3. F, 4. F, 5. F, 6. F.
LG 7.7:   1. Internet services and Web sites make it possible for small businesses to find and service customers all over the world, to keep an eye on the competition, and to make their own operations more efficient and competitive. Small business can serve as vendors or purchase inventory anywhere, doing business globally by means of the Net. In addition, many new businesses formed to bring new technologies to market.

2. Large companies can gain all of the above benefits. In addition, with their larger and more geographically dispersed workforce and operations, the Net offers opportunities for coordination and teamwork among workers all over the world and in different time zones.

Self Review

True or False: 1. T, 2. F, 3. T, 4. F, 5. F, 6. T, 7. T, 8. F, 9. T, 10. T, 11. T, 12. F, 13. T, 14. F, 15. F, 16. F, 17. T.

Multiple Choice: 1. d, 2. a, 3. c, 4. d, 5. b, 6. b, 7. b, 8. b, 9. d, 10. b, 11. d.

Application Exercises

Five concrete suggestions for Malcolm's Web site might include:

1. Consider using an outside firm to create and maintain the Web site. Their expertise ensures a more professional site, and as a busy entrepreneur that is one less thing he'll have to spend time doing.

2. Develop content that will bring people back to the site again and again, perhaps by providing links to other sites (good surf spots, surfing contests, etc.).

3. Make sure that contact information like address, phone number, fax number, etc., are clear and easy to find. Also promote the site by putting the Web address on business cards, brochure, stationary, etc.

4. Take advantage of the Internet's potential for interactivity: don't just put a copy of your brochure on the Web, allow for chat rooms or other interactive elements.

5. Update the site with fresh content to keep people coming back.

Short Essay Questions

1. This statement is plainly false. The Internet has provided so many new ways for people to communicate, exchange information, enjoy entertainment, and do business it is likely to grow rather than fade away. The ability to overcome distances and time differences, to access information anywhere in the world, to do research, and to conduct business transactions efficiently are all enhanced by the Internet. Other advantages of using the Net include people being able to do all this from anywhere they have an Internet connection: businesses and individuals can communicate and/or do work from a park or beach as well as from an office using these new technologies. People will not want to part with the freedom the Net has produced!

2. B2B is electronic commerce between businesses. It allows businesses to conduct research, transactions, and collaborative activities on the Net. This has led to incredible improvements in efficiency and productivity of businesses. The cost savings alone have made B2B a necessary tool in today's competitive marketplace. In addition, B2B allows business people in different locations and time zones to communicate and collaborate, again producing huge advantages necessary to today's competitive global environment. Today, many large businesses refuse to use suppliers unless they can integrate B2B into their operations. This growth is only expected to continue.

3. The key questions a business should answer as it develops a Web site are found in Figure 7.8.

CHAPTER 8

Vocabulary

1. Management
2. organizing
3. Directing
4. controlling
5. Vision
6. planning
7. mission statement
8. SWOT analysis
9. Objectives
10. Strategic planning
11. tactical planning
12. Operational plans
13. Leadership
14. contingency planning
15. Departmentalization
16. competitive differentiation
17. Delegation
18. decision making
19. Technical skills
20. human skills
21. Conceptual skills
22. programmed decision
23. nonprogrammed decision
24. autocratic leadership
25. democratic leadership
26. free-rein leadership
27. Empowerment
28. span of management
29. organization
30. line manager
31. staff managers
32. centralization
33. decentralization
34. organization chart
35. Top management
36. Supervisory management
37. Middle management
38. chain of command
39. line organization
40. line-and-staff organization
41. committee organization
42. matrix organization
43. corporate culture

Analysis of Learning Goals

LG 8.1: 1. T, 2. F, 3. T, 4. F.

The skills managers must have are:
5. Technical skills: the manager's ability to understand and use techniques, knowledge, and tools of a specific discipline or department.
6. Human skills: the people skills such as communicating motivating, and leading effectively.
7. Conceptual skills: the ability of a manager to see the organization as a unified whole and to understand how each part of the organization fits in and interacts with the other parts. Important components include the skills needed to acquire, analyze and interpret information.

LG 8.2: 1. T, 2. F, 3. F, 4. T, 5. F.
LG 8.3: 1. d, 2. a, 3. b, 4. c, 5. a.

LG 8.4:

1. Define the organization's mission: translating the organization's vision into an enduring statement of company purpose, highlighting the scope of operations, the markets to be served, and how it will set itself apart from competition.

2. Assess the organization's competitive position: SWOT analysis and forecasting are two important techniques.

3. Set objectives for the organization: concrete statements of specific objectives for profit, customer relations, social responsibility, etc.

4. Creating strategies for competitive differentiation: human resource management, product innovation, technology and financial management are sources, as is relationship management.

5. Turning strategy into action: action plans for achieving objectives should specify methods and deploy the resources necessary to implement the intended plans.

6. Monitoring and adapting strategic plans: establishing methods of securing feedback about actual performance, and ongoing use of SWOT and forecasting.

LG 8.5:

1. Programmed decisions involve simple, frequently occurring problems or opportunities for which solutions have been previously determined. When a decision is the result of an established policy, procedure, or rule we have a programmed decision. Nonprogrammed decisions involve more complex, relatively unique situations for which no procedure exists, such as a new problem with important consequences for the organization.

2. The five steps in the decision making process are:
   a. Recognition of a problem or opportunity.
   b. Development of alternative courses of action.
   c. Evaluation of alternatives.
   d. Selection and implementation of chosen alternative.
   e. Follow-up to determine effectiveness of decision.

LG 8.6:   1. T, 2. F, 3. F, 4. T, 5. F.

LG 8.7:   1. T, 2. F, 3. T, 4. T, 5. F.

LG 8.8:

1. Departmentalization is the process of dividing work activities into units within the organization. Workers can specialize, leading to more efficient performance.

2. The five major forms of departmentalization are:
   a. Product departmentalization: organizes work based on the goods or services offered.
   b. Geographic departmentalization: organizes work based on region. Especially common in sales and distribution work units.
   c. Customer departmentalization: different departments service different customer groups, allowing each department to focus on the specific needs of that customer group.
   d. Functional departmentalization: organizes work by business function, such as production, marketing, finance, etc.
   e. Process departmentalization: some goods and services require multiple work processes to complete their production. A separate department is formed for each process.

3. The line organization is the oldest and simplest organization structure in which authority flows directly down the chain of command.
   a. The advantages of the line organization include: clear lines of authority and communication, quick decisions, simple and easy to understand.
   b. The disadvantages of the line organization include: overburdening executives with details, lack of specialization.

4. The line-and-staff organization combines staff managers who advise, counsel, and aid line managers, bringing their specialized skills to bear as complex organizations pursue line functions. Line managers manage and have authority over line functions.
   a. The line-and-staff organization has the following advantages: specialists (staff) are there to advise line managers, yet each employee reports to only one supervisor.
   b. The line-and-staff organization may suffer from the following disadvantages: there may be conflict between line and staff unless relationships are clear, and staff managers have authority only to advise, but not to command, line managers.

5. In the committee form of organization, authority and responsibility are jointly held by a group of individuals.
   a. The advantages of this form of organization include: utilizing the combined judgment of several executives in decision making, and improved morale through participation in decision making.
   b. The disadvantages of this form of organization include: decisions may be the result of compromise rather than optimization, and committees are slow in making decisions.

6. The matrix organization structure brings specialists from different parts of the organization to work together on specific projects. This form is often used in conjunction with the line-and-staff organization to achieve flexibility and permit project groups to be formed for specific purposes and then disbanded.

    a. The advantages gained through matrix organization form include: flexibility, the ability to focus strongly on specific major problems or unique technical issues, and the ability to innovate without disrupting the regular organizational structure.

    b. The disadvantages that may arise when the matrix organization form is used include: difficulty in developing a cohesive team from diverse individuals recruited from various parts of the organization, and conflict that may arise when workers must answer to both project managers and their own department managers, or between line managers and staff managers.

Self Review

True or False: 1. T, 2. F, 3. T, 4. T, 5. T, 6. F, 7. F, 8. F, 9. T, 10. F, 11. F, 12. F, 13. T, 14. T, 15. T, 16. F, 17. F, 18. T, 19. T, 20. T., 21. T.

Multiple Choice: 1. a, 2. a, 3. b, 4. c, 5. b, 6. d, 7. a, 8. b, 9. b, 10. a, 11. d, 12. a, 13. a, 14. b.

Application Exercises

1. a. They should carefully follow the five step organizing process, focusing on how they can best serve their customers, what activities will be needed, and how to arrange them logically. They will have to decide which types of departments are needed, and carefully delegate work assignments to departments and their personnel.

    b. They should probably select the line-and-staff structure, which will enable line managers to have the authority they need while getting support from staff personnel.

2. a. Paul might do a bit of self analysis, consult with others who have been exposed to him while he was in a leadership role, and do his own evaluation of the advisability of the autocratic, democratic, and free-rein leadership style.

    b. In the event that Paul is asked this question again, he might point out that the leadership style is a function of the leader, the individuals involved, and the situation. The appropriate style also depends on the corporate culture of the organization. Although a leader may adopt one style for general use, it is important to remain flexible so that quick decisions can be made in emergencies or greater freedom can be given to subordinates when their creativity and input are essential.

Short Essay Questions

1. Planning is the process of anticipating future events and conditions and determining the courses of action for achieving organizational objectives. The five types of plans are:

    a. Strategic plans: establish overall objectives, position the organization within its environment for both the short- and long-term.

    b. Tactical plans: Implement activities and allocate resources to reach strategic objectives.

    c. Operational plans: set quotas, standards, or schedules to implement tactical plans.

    d. Contingency plans: prepare for emergencies.

2. Delegation is giving tasks to subordinates. Delegation is a big help in time management for supervisors, and allows employees to vary their work and perhaps develop new skills. The four basic issues that must be addressed are:

    a. Responsibility: the subordinate must accept the obligation to complete the assigned tasks.

    b. Power: subordinates must have their own sources of power to ensure that they will be able to get the job done. They need adequate resources, knowledge, and personal traits that will allow them to influence others around them as they complete their tasks.

    c. Authority: subordinates and their co-workers should know just what they have authority to do, so that their power and authority are well matched.

    d. Accountability: employees must understand that they will be judged on how well they complete their tasks, and will have to accept the consequences of their actions.

3. Corporate culture refers to the shared values within an organization, and can contribute to the level of worker satisfaction in the organization and the ability of the organization to develop a competitive differentiation. Leadership is the ability to direct and inspire employees to meet the organization's objectives. Leadership and corporate culture are related in that corporate culture begins with leaders who can clearly articulate the organization's vision and mission. Then those leaders help to clarify the organization's values, and must embrace those values themselves and insist others in the organization do the same. Without good leadership, corporate culture may be weak, and leadership may have to depend more on centralization of authority and autocratic leadership styles instead of benefiting from the rewards of empowerment and decentralization.

CHAPTER 9

Vocabulary

1. Human resource management
2. need
3. motive
4. Morale
5. Employment at will
6. Job enlargement
7. Theory X
8. Theory Y
9. Theory Z
10. employee benefits
11. Job enrichment
12. On-the-job training
13. management development programs
14. flexible benefit plan
15. performance appraisal
16. telecommuters
17. Flextime
18. Downsizing
19. job sharing
20. exit interview
21. Outsourcing
22. compressed workweek
23. flexible work plan
24. professional employer organization (PEO)
25. 360-degree performance review
26. Contingent workers
27. salaries
28. Wages
29. labor union
30. lockout
31. boycott
32. grievance
33. injunction
34. Arbitration
35. Employers' Associations
36. strikebreakers
37. collective bargaining
38. Mediation
39. strike
40. picketing
41. alternative dispute resolution (ADR) programs
42. grievance
43. paid time off (PTO)

Analysis of Learning Goals

LG 9.1: 1. F, 2. T, 3. F, 4. T, 5. T, 6. T, 7. F, 8. T.

LG 9.2: 1. The recruitment process is the search for applicants. Firms can look at current employees in an effort to enhance morale by hiring from within or they may conduct an outside search for candidates. Outside sources include colleges, advertisements in newspapers and professional journals, public employment agencies, unsolicited applications, and recommendations from current employees.

2. The steps in the selection process are:
   a. Identify job requirements
   b. Recruit applicants
   c. Review applications and resumes.

   d. Interview candidates

   e. Conduct employment tests and check references.

   f. Conduct follow up interviews.

   g. Select a candidate and negotiate an offer.

  An applicant may be rejected at any step in the process.

3. Human resource managers must be familiar with employment law (Chapter 2 and Part I Appendix). Inattention to labor law can lead to lawsuits from unhappy employees, and to bad publicity that hurts the firm's image.

4. First, a new hire must be oriented, that is acquainted with the organization. Next, initial training will take place. This may involve on-the-job training, apprenticeship programs, classroom training, and, management development programs. Training should be regarding as an on-going activity that continues as long as the employee is with the firm.

5. A performance appraisal defines acceptable employee performance levels, evaluates the employee's actual performance, then compares actual and desired performance levels. The findings can be used to aid in decisions about training, compensation, promotion, transfers, and terminations.

LG 9.3: 1. b, 2. c, 3. d, 4. d, 5. d, 6. c.

LG 9.4: 1. downsizing and outsourcing.

    2. outsourcing.

    3. outsourcing.

    4. downsizing and outsourcing.

    5. downsizing and outsourcing.

    6. downsizing.

    7. outsourcing.

    8. downsizing and outsourcing.

LG 9.5: 1. Maslow's three assumptions are:

    a. People are wanting animals whose needs depend on what they already possess.

    b. A satisfied need is not a motivator; only those needs that have not been satisfied can influence behavior.

    c. People's needs are arranged in a hierarchy of importance; once they satisfy one need, at least partially, another emerges and demands satisfaction.

2. The five needs in Maslow's hierarchy are:

   a. Physiological needs: the need for food, water, shelter, and other necessities of life.
   b. Safety needs: protection from harm, employee benefits and job security.
   c. Social needs: acceptance, affection, affiliation with work groups, family, friends, co-workers, and supervisors.
   d. Esteem needs: recognition, approval of others, status, increased responsibilities.
   e. Self-actualization needs: accomplishment, opportunities for advancement, growth, and creativity.

3. T, 4. F, 5. T, 6. a, 7. b, 8. d, 9. b.

LG 9.6: 1. T, 2. F, 3. F, 4. F, 5. T.
LG 9.7: 1. b, 2. e, 3. e, 4. c.
LG 9.8: 1. Alternative dispute resolution (ADR) techniques include:

   a. open-door policies: ensures employees that they will have access to managers and human resource representatives if they have questions or problems in the workplace.

   b. employee hot lines: employees have a number to call to air a complaint, get advice on how to file a formal complaint with management, or to have confidential conversations with someone outside the firm about the grievance process.
   c. peer-review boards: some organizations have developed a means for complaint resolution using a group made up of several of the employee's peers as well as representatives of management. These groups help build trust and ensure fair treatment of employees.

   d. mediation and arbitration: use of impartial third parties to suggest or impose solutions in employee-management disputes can help avoid costly litigation and ensure employees that they will get a fair resolution to their complaint.

2. Job security continues to be a concern for workers. Hence, employers needing to reduce staffing often try to provide alternatives to layoffs, including offering incentives for early retirement and /or resignation. While such programs cost the employer some of its most experienced workers, the change often replaces older workers with younger employees who are likely to come in at lower wages.

Self Review

True or False: 1. F, 2. T, 3. F, 4. T, 5. T, 6. T, 7. T, 8. F, 9. T, 10. F, 11. T, 12. F, 13. T, 14. T, 15. F, 16. F, 17. T, 18. T .

Multiple Choice: 1. c, 2. b, 3. b, 4. d, 5. c, 6. e, 7. a, 8. d, 9. b, 10. c, 11. a, 12. d, 13. e, 14. d.

Application Exercises

1   Anita should probably first be clear about the job description she wants the new employee to fulfill. Then she can begin a search for candidates by contacting colleges and universities, public and private employment agencies, asking current employees for possible leads, or perhaps by advertising in newspapers or professional journals. Once she has a pool of candidates, she should get an application form from each, and perhaps do a pre-employment skills test. Those candidates who perform well on the test should be called in for an interview. Once she has selected the top two or three candidates, she should contact previous employers or other references and do a background check. Before she makes an offer, it may be wise to have the applicant take a medical examination, perhaps including a test for substance abuse. At each step of the process she must be careful to obey the laws regarding equal opportunity discussed in Chapter 2 and Part I Appendix. She may reject applicants at any step in the process, and hopefully by following this careful process will find the right person for the job.

2.   Anita should do a complete orientation for the new worker, providing introductions to key personnel and a tour of the facility. If she has an employee manual that describes the organization's mission and benefit programs, this should be part of the orientation. Anita also needs to think about what training methods she will use to be sure the new worker is prepared to do the job initially, and so that the worker can advance to new tasks in future. Anita should consider several other factors. First, pay: what can she afford to pay, and what are competitors for this skilled labor paying in her area?. If possible, she should enrich the job so that a talented employee will be challenged, and find the opportunity to meet higher order needs in the workplace. Anita might also consider offering employees a flexible work schedule or work plan. Finally, she needs to consider how she will tailor benefits to meet the differing needs of her workers.

Short Essay Questions

1. Human resource management is a complex set of activities designed to acquire, train, develop, compensate, motivate, and appraise a sufficient quantity of qualified employees to perform the activities needed by the organization. It also involves developing an organizational climate conducive to maximum efficiency of workers and to high worker satisfaction and morale. People are the key resource of any organization, and represent a significant cost factor. The right people, trained in the right way, compensated and motivated in a way that produces worker satisfaction, are all essential steps in making any organization a success.

2. Human motivation is based on needs. Where people lack something useful, they are motivated to do something about it. Maslow identified a hierarchy of needs that managers can use in understanding human motivation. The first and most fundamental level of need are the physiological needs, those needs that must be met if the person is to survive. Included at this level are food, shelter, water, etc., One way to meet these needs in the workplace is to provide adequate pay. The next level in Maslow's hierarchy are the safety needs. Organizations can help meet these needs by offering good benefit programs, job security, and a safe work environment. The third level of needs identified by Maslow are the social needs. Organizations need to be attentive to providing a climate that is conducive to both effective work and personal satisfaction. Next, Maslow identified the esteem needs. These are the needs people have for respect, recognition and responsibility. Finally, Maslow identified the self-actualization needs, those needs met by challenge, being creative, and accomplishing something important. These needs can be met by devising enriched jobs that challenge workers, and requires constructing job descriptions that will take advantage of higher level need gratification. Theory X is the belief that people are lazy and need to be coerced or threatened if they are to do a good job. This theory has largely been replaced by Theory Y, which assumes that workers like work, will accept responsibility under the right circumstances, and seek to meet their higher level needs on the job. Theory Z builds on Theory Y, emphasizing employee participation as the key to increased productivity and improved quality of work life.

    The essential lessons we can learn from these theories is that good pay is not enough. Workers must have their lower level needs met to an acceptable degree as a basis for motivation, so good pay and benefits, safe and pleasant working conditions are extremely important. But we must go further: managers should realize that most people want to meet their higher level needs on the job, and that Theory Y and Theory Z management assumptions should be adopted whenever possible. The most important lesson in motivating employees is that jobs must be constructed so that workers have an opportunity to meet their higher level needs at work. Challenge, creativity, and other job enriching activities are the key to motivation in the future.

CHAPTER 10

Vocabulary

1. team
2. Team cohesiveness
3. problem-solving teams
4. conflict
5. work team
6. task-specialist role
7. socio-emotional role
8. Communication
9. listening
10. formal communication channel
11. informal communication channel
12. nonverbal communication
13. internal communication
14. grapevine
15. centralized communication network
16. external communication
17. decentralized communication network
18. stock options
19. norm
20. high-context culture
21. low-context culture
22. Empowerment
23. employee stock ownership plan (ESOP)
24. teamwork

Analysis of Learning Goals

LG 10.1:   1. d,   2. a,   3. c,   4. d.
LG 10.2:   1. T,   2. T, 3. T,   4. T.
LG 10.3:   1. b,   2. d,   3. d,   4. b.
LG 10.4:   The five stages of group development are:

1. Forming: orientation, breaking the ice; leader facilitates social interchanges.

2. Storming: conflict, disagreement; leader encourages participation, differences surface.

3. Norming: establishment of order and cohesion; leader helps clarify team roles, norms, and values.

4. Performing: Cooperation, problem solving; leader facilitates task accomplishment.

5. Adjourning: Task completion; leader brings to closure and signifies completion.

LG 10.5:   1. F, 2. T, 3. T, 4. T, 5. F.

LG 10.6:   1.   Team conflict can be caused by competition for scarce resources, personality clashes among members, poor communication, unclear job responsibilities or ambiguous team roles.

                 2.   The five styles of conflict resolution are:

                     a.   Competing style: a decisive assertive approach. "Do it my way."

                     b.   Avoiding style: neither assertive nor cooperative; most effective when conflict results from some trivial cause or creates a no-win situation, when more information is needed, or when open conflict would be harmful.

                     c.   Compromising style: blending moderate degrees of assertiveness and cooperation; works well when two opposing goals are equally important, when combatants are equally powerful, or when the team feels pressure to achieve some sort of immediate solution.

                     d.   Accommodating style: emphasizing a high degree of cooperation, this style can help to maintain team harmony. A team member may choose to back down if an issue is more important to others in the group.

                     e.   Collaborating style: high assertiveness and cooperation; can be time-consuming and require lengthy negotiation aimed at achieving a win-win solution. Used when consensus from all parties is important.

LG 10.7:   1. T, 2. F, 3. F, 4. T, 5. F.

LG 10.8:   1. T, 2. F, 3. T, 4. T, 5. F, 6. F.

Self Review

True or False: 1. F, 2. T, 3. T, 4. T, 5. T, 6. T, 7. T, 8. T, 9. F, 10. T, 11. F, 12. T, 13. T, 14. T, 15. F, 16. T, 17. F.

Multiple Choice: 1. a, 2. b, 3. c, 4. d, 5. b, 6. b, 7. e, 8. d, 9. a, 10. d.

Application Exercises

1.   The team approach, especially a problem-solving or cross-functional team would probably be very helpful here. New product development is a natural place to bring people from different areas of the organization together so that the expertise of each can be applied to solving problems.

2.   a.   Jill is probably excited.

   b.   Jim should work on his listening skills and learn to solicit feedback to be sure he has been understood.

   c.   Gina is not receptive to what Tom is saying.

   d.   David has not seized the attention of his audience--their inattention is a form of feedback he cannot afford to ignore.

   e.   Your professor is trying to engage your interest, and solicits feedback by looking into students' faces. When the professor moves around the room it may be more interesting to listen to the lecture; if so, this movement is a communication aid.

Short Essay Questions

1.   A sender must come up with some idea to communicate, then encode that idea into a form that can be transmitted through some channel. When the audience receives the message it must be decoded, and its meaning extracted. Throughout this process there is the likelihood that noise (a sound, someone's defensiveness, or anything else that may distort the meaning of a message) may interfere with the process. It is extremely important that feedback be solicited so that the sender can be sure the receiver understood the intended message. Good listening is critical to good communication. In every communication, there is both a sender *and a receiver*. Listening skill helps you get feedback when you are the sender, and is crucial to making the appropriate response, asking the right question, or giving sensitive input that will quell conflict. You can't be a good communicator until you become a good listener!

2.   Teams are groupings of workers formed to achieve organizational objectives. The two main types of teams are work teams (relatively permanent groupings of people with complimentary skills who perform the day-to-day activities of the organization) and problem-solving teams (groups formed to bring together diverse skills for the

purpose of solving some particular issue, then disbanded). The team concept is of growing importance in modern organizations. The team concept makes use of empowered employees who collaborate and hold themselves mutually accountable for results. This not only makes good use of an organization's human resources, but also motivates people to do a better job, generates more creativity, and maximizes the contributions of a diverse work force.

CHAPTER 11

Vocabulary

1. Production
2. mass production
3. assembly line
4. flexible manufacturing system (FMS)
5. computer-aided design (CAD)
6. computer-aided manufacturing (CAM)
7. computer-integrated manufacturing (CIM)
8. Inventory control
9. Benchmarking
10. Materials requirement planning (MRP)
11. make, buy, or lease decision
12. Scheduling
13. production and operations management
14. production planning
15. Routing
16. quality control
17. environmental impact study
18. Program evaluation and review technique (PERT)
19. follow-up
20. just-in-time (JIT)
21. perpetual inventory
22. critical path
23. dispatching
24. robot
25. Production control
26. International Organization for Standards (ISO)
27. vendor-managed inventory (VMI)
28. CPFaR

Analysis of Learning Goals

LG 11.1: 1. T, 2. F, 3. T, 4. F, 5. F, 6. T.

LG 11.2: 1. T, 2. T, 3. F, 4. T, 5. T, 6. T, 7. T.

LG 11.3:
1. Proximity to markets.
2. Proximity to raw materials
3. Availability of transportation alternatives
4. Labor supply
5. Local regulations
6. Community living conditions and environmental impact
7. Water supply
8. Energy
9. Hazardous wastes

LG 11.4:
1. Plan the overall production process.

2. Determine the most efficient production facility layout (process, product, fixed-position, or customer-oriented).

3. Implement the production plan, including selecting suppliers and deciding how to control inventory.

4. Control the production process to maintain the highest quality of output and greatest efficiency of production, while simultaneously evaluating the results.

LG 11.5:   1.   process layout
2.   product layout
3.   fixed-position layout
4.   customer-oriented layout

LG 11.6:   1. T, 2. T, 3. F, 4. F, 5. T.
LG 11.7:   1. T, 2. F, 3. F, 4. T, 5. T.
LG 11.8:   1.   production planning
2.   follow-up
3.   dispatching
4.   routing
5.   scheduling

LG 11.9:   1. T, 2. F, 3. T, 4. T.

Self Review

True or False: 1. T, 2. T, 3. T, 4. T, 5. T, 6. F, 7. T, 8. F, 9. T, 10. T, 11. F, 12. T, 13. T, 14. T, 15. F.

Multiple Choice: 1. b, 2. a, 3. e, 4. c, 5. c, 6. d. 7. e, 8. a, 9. e, 10. c, 11. a, 12. b, 13. d.

Application Exercises

Specialization of labor is the breaking down of an assembly process into individual tasks. Each task is performed by a different worker.

1. The advantages of specialization:

    a. A worker can be trained to be a specialist in performing one task, hopefully making it possible for that worker to perform the task more quickly and accurately.
    b. The cost of training is low compared with training a person to function in several areas.

2. The disadvantages of specialization:

    a. Specialization may lead to worker boredom.
    b. Attention may wander, thus increasing the number of errors.
    c. Employee turnover may increase due to lack of challenge.

3. Suggestions:

    a. Have present employees train new employees.
    b. Divide total process into small units and use a team concept for each unit.
    c. Have the employees determine a team rotation schedule.

Short Essay Questions

1. Production and operations managers must plan the production process, select the most appropriate layout, implement the production plan, and control the production process. Each of these activities is crucial to producing high quality services that meet customer needs and expectations. A bank or beauty salon must determine what products to offer, design a layout, decide what to make and what to buy and from whom, and then plan, route, schedule, dispatch, and do a follow-up every time a loan application is processed or an individual client buys service.

2. Computers are useful in planning, implementing, and controlling operations. Robots are especially useful since they can be programmed to repeat the same tasks over and over. CAD/CAM software improves the product design and development process by making it faster and more responsive to changing customer demands. A Flexible Manufacturing System (FMS) backed by a computer system allows a company to

be more flexible in retooling producing processes. CIM places all manufacturing processes under centralized computer control. Computers have also helped significantly in inventory control (computerized perpetual inventory systems and MRP are examples), and in quality control (robots and electronic sensors are examples).

CHAPTER 12

Vocabulary

1. market
2. marketing mix
3. seller's market
4. utility
5. exchange process
6. Marketing research
7. data mining
8. Marketing strategy
9. target market
10. buyer's market
11. Consumer products (B2C)
12. marketing concept
13. Market segmentation
14. Business products (B2B)
15. Marketing
16. data warehouses
17. Buyer behavior
18. consumer behavior
19. Customer satisfaction
20. frequency marketing
21. Value-added
22. lifetime value of a customer
23. transaction marketing
24. relationship marketing
25. affinity program
26. co-marketing
27. co-branding

Analysis of Learning Goals

LG 12.1:   1. T, 2. T, 3. T, 4. T, 5. F.
LG 12.2:   1. T, 2. F, 3. F, 4. F, 5. T, 6. F, 7. T, 8. F.
LG 12.3:   1. T, 2. F, 3. T, 4. F.
LG 12.4:   1. b, 2. a, 3. d, 4. c, 5. e.
LG 12.5:   1. T, 2. F, 3. F, 4. T, 5. F, 6. T.
LG 12.6:   1. b, 2. a, 3. b, 4. d, 5. b.
LG 12.7:   1. T, 2. F, 3. F, 4. T, 5. F
LG 12.8:   1. T, 2. T, 3. T, 4. T, 5. F.

Self Review

True or False: 1. F, 2. T, 3. T, 4. F, 5. T, 6. T, 7. T, 8. F, 9. F, 10. T, 11. T, 12. F, 13. T, 14. F, 15. T, 16. T, 17. T, 18. T, 19. T.

Multiple Choice: 1. e, 2. c, 3. e, 4. d, 5. d, 6. d, 7. b, 8. d, 9. e, 10. e, 11. a, 12. d.

Application Exercise

1. You should probably start by defining market segmentation as the division of a total undifferentiated market into specific homogeneous market segments. You might note that the bases used to segment consumer markets can differ from those used to segment business markets. Since toys are consumer goods, your group would be concerned with market segmentation by demographics (i.e., sex, income, age, education, and stage of family life cycle); by geographics, based perhaps on regional lines; by psychographics, which centers on life styles; and by product-related segmentation, which deals with the benefits that the potential buyers will expect to derive from the product.

2. The five questions the speaker should be asked might include:

    a. How does education level of purchasers affect the type of toys that are purchased?

    b. What are the external environmental factors with the most impact on segmenting a toy market?

    c. Are there any regional differences in the type of toys preferred?

    d. How does ethnic origin affect the purchasing of toys?

    e. Have the toy manufacturers done much research in applying the concept of product-related (benefit) segmentation to their marketing strategies?

Short Essay Questions

1. The marketing concept is a customer oriented philosophy that demands that organizations take a customer orientation in all activities. This includes designing the product the customer wants, distributing it where and when the customer wants it, promoting it in ways that will reach the target market, and pricing it so that it will be affordable for and perceived as a good value by the target market.

    The marketing concept arose after World War II when, for the first time, there were significant surpluses in consumer goods. Once a buyer's market exists, just being able to produce and then sell a product is no longer enough: marketers have to identify and meet customer needs in order to sell anything.

The marketing concept means that producers must give up the "production" orientation whereby they produce what they want and then try to sell it. It means they must do market research to determine customer needs, and then develop a marketing strategy aimed at well defined target markets, adopting product, price, promotion, and distribution strategies dictated by customer expectations.

Customers benefit from the marketing concept, since they are now at the center of all the organization's activities. Customer service objectives, as well as quality objectives, must be met if the organization is to be successful. This customer orientation will benefit customers in all segments of the economy, whether we are talking about products or services, and whether the organization attempting to attract customer patronage is in the profit or not-for-profit sector.

2. The marketing mix is the combination of four strategies designed to meet the needs and expectations of customers. First there is product strategy, which deals with finding the right tangible and intangible product characteristics to meet customer needs, then packaging and labeling the product so that it will be attractive to customers. Product strategy also includes new product development and designing customer service. Next is pricing strategy. Marketers must price the product so that it is affordable to the target market, and is perceived by that intended market as representing a good value for their money. The price strategy must also generate adequate revenues to earn a profit for businesses, or to permit the continued operation of not-for-profit organizations. The third component of the marketing mix is distribution, in which the marketers must determine the middlemen they will use to get the product to market, and plan and execute a physical distribution strategy. Finally, the marketing mix must address promotional issues including how and where to advertise, whether or not to use personal sales, what sales promotional activities will be used, and what public relations objectives must be met. All of these components are interrelated and must be aimed at well defined target markets.

3. Marketing research is done to improve marketing decisions. It provides the information about potential target markets that planners need to design effective marketing mixes. Data can be obtained by examining internal data, or from external sources, such as previously published data, or by conducting the firm's own observation, surveys, or other external studies. The five basic reasons to conduct marketing research include:

    a. Identifying marketing problems and opportunities.
    b. Analyzing competitors' strategies.
    c. Evaluating and predicting consumer behavior.
    d. Gauging the performance of existing products and package designs, and assessing the potential of new ones.
    e. Developing price, promotion, and distribution plans.

CHAPTER 13

Vocabulary

1. product
2. brand
3. brand name
4. product life cycle
5. private (store) brand
6. trademark
7. product mix
8. product line
9. manufacturer's (national) brand
10. brand loyalty
11. individual branding
12. family brand
13. Brand equity
14. label

15. warranty
16. category manager
17. distribution strategy
18. distribution channels
19. physical distribution
20. Wholesalers
21. Retailers
22. supply chain
23. Logistics
24. direct distribution channel
25. wheel of retailing
26. intensive distribution
27. selective distribution
28. exclusive distribution

Analysis of Learning Goals

LG 13.1:   1. T, 2. F, 3. T, 4. F, 5. T.
LG 13.2:   1. c, 2. c, 3. e, 4. b, 5. a, 6. c.
LG 13.3:   1. F, 2. F, 3. T, 4. T, 5. F.
LG 13.4:   1. a, 2. b, 3. c, 4. d, 5. d.
LG 13.5:   The stages of the new-product development process are:

1. Stage One: New-product idea generation. Ideas may come from many sources, including customers, suppliers, employees, research scientists, marketing research, inventors outside the firm, and competitive products. The best ideas focus of satisfying customer needs or resolving customer complaints.

2. Stage Two: Screening. This stage deals with eliminating ideas that do not fit into the firm's objectives, or cannot be developed given the firm's resources.

3. Stage Three: Business analysis. This stage involves assessing potential sales, profits, distribution, and promotional resources, as well as considering the competitors' strengths and weaknesses.

4. Stage Four: Product development. The product is manufactured, tested, and revised. This may involve use of CAD or an actual prototype. At this point, the product's features and potential customer reactions are studied. Based on the findings, the product may be further modified.

5. Stage Five: Testing. The product is sold in a test market. This is done to help determine the likelihood of success in the total market.

6. Stage Six: Commercialization. This is the all-out introduction of the product, complete with promotion, distribution, and pricing strategies in place.

LG 13.6: 1. T, 2. F, 3. F, 4. T, 5. F, 6. F, 7. T, 8. T.

LG 13.7: 1. T, 2. T, 3. T, 4. F, 5. T, 6.T, 7. T, 8. T, 9. T.

LG 13.8:

1. In direct distribution, producers sell directly to end users. Direct distribution can be used for consumer goods, business goods, and services. Direct distribution is most common in business to business transactions, and also is a dominant method of distributing services.

2. Consumer goods can be distributed directly, or purchased through a retailers. Some retailers buy directly from producers, others buy from wholesalers, and still others buy from wholesalers who themselves used agents or brokers to acquire their goods.

Business goods can be distributed directly, and this is very common. However, producers sometimes reach business customers through agent/brokers, wholesalers, or a combination of the two.

Services are either directly distributed to business users or consumers, or they may be distributed via an agent/broker.

The channel used depends on the type of good or service offered, the efficiencies that may be realized through using marketing intermediaries, and the needs of the final customer. For example, some consumers prefer to order directly from a producer while others enjoy the retail shopping experience. Business users tend to buy services and installations directly from producers, but rely on marketing intermediaries for supplies or accessory equipment. Most services are directly marketed, unless efficiencies can be realized by inserting a marketing intermediary.

3. The four important factors that impact the selection of the appropriate distribution channel are:

    a. Market factors: target market the producer is trying to reach.

    b. Product factors: in general, products that are complex, expensive, custom-made, or perishable move through shorter distribution channels. Inexpensive or standardized products are typically sold through longer channels.

    c. Producer factors: a producer that offers a broad product line and has the financial and marketing resources to distribute its own output may use a short channel. Producers without such resources will need the help of marketing intermediaries and therefore select longer channels.

    d. Competitive factors: channel members must be able to provide those services that allow the producer to compete effectively.

Self Review

True or False: 1. T, 2. T, 3. T, 4. T, 5. F, 6. F, 7. F, 8. T, 9. T, 10. F, 11. T, 12. T, 13. T, 14. T, 15. T, 16. F, 17. F, 18. F, 19. F, 20. F, 21. T, 22. T.

Multiple Choice: 1. b, 2. c, 3. b, 4. a, 5. b, 6. d, 7. c, 8. a, 9. c, 10. d, 11. e, 12. b, 13. b.

Application Exercises

1. a. The product is apparently in the late maturity stage. We know that competition has entered, and that sales have been declining for some time, and that industry sales are also suffering.

    b. Sara should explore several options. She might look at increasing the frequency of her product's use, or try to find new users, perhaps abroad. She might consider what new uses can be found for the product, or consider altering the package. Perhaps an aggressive promotion program, coupled with changes in the product itself, would allow the firm to sell the product as "new and improved." If she feels none of these options are viable, she may have to recommend that the product be discontinued.

2. He will probably achieve only limited distribution if he follows his current plan. He might do better to find a marketing intermediary who can market his music either through retailers, or perhaps by mail order catalogue. He should also be aware that since middlemen are specialists, they may be able to do the distribution work more economically than he can. While he will have to share some of the proceeds, more sales and lower costs of distribution could end up producing much better profits in the long run.

Short Essay Questions

1. Products are divided into consumer and business products on the basis of their intended use: are they destined for business, non-personal use, or for personal, non-business use? The classifications of consumer goods are: a) convenience goods--frequently purchased items for which the consumer will expend a minimal shopping effort; b) shopping goods--products about which the customer lacks complete knowledge and for which the buyer now wants to shop and compare; 3) specialty goods--those goods that the customer wants enough to make a special shopping effort and for which the buyer will not accept a substitute. Business goods are classified by how they are used and by their basic characteristics. Products that will be used for a longer period of time are known as capital items, and include installations and accessory equipment. Business goods that will be used over the short-term are known as expense items, and include raw materials, component parts and materials, and supplies.

2. Distribution strategy involves getting the right product to the right place at the right time for its target market. It involves selecting the appropriate distribution channel, developing and maintaining effective relationships among channel members, and working out the details of effective physical distribution.

3. Physical distribution includes transporting goods, warehousing them, inventory control, materials handling, order processing, and setting and achieving customer service standards. In transportation, type of carrier and mode of transport must be determined. Warehousing may be purely for storage, or may concentrate goods for eventual distribution. Inventory control is critical both to providing customer service and holding costs down. Materials handling should make it easy to move quantities of product economically and with a minimum of damage or loss. A key component of distribution's contribution to customer service is efficient and effective order processing. All of these activities are designed to get the right amount of product to the right place at the right time while holding down total costs.

CHAPTER 14

Vocabulary

1. sales promotion
2. Advertising
3. pushing strategy
4. promotional mix
5. Positioning
6. pulling strategy
7. Promotion
8. telemarketing
9. order processing
10. Point-of-purchase (POP) advertising
11. Advocacy advertising
12. Comparative advertising
13. Personal selling
14. missionary selling
15. Creative selling
16. trade promotions
17. Product advertising
18. institutional advertising
19. Promotional products
20. public relations
21. Cooperative advertising
22. Sponsorship
23. Integrated Marketing Communications (IMC)
24. Sales Force Automation (SFA)
25. publicity
26. Relationship selling
27. consultative selling
28. team selling
29. infomercial
30. nonpersonal selling
31. product placement
32. price
33. profitability objectives
34. volume objectives
35. Cost-based pricing
36. Breakeven analysis
37. breakeven point
38. skimming price strategy
39. penetration pricing strategy
40. Competitive pricing
41. Every day low prices (EDLP)
42. odd pricing

Analysis of Learning Goals

LG 14.1: 1. Integrated Marketing Communications (IMC) is the marketing strategy designed to ensure that all promotional activities are integrated and coordinated to execute a unified, customer-focused message. Components of the promotional strategy that are coordinated include traditional print and electronic media, as well as packaging, store displays and other sales promotions, sponsorships, and online information. This strategy permits development of promotional strategies to reach many different market segments with a unified message.

2. a. Identify the target markets
   b. Set goals for the firm's promotional strategy with overall organizational objectives and marketing goals in mind.
   c. Weave together the components of the promotional mix into an integrated marketing communications plan.
   d. Solicit and evaluate feedback on how IMC is working.
   e. Use feedback to improve the IMC plan.

LG 14.2:   1. T, 2, F, 3. F,
   4. The five objectives of promotional strategy are:
      a. Providing information: A customer must know what your product is and where to find it. While this is important throughout the life of a product or service, it is crucial to stress informative advertising objectives in the introductory stage of the product life cycle.
      b. Differentiating the product: You must show how your product is the right one for the target customer. Techniques like positioning or comparative advertising can help here.
      c. Increasing sales: Whether focusing on primary or selective demand, increasing sales volume is the most common objective of promotional strategy.
      d. Stabilizing sales: Virtually every product and service has a "high" and a "low" season. Promotion can even out these cycles and help make operations smoother.
      e. Accentuating the product's value: You must tell the customer how you offer them more for their money. Stressing warranties or convenience can achieve this end.

LG 14.3:   1. F, 2. T, 3. T, 4. T, 5. F, 6. F, 7. T, 8. T, 9. T, 10. F, 11, T.
LG 14.4:   1. T, 2. F, 3. T, 4. T, 5. T, 6. T, 7. F.
LG 14.5:   1. F, 2. F, 3. T, 4. T, 5. T, 6. F.
LG 14.6:   1. F, 2. F, 3. T, 4. F, 5. T, 6. F.
LG 14.7:   1. c, 2. c, 3. b, 4. d, 5. b, 6. b, 7. b, 8. d, 9. d.
LG 14.8:   1. F, 2. T, 3. T, 4. F, 5. F.
LG 14.9:   1. While consumers expect value for their money, they are also often persuaded that higher price means better quality.
   2. Odd pricing uses odd amounts, such as $2.99 or $6.77, to make a price seem lower than it really is.

Self Review

True or False: 1. F, 2. F, 3. T, 4. T, 5. T, 6. T, 7. T, 8. F, 9. T, 10. T, 11. T, 12. T, 13. F, 14. T, 15. T, 16. F, 17. T, 18. T, 19. T.

Multiple Choice: 1. b, 2. b, 3. e, 4. c, 5. a, 6. e, 7. c, 8. a, 9. d, 10. b, 11. d, 12. c, 13. e, 14. a, 15. b., 16. c.

Application Exercises

There are many possible answers to each of these situations. Some suggestions might include:

1. Since this is a low cost item with wide distribution, product advertising will probably be a key focus of the promotional effort. Sponsorships and trade promotions might also be useful.
2. While some advertising in a local newspaper, radio station, or by direct mail might be worthwhile, this business probably should concentrate on patronage loyalty of its customer base. The owners might focus on offering some kind of premium for continued patronage and good in-store customer service.
3. Local advertising might be the best bet here, perhaps in conjunction with a free trial (sample) or a coupon offer to bring in initial customers.
4. While product advertising will almost certainly be needed, this company should also focus on a pushing strategy to encourage foreign middlemen to distribute the product. Again, sponsorships might help penetrate the foreign market.
5. Since this product is expensive, highly technical, and aimed primarily at business users, a sales force well trained in creative and missionary selling is essential.
6. This organization must overcome possible concerns of the surrounding community, so public relations campaigns, perhaps coupled with institutional advertising, might be used.

Short Essay Questions

1. Promotion consists of two distinct components: personal selling and nonpersonal selling. Personal selling will entail order processing, creative selling, and missionary selling. Modern trends in personal sales include relationship selling, consultative selling, and team selling, all of which use expertise, information, and resources outside of the traditional sales force to enhance the long-term prospects of the firm while providing service that creates a competitive differentiation.

   Nonpersonal selling involves advertising, sales promotion, and public relations. Advertising can aim at promoting the product, building the image and reputation of the firm, or advocating a position on some topic. Sales promotion efforts can be aimed at increasing customer purchases or enhancing dealer effectiveness. Public relations is designed to build positive relationships with not only customers, but also vendors, government, and the public at large.

The promotional mix is the combination of these various elements a firm uses to achieve it promotional objectives. This combination must be well coordinated to ensure that a unified, customer-focused message reaches various target markets. Modern Integrated Marketing Communications (IMC) can lower costs while integrating information from many sources, and promotions in all areas of the mix, to reach a common objective.

2. While we do recognize the right to freedom of speech, advertising practices have been regulated due to previous excesses. First, since consumers should have a right to make an informed choice, truth in advertising has been deemed essential and is legally mandated. Likewise, we have passed laws to limit the kind and amount of advertising children will see. Certain products whose use can produce harmful consequences (tobacco products, alcoholic products) have had their advertising options limited. Other concerns include whether consumers can differentiate from entertainment and the advertising contained therein. Some feel that advertising exercises an undue influence on customer buying patterns, "forcing" people to buy things they don't really need. While marketers naturally want to increase sales, making exaggerated claims or misleading the public is unethical. Limitations on the use of advertising and various advertising practices are not uniform internationally, so global marketers must make a special effort to understand the culture and laws in other countries.

3. Marketers can achieve many objectives through pricing strategy. Among them are:

   a. Profitability objectives. If the firm is pursuing profit maximization, the price must be based on what will produce the greatest profit for the product as a whole, rather than on a profit-per-unit basis. Other profitability objectives including seeking a target-return on sales or on investment.

   b. Volume objectives. Firms can price to seek sales maximization, or to improve market share.

   c. Pricing to meet the competition. This strategy simply meets the competitors' prices, and focuses competition on non-price variables such as adding value, improving quality, educating consumers, and establishing relationships.

   d. Prestige pricing objectives. A producer of high quality goods may decide to price the product higher rather than lower to achieve the image of top quality and exclusiveness.

CHAPTER 15

Vocabulary

1. management information system (MIS)
2. chief information officer (CIO)
3. application software
4. personal computer (PC)
5. Wi-Fi
6. Word processing
7. operating system
8. local area network (LAN)
9. desktop publishing
10. Spreadsheet
11. decision support system (DSS)
12. intranet
13. executive information system (EIS)
14. expert system
15. Hardware
16. Software
17. Interactive media
18. multimedia computing
19. Groupware
20. database
21. presentation software
22. disaster recovery plan
23. firewall
24. computer virus
25. mainframe computer
26. Supercomputers
27. minicomputer
28. wide area networks (WAN)
29. Application service providers (ASPs)
30. broadband technology
31. enterprise resource plan (ERP)
32. virtual private network (VPN)
33. Encryption

Analysis of Learning Goals

LG 15.1: 1. T, 2. T, 3. F.
LG 15.2: 1. T, 2. T, 3. F, 4. T, 5. T, 6. F.
LG 15.3: 1. d, 2. a, 3. b, 4. b, 5. a, 6, d, 7. c.
LG 15.4: 1 F, 2. T, 3. T, 4. F, 5. T. 6. T.
LG 15.5: 1. b, 2. d, 3. a, 4. d.
LG 15.6: 1. c, 2. a, 3. a, 4. c.
LG 15.7: 1. F, 2. T, 3. T, 4. F, 5. F.
LG 15.8: 1. T, 2. T, 3. T, 4. F, 5. T.

Self Review

True or False: 1. T, 2. F, 3. F, 4. T, 5. T, 6. T, 7. T, 8. F, 9. F, 10. F, 11. F, 12. T, 13. T. 14. F, 15. F.

Multiple Choice: 1. d, 2. c, 3. d, 4. e, 5. a, 6. e, 7. d, 8. d, 9. d, 10. a.

Application Exercises

1. word processing.

2. desktop publishing.

3. spreadsheet.

4. database.

5. e-mail.

6. presentation software.

Short Essay Questions

1. Information management is a key element in the success of any organization. Managers must make decisions and allocate resources, and information management is crucial to making the right choices. Information technology supports decision making by providing data about internal and external activities, including forecasts. Data can be stored on a database. Then decision support systems (DSS), executive information systems (EIS), expert systems, spreadsheets and other applications can help use that data to make better decisions.

   Information management also aids in sales and customer service. Presentation software makes it possible to produce graphic visual aids, while desktop publishing can help produce brochures and marketing materials. Sales people who need quick answers to detailed questions rely on information technology to do their job.

   Information management also makes a major contribution to management of human resources for an organization's success. Employees are empowered when they have the necessary information at their fingertips. And teamwork can be enhanced through groupware and intranet technology, allowing employees in different locations or time zones to work collaboratively.

2. The use of modern Management information systems has significantly improved business effectiveness and efficiency. However, important security issues have arisen, and will continue to provide challenges to users of computer systems in future. First, natural disasters, power failures, equipment malfunctions, and the like can crash a computer system. This means organizations must have backup systems and disaster recovery plans in place. For example, it is crucial that regular backups of data and documents be part of any electronic office.

    Another important concern is computer crime, which falls into three general categories:

    1. data can be changed or invented to produce inaccurate information.
    2. computer programs can be changed to create false information or illegal transactions.
    3. unauthorized people can get access to computer systems for their own illicit benefit.

    As a result, modern organizations must take steps to protect hardware, software, data security, and to manage operations, systems development and access to information in a way that minimizes opportunities for error, fraud, and theft. These efforts include using passwords for access to groupware and intranets, encrypting sensitive data, building electronic firewalls to prevent unauthorized access, and training employees to keep a close eye on computing devices, especially portable electronic devices they have with them when they are away from the office.

    A final concern is the problem of computer viruses. These are programs that secretly attach themselves to other programs and change them or destroy data. They are spread when infected software exchanges files with other users, as by means of electronic bulletin boards or trading disks. Viruses can be programmed to remain dormant for a long time, and then suddenly activate themselves. Many of these viruses result from simple pranks, but others involve deliberate crime. In either case, it is crucial that computer users understand the risks and take appropriate measures to protect their systems.

Notes:

CHAPTER 16

Vocabulary

1. Accounting
2. certified public accountant (CPA)
3. public accountant
4. asset
5. owners' equity
6. Liability
7. government accountant
8. balance sheet
9. management accountant
10. income statement
11. accounting process
12. bottom line
13. budget
14. cash budget
15. basic accounting equation
16. Ratio analysis
17. liquidity ratio
18. profitability ratio
19. leverage ratio
20. activity ratio
21. statement of cash flows
22. Accrual accounting
23. free cash flow
24. Public Company Accounting Oversight Board

Analysis of Learning Goals

LG 16.1: 1. T, 2. T, 3. F, 4. T, 5. F.

LG 16.2:
1. Financing activities: these activities are necessary to provide the funds to start a business and to expand it in the future. Lenders, investors and even those attempting to take over a firm will all have an interest in the financial information about the firm.
2. Investing activities: these activities are needed to provide the valuable assets required to run a business. Businesses seeking to install new equipment or purchase a subsidiary will need to see financial information to help them make the investment decision and understand how new investments will be funded and what returns they will be expected to generate.
3. Operating activities: these activities focus on the sale of goods and services, but also consider expenses. If a firm needs to cut costs accounting data will help them see where potential savings can come from. In pricing decisions, costs must be calculated using accounting data. Operations such as promotion will also be budgeted based on accounting data, and operations will be controlled in part on the basis of this information.

LG 16.3: 1. F, 2. T, 3. T, 4. T, 5. T.

LG 16.4: 1. c, 2. a, 3. a, 4. d.

LG 16.5:
1. the accounting profession.
2. Public Company Accounting Oversight Board

3. five.
4. Securities and Exchange Commission.

LG 16.6: 1. T, 2. F, 3. T, 4. T, 5. F, 6. T, 7. F, 8. T, 9. T.

LG 16.7: 1. Current Ratio:
    a. it measures the firm's liquidity, that is, its ability to meet its short-term obligations.
    b. Current assets/current liabilities
    c. balance sheet/balance sheet
    d. A current ratio should be at least 2/1, that is, a firm should have at least twice as much in current assets as it has in current liabilities.

2. Acid-test (quick) ratio:
    a. it also measures the firm's liquidity, but excludes inventory and prepaid items from current assets and counts only "quick" assets.
    b. quick assets/current liabilities
    c. balance sheet/balance sheet
    d. A quick ratio should be at least 1/1, that is, a firm should have at least as much in quick assets as it has in current liabilities.

3. Earnings per share:
    a. measures a firm's profitability, specifically, how much profit was earned for each share of common stock.
    b. net income / # of common shares outstanding
    c. income statement (bottom line)/balance sheet (equity section)
    d. evaluated by comparing to firm's own record and to industry standards.

4. Net Profit Margin:
    a. measures how much of each dollar in sales ends up as profit.
    b. net income / sales
    c. income statement/income statement
    d. evaluated by comparing to firm's own record and to industry standards.

5. Return on equity:
    a. measures the return earned (profitability) on firm's equity.
    b. net income / total owners' equity
    c. income statement (bottom line)/balance sheet (equity section)
    d. evaluated by comparing to firm's own record and to industry standards.

6. Total liabilities to total assets:
    a. this is a leverage ratio, that is, it calculates the extent to which a firm is relying on debt financing.
    b. total liabilities / total assets
    c. balance sheet (liabilities section)/balance sheet (assets section)

      d.   In general, lenders and investors prefer to deal with a firm whose owners have invested more of their own money than they hope to borrow from others.

    7.   Inventory turnover ratio:

      a.   this is an activity ratio, and measures how effectively the firm is using its resources, in this case, its inventory.

      b.   cost of goods sold/average inventory

      c.   cost of goods sold is found on the income statement; average inventory can be found by adding beginning inventory to ending inventory (from the income statement) and dividing it by two. If a firm takes more frequent inventories, adding them together and finding the average can help even out seasonal differences in the firm's operations that would be missed using only the beginning and ending inventory figures.

      d.   This figure varies greatly by industry: a bakery would have a higher inventory turnover ratio than would a car dealer. A firm should also compare this ratio to its own history.

LG 16.8:   1. F, 2. T, 3. T, 4. T, 5. F, 6. T, 7. T.

LG 16.9:   1. F, 2. T, 3. F, 4. T.

Self Review

True or False: 1. T, 2. T, 3. F, 4. T, 5. T, 6. T, 7. F, 8. F, 9. F, 10. T, 11. T   12. T, 13. T, 14. T, 15. T, 16. F, 17. T.

Multiple Choice: 1. b, 2. b, 3. b, 4. a, 5. a, 6. c, 7. d, 8. a, 9. d, 10. a.

Application Exercises

1.   Sales
    Minus: Cost of goods sold
    Equals: Gross income

    Minus: Operating expenses
    Equals: Operating income

    Minus: Income taxes
    Equals: Net income

2.   The current ratio is found by dividing current liabilities into current assets:

    $46,000/$10,000 = 4.6 to 1. This is acceptable, since the ratio should be 2 to 1 or better.

3. The total liabilities to total assets ratio is

   $50,000/$150,000 = approx. 33%. This is acceptable, since the firm has borrowed only one third as much as it has in assets.

4. The current ratio is: $60,000/$20,000 or 3 to 1, which seems fine. The quick ratio first requires us to calculate the quick assets: Current Assets ($60,000) less inventory and prepaid expenses ($50,000) = $10,000. Now the quick ratio is found by dividing quick assets by current liabilities: $10,000/$20,000 = 1 to 2. This firm's liquidity position is not as good as it first appeared when we did the current ratio, since so much of its current assets are in inventory. This firm will have to move a lot of inventory quickly if it is to meet its short-term obligations.

Short Essay Questions

1. The accounting process involves the recording, classifying, and summarizing of accounting transactions and using this information to produce financial statements for the firm's management and other interested parties. Transactions are recorded chronologically in journals, then posted to ledger accounts, and then summarized in accounting statements. With modern accounting software, the transaction data is entered once, and the journal, ledger accounts, financial statements, and ratios can then be automatically accessed.

   The three most important accounting statements are: 1) the balance sheet, which is like a snapshot of the business on a given day, and which makes the accounting equation explicit, that is, it shows assets = liabilities and equity; 2) the income statement, which is more like a moving picture of a business over a period of time and shows the firm's revenues, less cost of goods sold, less operating expenses, and less taxes, to give the firm's net income (or loss); and 3) the statement of cash flows which summarizes the cash effects of a firm's operating, investing, and financing activities during a specific accounting period. It is sometimes called the "where got/where gone" statement since it shows cash inflows and outflows.

2. Budgets are financial guidelines for future periods reflecting expected sales revenues, operating expenses, and/or cash receipts and outlays. They represent management's expectations of future occurrences based on plans that have been made. They serve as important planning and control tools by providing standards against which actual performance can be compared.

CHAPTER 17

Vocabulary

1. Finance
2. financial managers
3. risk-return trade-off
4. Money
5. financial system
6. debt capital
7. equity capital
8. financial plan
9. Bonds
10. VP for Financial Management
11. Leverage
12. treasurer
13. controller
14. electronic funds transfer system (EFTS)
15. Federal Reserve System (FED)
16. monetary policy
17. check clearing
18. discount rate
19. Open market operations
20. reserve requirement
21. Commercial paper
22. trade credit
23. Treasury Bills (T-Bills)
24. depository institutions
25. Venture capitalists
26. private placements
27. Federal Deposit Insurance Corporation (FDIC)
28. demand deposits
29. certificate of deposit (CD)
30. commercial banks
31. M1
32. M2
33. Chief Financial Officer (CFO)
34. underwriting
35. federal funds rate

Analysis of Learning Goals

LG 17.1:   1. T, 2. T, 3. F, 4. F. 5. T.

LG 17.2:   1.   The characteristics of modern money are:
   a.   divisibility: partial value can be spent and change can be made.
   b.   portability: easy to carry and conceal.
   c.   durability: the money should last rather than being perishable.
   d.   difficult to counterfeit: since counterfeit money increases the supply of money it can undermine a nation's monetary system.
   e.   stability: money should hold its value over time.

2.   The functions of money are:
   a.   medium of exchange: makes exchange easy and eliminates the need for a barter system.
   b.   unit of account: money is the common denominator by which we measure and compare value in the marketplace.
   c.   store of value: money retains its value over time, making it possible to save for future expenditures, yet it is liquid, which means it can be easily spent when the time comes.
   d.   liquidity: money allows quick, easy and immediate transactions.

LG 17.3:   1. T, 2. T, 3. F, 4. F.
LG 17.4:   1. T, 2. T, 3. F, 4. F, 5. F, 6. T.
LG 17.5:   1. d, 2, c, 3. c, 4. a, 5. a.
LG 17.6:

1.	Private placements	5.	Short-term
2.	commercial paper	6.	after a year or longer
3.	trade credit	7.	long-term sources of capital
4.	unsecured loan	8.	venture capitalists

LG 17.7:   1. a, 2. d, 3. c, 4. e, 5. b, 6. a.
LG 17.8:   1. T, 2. F, 3. T, 4. T, 5. F, 6. F.
LG 17.9:   1. T, 2. F, 3. F, 4. T.

Self Review

True or False: 1. T, 2. F, 3. T, 4. T, 5. T, 6. T, 7. F, 8. F, 9. T, 10. F, 11. T, 12. T, 13. T, 14. F, 15. T, 16. T, 17. T, 18. F, 19. F, 20. T.

Multiple Choice: 1. e, 2. d, 3. b, 4. b, 5. b, 6. c, 7. c, 8. b, 9. a, 10. c, 11. b, 12. e.

Application Exercises

1. Mrs. Brown should be certain that the deposit institution she selects is a federally insured institution, and that she does not allow any one account to exceed $100,000. This will protect her, since such institutions insure each account up to $100,000, and are required to undergo regular, unannounced inspections by bank examiners who evaluate the financial practices of the deposit institution. She should also be careful that she puts her money in an account, rather than buying stocks, bonds, or funds offered by the institution. It is important for her to know that within the limits of the insurance, depositors are protected in bank failures, while lenders and investors may suffer some loss.

2. a. Stock $80,000
        Earnings $40,000
        Return to stockholders = $40,000/$80,000 = 50%

    b. Stock $60,0000
        Bonds   20 ,000
        Earnings   40,000
        Interest on bonds: $20,000 x 8% = $1600
        Net earnings are $40,000 - $1600 = 38,400.
        Rate of return to shareholders = $38,400/60,000 = 64%

c. Stock $80,000
    Bonds   40,000
    Earnings   50,000
    Interest on bonds: $40,000 x 10% = 4,000
    Net earnings are $50,000 - $4,000 = 46,000
    Rate of return to shareholders = $46,000/80,000 = 57.5%

Short Essay Questions

1. Financial management is the business activity of developing and implementing the firm's financial plan and finding the best sources and uses of funds. Financial managers are responsible for producing a financial plan, noting what sources of funds the firm will seek and how the funds will be used. Financial managers must then perform the activity of financial control, that is, periodically checking actual revenues, costs, and expenses against the forecasts. A financial manager must obtain funds in the most efficient manner, and use funds to maximize the total value of the firm. A firm with a great product aimed at a willing market can still fail if it runs out of cash, or lacks the financial resources to seize an opportunity or solve a significant problem.

2. Debt capital is borrowed money. Firms have access to many short-term sources of debt capital, such as taking out short-term loans, selling commercial paper, or using trade credit. Firms may also use long-terms sources of debt capital, such as long-term loans from banks or equipment vendors, and the sale of bonds. Debt capital has a prior claim to assets in the event the firm fails. The firm is legally required to pay interest to the lender, and to repay the principal at debt maturity. So long as the firm meets these obligation, lenders will not normally have a say in managing the affairs of the firm.

    Equity capital is invested money. Investments can come from owners, plowing back retained earnings, selling shares of stock, or attracting investment from venture capitalists. Equity capital is generally long-term, since there is no date at which an investment has to be repaid, i.e., investment capital has no maturity date. Investors have a claim to assets after the claims of lenders have been satisfied. There is no contractual obligation to pay interest on equity capital, though most investors hope to earn some return for their investment. Investors, unlike lenders, do have management authority over the firm.

3. The Federal Reserve System (the "Fed") is a system of 12 district banks that regulates banking, acts as a clearinghouse for checks, and regulates the supply of money and credit in order to promote economic growth and a control inflation. The major tools of the Fed are:

a. the reserve requirement: the Fed requires member banks to hold aside some deposits rather than lending them all. If the reserve requirement is raised, banks have less money to lend, and if the Fed lowers the reserve requirement, banks will have more money to lend.

b. the discount rate: this is the interest rate the Fed charges member banks to borrow reserves. If the discount rate is raised, banks will have to charge a higher rate of interest on their loans, which will discourage lending and reduce the money supply. If the Fed lowers the discount rate, banks can charge lower rates, which encourages borrowing and can stimulate the economy.

c. open market operations: the Fed can buy and sell government bonds on the open market. When it buys bonds, it puts money into the money supply in exchange for the bonds it purchases; when it sells bonds it takes money out of circulation, reducing the money supply.

d. selective credit controls: The fed also has the authority set margin requirements in the purchase of stocks and bonds.

The Fed also plays a major role in international commerce by holding and selling reserves of foreign currencies, thereby influencing the exchange rate of the dollar.

CHAPTER 18

Vocabulary

1. brokerage firm
2. investment bankers
3. Insider trading
4. secondary market
5. bond rating
6. price-earnings ratio (P/E)
7. Electronic Communications Network (ECN)
8. limit order
9. market order
10. prospectus
11. securities
12. Municipal bonds
13. full and fair disclosure
14. yield
15. book value
16. Common stock
17. Preferred stock
18. call provision
19. Institutional investors
20. Money market instruments
21. primary market
22. Mutual funds
23. Initial Public Offering (IPO)
24. underwriting
25. debenture
26. secured bond
27. stock exchange (market)
28. government bonds
29. convertible security
30. Regulation FD

Analysis of Learning Goals

LG 18.1:   1. a, 2. b, 3. d, 4. a.

LG 18.2:   1. d, 2. a, 3. a, 4. c, 5. b.

LG 18.3:   1. Growth in capital. Sometimes also called capital appreciation, it means the value of your investment goes up over time. The best selection to meet this objective would be common stocks, which have outperformed all other asset classes in meeting this objective.

2. Stability of principal. Investing to preserve the amount you started out with. Money market instruments generally do best here, since over their short life, the odds of the instrument declining in value are virtually zero.

3. Liquidity. This is the speed at which assets can be converted into cash without loss of value. Again, money market instruments are the best choice to pursue this objective.

4. Current income. Since interest rates on longer term bonds are higher than on money market instruments, these bonds would be the best choice for this objective.

5.   Growth in income. For an investment with the best chance of income increasing over the long term, common stocks that pay dividends may be the best choice. While bonds pay a set income until they mature, common stock dividends may increase over time with good profit performance.

LG 18.4:   1. F, 2. F, 3. T, 4. T, 5. F.
LG 18.5:   1. e, 2. e, 3. c, 4. c, 5. a.
LG 18.6:   1. F, 2. T, 3. T, 4. T. 5. T.
LG 18.7:   1.   Securities and Exchange Commission (SEC)
2.   prospectus
3.   full and fair disclosure
4.   insider trading
5.   Regulation FD
6.   industry self-regulation

Self Review

True or False: 1. T, 2. F, 3. F, 4. F, 5. F, 6. T, 7. T, 8. T, 9. F, 10. F, 11. F, 12. T, 13. T, 14. T. 15. T.

Multiple Choice: 1. c, 2. a, 3. a, 4. a, 5. d, 6. a, 7. d, 8. a, 9. a, 10. b, 11. a.

Application Exercises

1.   This investment is best suited to an investor seeking growth in capital.

2.   This investment is best suited for an investor who is interested in current income.

3.   This investment is suited for investors who want current income and who are in high tax brackets, since the interest earned is exempt from federal income tax, and may also be exempt from state income tax.

4.   This investment is suited for more speculative investors, who are willing to take a significant risk in hopes of earning a higher current income.

5. These instruments are good for stability of principal and liquidity.

6. This investment allows an individual investor to purchase a diversified basket of securities in the global marketplace.

Short Essay Questions

1. Common and preferred stocks, money market instruments, and bonds of all kinds are collectively referred to as securities. The rewards of investing in securities include capital appreciation (growth in the value of the invested principal), and income (interest on bonds or dividends on stocks). While investors can earn income from bank accounts, the rates are generally lower than securities will provide, and there is no opportunity for capital appreciation in bank deposits. Likewise, bank deposits, because they are insured, are generally risk free, while securities investments are not. Since the prices of securities vary widely over time, investors cannot know in advance what their investment will be worth when they want to withdraw the money. Still, over the long run, stocks in particular have outperformed bank deposits as investment vehicles.

   Investors should carefully study any security before investing. They should know, for example, that good quality bonds are generally safer than stocks, and that preferred stocks offer greater safety than do common stocks. If their main goal is stability of principal and liquidity, money market instruments may be best. If they want high current income, they will should consider bonds, and must carefully evaluate the bond ratings to understand their level of risk. Finally, individual investors might consider investing in mutual funds to achieve the benefits of diversification and professional financial management of their investment.

2. The primary market is used by businesses and government units to sell new issues of securities. Announcements of these security offerings appear daily in such business publications as the Wall Street Journal in the form of simple black-and-white advertisements called "tombstones." Although an organization seeking to generate funds through the sale of securities could market its offering directly to the public, most large offerings are handled by investment bankers who acquire the total issue and then resell it to other investors.

   The secondary market is made up of the various major exchanges, the NASDAQ, and the new, "fourth" market, whereby traders bypass the exchanges and NASDAQ system and make direct transactions via computer network. No new funds are generated for issuers of stocks and bonds in the secondary market. Instead, previously issued securities are traded between investors, who realize all the profits (and losses) from these transactions.

APPENDIX A

Vocabulary

1. Risk
2. speculative risk
3. pure risk
4. insurance
5. law of large numbers
6. actuarial tables
7. insurable interest
8. Property and liability insurance
9. self-insurance fund
10. life
11. Disability income insurance
12. Health insurance
13. Health maintenance organization (HMO)
14. insurable risk
15. Key executive insurance
16. premium
17. public insurance agency
18. unemployment insurance
19. workers' compensation insurance
20. Liability insurance
21. managed care plans
22. fee-for-service
23. preferred provider organization (PPO)
24. Term policies
25. cash value policies
26. Medicare
27. business interruption insurance
28. Underwriting

Self Review

True or False: 1. T, 2. F, 3. F, 4. F, 5. T, 6. F, 7. T, 8. F, 9. T, 10. T, 11. T
12. F, 13. T, 14. T, 15. T, 16. T, 17. T, 18. F, 19. T.

Multiple Choice: 1. b, 2. a, 3. a, 4. c, 5. c, 6. c, 7. b, 8. c, 9. e, 10. b, 11. d.

APPENDIX B

Vocabulary

1. Personal finance
2. standard of living
3. lifestyle
4. net worth
5. credit
6. revolving credit
7. installment loan
8. defined benefit plans
9. defined contribution plan
10. financial plan

Self Review

True or False: 1. T, 2. T, 3. F, 4. F, 5. T, 6. T, 7. T, 8. T, 9. F, 10. T.

Multiple Choice: 1. a, 2. d, 3. b. 4. c, 5. b, 6. c, 7. d, 8. d, 9. d, 10. d.

APPENDIX C

Vocabulary

1. business plan
2. executive summary
3. introduction
4. marketing strategy
5. demographics
6. trends
7. Market penetration
8. potential sales revenue
9. financial section

Self Review

True or False: 1. F, 2. F, 3. F, 4. T, 5. T, 6. T, 7. F, 8. T, 9. T.

Multiple Choice: 1. a, 2. d, 3. b, 4. c, 5. d, 6. d. 7. d, 8. d.